CREDO

GUSTAF WINGREN

CREDO

The Christian View of Faith and Life

Translated by
Edgar M. Carlson

Augsburg Publishing House

Minneapolis, Minnesota

Contents

Translator's Preface 8

Foreword 11

The Apostles' Creed 16

The Nicene Creed 17

INTRODUCTION 18
    Three Aspects of the Whole—
        Three Articles   18
        The Creator at Work in Everything
          (The First Article)
        Humanity Present in Everything
          (The Second Article)
        Eternal Dominion the Aim in Everything
          (The Third Article)
    God's Activity Encounters Opposition   26
    The Hazard for Doctrine: Theorizing   29
        The View that the Concept of Revelation
          Is Dominant Is a Misconception
        The View that the Authority of Scripture
          Is Dominant Is a Misconception

THE FIRST ARTICLE: THE FATHER
Creation and Law

 I. CREATION 37
    Creation Is Happening Now   37
        To Live Is to Be in Relationship to God
        Hope Is Prayer
    Destruction Is Happening Now   43
        This Destruction Cannot Be Terminated
          During the Course of History
        In Destruction One Perceives
          What Creation Is
        To Find Meaning Is to Interpret Death
    Human Beings and Their Environment   50
        The Human Is a Part of the Created
        Human Dominion
        Man and Woman
        Prayer

II. THE LAW 58
    God Compels   58
        The Bible and Our Neighbor
        Legislation Constitutes Our Neighbor's
          Demand-Note Against Us
        No Law Is Eternal

God Accuses   66
   Memories and the Irreparable
   The Conscience
Caricatures and Images   72
   Guilt Is a Negative Imprint
   That Which Is Forced Is an Imitation
   "God's Image"
   Prayer

THE SECOND ARTICLE: THE SON
Christ

III. WORKS 81
   The Restored Creation   81
     Jesus' Birth
     His Ministry
   Deeds Are Signs Pointing to the Future   86
     Healing and Proclaiming
     Short-term Resurrection
     Hope
   Deeds Are Acts of Service   92
     To Heal and to Give
     The Unity of Cross and Deeds
     Prayer

IV. THE CROSS 97
   The Humiliation   98
     Repudiated by God's People
     Condemned by God's Law
   The Victory   103
     No Personal Gain
     Creation's Spring
     The Harvest
     God Becomes Different
     Prayer

V. THE RESURRECTION 113
   He Who Comes from the Future   113
     The Unbiblical Injection Idea
     Christ Is Ahead of Us
     "Judge" and "Author of Life"
   Ethical and Physical   120
     The Visions and the Empty Grave
     Resurrection and Forgiveness
     Peter
     Prayer

VI. THE GOSPEL 128
   The Sending Forth   128
     The Ascent into Heaven
     The Spoken Word

The Image   133
   To Preach Is to Tell
   "God's Fingers"
Ev Means Rejoicing   137
   The Will to Live
   The Eucharist
   Prayer

THE THIRD ARTICLE: THE SPIRIT
The Congregation and the Promise

VII. THE CONGREGATION IN THE WORLD 144
   "I Will Pour Out My Spirit
      on All Flesh"   145
      The Church and the World
      Salt and Light
      Comparison with Marxism
   "By One Spirit We Were All Baptized
      into One Body"   151
      The Dissimilarity among Individuals
      Comparison with Humanism
   "The Spirit Says to the Churches"   157
      The Word and the Church
      The Views of Various Confessions
      Comparison with Existentialism
   "All Were Made to Drink of One Spirit"   165
      Body and Mealtime
      Comparison with Mysticism
      Prayer

VIII. ETERNAL LIFE 171
   Eternal Life   171
      The Spontaneous Expressions of Life
      Christ's Resurrection
   Baptism   175
      That Which Happened Once
      The Forward Movement
   Judgment   180
      Death as Judgment
      To Assert and to Pray
      Comparison with Naturalism
   The Song of Praise   187
      In the Present
      In Heaven
      Prayer

Notes 195
Index of Biblical Passages 203
Index of Names 206

Translator's Preface

This volume offers a fresh and invigorating journey through the theological landscape of the historic Creeds. Those acquainted with Wingren's writings will find in this volume an integrated and comprehensive presentation of his theology. Wingren has described *Credo* as "a fairly complete dogmatics, useful at an academic level."

What makes this such a fresh and stimulating discussion of the traditional statements of the Creed is Wingren's unusual sensitivity both to the historical circumstances in which doctrinal positions developed, and to the contemporary moods and movements which form the context of our own thinking and acting. Comparisons with Marxism and Existentialism seem as natural and germaine as descriptions of the encounter with Gnosticism in the Creed-making era of the early centuries.

The particular emphasis in this work, as in most of Wingren's writings, is the doctrine of creation. God is at work in every birth and in each moment of life, whether we recognize it or not. Like the new-born child who is sustained by oxygen which it breathes in without knowing it, we are sustained by God's creative action whether we acknowledge it or not. So the Creed has something to say to our time. Even though we have come to blush when we use religious words, we cannot avoid the religious dimension of existence. We talk about what "life offers" or what "life has given" the way earlier generations talked about God. We know life is vulnerable—that we are not the lords over our existence—and we cannot avoid fearing and hoping, being sorrowful and grateful, in response to what "life brings." Even a secularized generation continues to show some respect for the religious rites connected with birth, marriage, and death. It has no substitute for them, and it cannot dispense with some recognition of powers beyond itself.

This kind of engagement with the realities of our human existence is characteristic of Wingren's treatment of all aspects of the Creed. He insists throughout on the inter-relatedness of the three articles but freely acknowledges that in this presentation the first article is given the primary focus. He believes that this pivotal emphasis on creation is a much needed counterbalance to the one-sidedness of the widespread concentration on Christology and the emerging concentration on the Holy Spirit.

Professor Wingren is a creative theologian whose academic credentials are of a very high order. He does not fit into any of the theological schools, but has charted his own course. Although he was a student of the leaders of the Lundensian school (Aulen, Nygren, Bring, and others), his theology has been shaped in controversy with many of the positions taken by his mentors. He has expressed particularly strong dissent from what he considered to be the neo-Kantian assumptions of Anders Nygren, whose successor he became in the chair of theological ethics at Lund in 1951. He has defined his theology in sharp conflict with the Barthian concentration on Christology. Although he strongly affirms the values of biblical criticism (including demythologization) he has taken strong exception to Rudolf Bultmann's biblical interpretation and general theological postures. He is sharply critical of the influence of Kierkegaard in recent theology. He identifies himself at the philosophical level with Knud Løgstrup of Denmark, who represents a far more positive view of human existence. Although he draws freely from many sources (including several American writers) and from many theological traditions, Wingren takes an independent stance which relies heavily on his own exploration of the biblical and historical sources, and on his own reading of the world to which the gospel is addressed in our time.

In at least one respect, this translation does not constitute an exact rendition of the original. Each of the eight chapters concluded with a prayer and a hymn, both of which were the author's own compositions. We have translated the prayers, but have not felt that we could do justice to the hymns. They were written to accompany Swedish hymn tunes and in some respects were indigenous to the Swedish situation. Nonetheless, something valuable has been lost by this omission. It is Wingren's contention that the Creed belongs in the worship service, where it arose, rather than in the arena of debate. It has become customary for theologians to debate the tenets of the Creed, and to compare them with the tenets of other religions.

When we do this we apply to them certain criteria which are appropriate to debate but which have no place in worship. We need to look at the Creed within the worship setting, where it belongs. The prayers and the hymns were intended to provide such a setting for the reader.

They also served a further purpose: they demonstrate that theological positions which conflict with one another can be transcended in worship. In the history of the church, rival theologians have been able to pray together and to sing praises together. Some of the hymns illustrate how motifs can be drawn from different patterns of thought and combined into a common act of worship. Although we have not translated the hymns we have retained Professor Wingren's explanation of the purpose they were intended to serve, since this is clearly germaine to the general position taken. We hope that the prayers will provide some suggestion of the larger contribution which would have been made had it been possible to include the hymns as well. It is clear that the point which he makes concerning the way in which worship transcends and incorporates conflicting points of view is certainly valid and could be illustrated from the hymnody of every Christian communion.

We have also retained his references to peculiarities of the Swedish translation of the Creed, which makes its own contribution to our ecumenical understanding.

EDGAR M. CARLSON

Foreword

"Credo" is an old name for the confession of the faith. It is also the designation of a portion of the worship service. Credo is a Latin term meaning "I believe," hence it is the first word of the Creed. This "faith-word" is found in both the worship liturgy and the baptismal rite of the Swedish church at a point where it introduces a song of praise. This is how the Creed was conceived from the very beginning—as a song of praise in which God's deeds are recounted with thanksgiving. The setting is the worship service, either baptism (in the case of the Apostles' Creed) or the Lord's Supper (in the case of the Nicene Creed). The setting is *not* a debate in which a person defines one point of view over against other people with other points of view.

One who wishes to describe the Christian understanding of faith and life in our time could hardly choose a better basis than this ancient tripartite Creed. But now this text, which originated as a song of praise, is moved out of that original context into a new and foreign arena, the arena of debate. Christianity says one thing, Marxism says something else and Islam has a third position. When this happens a peculiar shift occurs with regard to the content of the Creed: the words in the text are now understood to apply to Christians in distinction from other people. The words in the Creed now describe one particular religious group. In spite of the fact that a change in perspective has occurred, everything seems completely objective and factual. If the confession of faith is typical of Christianity, it must be characteristic of Christians.

This modification does not at first glance seem to be a flaw. But such a shift in perspective results in a historical falsification, and

that is a very serious flaw. As a general rule, it is the starting point,
or the angle from which something is approached that most often
accounts for the distortion of historical material. A quick look at
Marxism will be enlightening.

Class interest is a central concept in Marxist ideology. It has its
assigned place both in the exposure of "the anatomy of the bour-
geoisie community" and in the liberating, forward-looking aspect of
its theory, namely the political victory of the working class. The
working class *ought* to be driven by class interest; it is thus that
the whole society is to be rescued. If one would conclude from this
premise that the other groups in society are not driven by their class
interest, one would falsify the very core of the Marxist system. This
is precisely the point: everybody is driven by class interest. Class
membership is therefore decisive for everybody. Marxism is a universal interpretation of human history. The premise from which all
Marxist ideas are derived is that all people are determined by their
economic circumstances.

It is the same with the doctrine of creation in Christianity, which
we will call *creation faith*:[1] it is a faith that includes everyone and is
applied to everyone, even atheists and followers of other religions.
God is at work in every childbirth and it is this same God who speaks
through Jesus. God is at work in every community-creating activity
that serves the well-being of people, regardless of who carries out
the activity, and it is the same God whom we praise in the Lord's
Supper. When the statements in the Creed are seen as *Christian*
statements about the *Christian's* God, this aspect of the Creed is
easily obscured. It is even more likely to be the case when one sets
alongside the Christian confession of faith Islamic statements about
the Muslim God or Platonic statements about True Being.

When we are dealing with all human beings as instruments in the
hand of the Creator, as in Christianity, certain considerations enter
in which do not appear when we are dealing with human beings as
determined by their class membership, as in Marxism. If the church
affirms that God works through creation (creation faith), then the
church must acknowledge that something good can come from the
heathen. Marxism, on the contrary, does not surrender any of its
grounds for claiming that the working class has unique responsibility for the whole of society when it grants that class interest is a
universal phenomenon. Indeed, the fact that the bourgeois members
of a society are governed by their class interest makes it all the more
legitimate to overthrow them. They contribute nothing to others, but
only exploit the workers in their need.

We may now understand more clearly why Christianity's belief in creation has become obscured. When one observes the structure of classical Christianity, one quickly realizes that what is believed about creation (first article) makes an impact also on what is believed about the Son (second article) and what is believed about the Spirit (third article). The reverse relationship is also true. The term *creation* comes to mean something new and different when it is filled with content drawn from Jesus' giving of himself on the cross, or when seen from the viewpoint of God's action in *creating* a new person through the gospel. The entire discussion which follows will testify to this inner relationship between the various parts of the Creed.

Other examples could be given of how setting the Creed into the context of debate actually distorts and obscures its content. Creation is not the only place where this happens. What we need to do to correct these distorting effects is to restore the Creed to its proper setting as a part of the worship service. An attempt is made in this book to accomplish this through a pedagogical device which will surely surprise many of the book's readers. The volume has three large sections, corresponding to the three articles of the Creed, and eight chapters. Four of these deal with the second article (about Christ) and two each deal with creation (the Father) and the congregation (the Spirit). These eight chapters conclude with a prayer.

The prayers are regarded as having pedagogical rather than artistic value, but they also serve another function. An essential point in my work, *Change and Continuity*, 1972, was a thesis about the variety of views in the New Testament. If the evangelists Matthew and John had engaged in a debate, they would soon have been at odds with each other in several respects. But there was no such meeting between them. Their two gospels apparently functioned in relation to two different groups of readers (or listeners) until they were brought together in the New Testament canon and began to function together in worship services. That is to say, they came together in exactly that setting which is the proper setting for the Creed. In a comparable way, we must allow the pluralism in Christian faith to remain in the twentieth century, but we can find unity in prayers and hymns.

In the analytic sections of this book, the reader will notice the assertion that two or more positions on some questions of faith are Christian, in spite of the inconsistency between them. That there should be variant positions and interpretations is no more remarkable than that there are four gospels. In the prayer which follows such an analytical section the different positions are freely incorporated. The prayers are intended to demonstrate the unity that prevails in the midst of the pluralism which characterizes the views described in the preceding chapter.

The reader will also observe that there are some positions with respect to the question under review, some formulations of the faith, which cannot be included in the prayer. This, too, is intentional. There are religious beliefs which cannot be included in the worship service; they are shut out by the Creed. The Apostles' Creed would never have come into existence if there had been no Gnostics who rejected creation, the humanity of Jesus, and the body's participation in redemption. We must recognize that there is a "No" in the Creed!

This function that the Creed serves of drawing boundaries and saying "No" is further strengthened and undergirded in our time by the debate setting in which discussion normally occurs, and by the fact of pluralism, and the inevitable comparison of the content of the various views held by the different faiths. When several different formulations of faith are compared with one another, each formulation gets a sharper contour than it would otherwise have. I hope to have occasion in this book to compare Christianity with other beliefs, and thereby also to illustrate the nay-saying element in the Creed. Putting the discussion of the Creed into the modern setting of debate has had two quite different effects. On the one hand, the tendency is to water down the belief in creation, but on the other hand the tendency is to sharpen the profile when it is a question of Christology, or some other doctrine.

I have hesitated about which text of the Creed I should use. Admittedly, the Creed becomes somewhat provincial through this choice of language. But it does not thereby become "confessional" as some have mistakenly argued. If the Lutheran Confessions had actually dominated in Sweden, it would never have occurred to anyone to change the original "resurrection of the body" to "the resurrection of the dead" (as we now say in Swedish not only in the Nicene Creed but also in the Apostles). Many Lutherans in neighboring countries continue to confess their faith in *die Auferstehung des Fleisches,* and in *kødets opstandelse,* while the English and the Americans use "the resurrection of the body" in the Apostles' Creed. These variations are not conditioned by confessional views and do not have any practical significance for the central position of the Creed.[2]

The most troublesome consequence of the choice of the contemporary Swedish text is the loss of the singular pronoun in the case of the Apostles' Creed. We say "We believe," instead of the original "I believe." As a result, the title of the book *Credo,* sort of hangs in the air. But that cannot be helped. In baptism and in the worship service, the confession is designated now as always—Credo (I believe). The plural form is quite recent in Sweden, a product of the nineteenth century. It has not yet intruded itself into the Nicene Creed. Even a modern Swede says "I believe" when reciting the Nicene form. This is somewhat peculiar since when this confession began to be recited by the congregation in the sixth century, it had a plural form as the first word—*credimus*.

To write a book on dogmatics is a task for which I have not been trained. But I have been permitted to live in the same city as Sweden's foremost author of dogmatics textbooks and I have been able to speak with him often. It is a priceless privilege for me to be able to publicly thank Bishop Aulen for this.

The two colleagues with whom I consult the most are the New Testament exegete, Birger Gerhardsson, and the systematic theologian, Per Erik Persson. I have profited much from these conversations. I have also been helped by my good friend Greta Hofsten, who is not afraid of being nonconformist. I thank all three.

With regard to modern philosophy, I am less well read than is the docent in my field. Lars-Olle Armgard and I engaged in a continuous exchange of ideas, and I think that I received more from him than he did from me. The amanuensis at my institution, Lennart Molin, is a constant support to me in all my work, even in the writing of books. He has put together the index and done much more. I am thankful that I can work together with these friends.

Miss Ingrid Lilliehook typed my manuscript. She understands all my corrections—often one correction on top of another, sometimes a third on top of the previous two. I do not know how she does it but I want her to know how much I appreciate her and her work.

GUSTAF WINGREN

THE APOSTLES' CREED

I believe * in God, the Father almighty, maker of heaven and earth:

And in Jesus Christ, his only Son, our Lord: who was conceived by the Holy Spirit, born of the virgin Mary, suffered under Pontius Pilate, was crucified, dead and buried: he descended into hell, the third day he rose from the dead, he ascended into heaven, and is seated on the right hand of God, the Father almighty, whence he shall come to judge the living and the dead.

I believe in the Holy Spirit, the holy Christian church, the communion of saints, the forgiveness of sins, the resurrection of the body,** and the life everlasting. Amen.

(*The Book of Concord*, Tappert, ed. Philadelphia: Fortress, 1959)

---

* The Swedish text reads *We believe.*
** The Swedish text reads *resurrection of the dead.*

THE NICENE CREED

I believe in one God, the Father almighty, maker of heaven and earth and of all things visible and invisible.

And in one Lord Jesus Christ, the only-begotten Son of God, begotten of the Father before all ages, God of God, Light of Light, very God of very God, begotten not made, being of one substance with the Father, through whom all things were made: who for us men and for our salvation came down from heaven, was incarnate by the Holy Spirit of the virgin Mary, and was made man: who for us, too, was crucified under Pontius Pilate, suffered, and was buried: the third day he rose according to the Scriptures, ascended into heaven, and is seated on the right hand of the Father: he shall come again with glory to judge the living and the dead, and his kingdom shall have no end.

And in the Holy Spirit, the lord and giver of life, who proceeds from the Father and the Son: who together with the Father and the Son is worshiped and glorified: who spoke by the prophets.

And I believe one holy, Christian, and apostolic church.

I acknowledge one Baptism for the remission of sins, and I look for the resurrection of the dead and the life of the age to come. Amen.

(*The Book of Concord*, Tappert ed. Philadelphia: Fortress, 1959)

Introduction

THREE ASPECTS OF THE WHOLE— THREE ARTICLES

The three articles do not deal with three separate and distinct subjects. A separation of this sort would imply that everything that can be said about God's creative activity would be said before one had even begun to talk about the work of Christ or about the Spirit. In the same way, if that were the case, nothing could be said about the Spirit until after we had spoken of Christ's death and resurrection. This understanding becomes absurd on the basis of even the most elementary review of the biblical texts.

The Spirit was present in creation (Gen. 1:2) and at decisive moments in Jesus' life, such as when he was baptized in the river Jordan and when he was driven out into the desert to be tempted (Mark 1:12-13). The divine creative power does not cease to be at work when the world has been created but continues to work in Christ—indeed, it is on the cross that "one new man" is created (Eph. 2:15). Every person who is in Christ can consequently be designated "a new creation" (2 Cor. 5:17). To divide up the Christian faith into three parts, with the three articles as dividing lines, is therefore quite impossible.

Instead one could describe the whole of the Christian faith as faith in the Creator. Nothing would fall outside of that. The cross of Christ, baptism, the resurrection of the dead, would all find a place within that whole; all of these are acts of creation which the Father carries out. But one could also call the whole of the Christian faith "believing in Jesus." Also then nothing would fall outside.

The lilies of the field (Matt. 6:28), the miracle of the lame walking and the blind seeing (Matt. 11:2-6), all of these are given a dimension through Christ's activity which from one point of view they have always had, and everywhere have today, but a dimension which from another point of view was first given with Christ's coming. The Son makes new because the Creator dwells in him.

In the same way one could give a complete description of the Christian faith under the single rubric: the Spirit. Also then nothing need be left over. When God sends forth his Spirit, life is created, and then the face of the earth is renewed (Ps. 104:30). The Spirit was at work in the bosom of Mary (Luke 1:35), in Christ's resurrection from the grave (Rom. 8:11), in prayer even when the one who prays does not know how to pray (Rom. 8:26), indeed in everything.

The three articles then show us three aspects of the *whole* Christian faith. This is the chief thesis of this book which is presented under the title of *Credo*. Such a thesis cannot be established until we have gone through the three articles in a definitive fashion—that is, until we come to the close of the final chapter (about eternal life). To present this main thesis in an outline form is the purpose of this introduction, and then to conclude with a few negative demarcations.

The Creator at Work in Everything
(The First Article)

When the first article calls God the "maker of heaven and earth," it is speaking of God as being active in all that is recounted in the entire confession—including the resurrection of the dead and eternal life. Moreover, he is active precisely in his role as Creator. There is a great problem implicit in the fact that the life which is created by God is given without the recipient knowing who the giver of it is. God's creative action is received by us in the same way that a newborn child receives oxygen through breathing. One can breathe without any idea of what breathing is. One lives in a relationship to God without using his name and without using any religious labels.

This flight from religious language has been consciously pursued in our own time. But it has not always been so. When the gospel was proclaimed in missionary sermons around the Mediterranean or up in the North, such words as "Lord" or "Messiah" were substituted for earlier terms which were equally concrete and which had the same religious-historical character—such as Zeus and Odin. Today we almost blush when we hear any direct religious overtones in one's attitude toward existence. This about-face is part of our

heritage from the Enlightenment. The result of this attitude is that
we come to load abstract words such as "life" with the same content
as was previously represented by the term "God."

For instance, when a young person wants to see "what life has to
offer," or an old person talks about "what life gave," they are using
mythical language. There is no "life" which can be regarded as a
subject over against us which is able to give or take. If we speak
thus, we are speaking religiously about God. It was precisely in this
way that, prior to the Enlightenment, prayers were formulated to
be offered to God, complaints directed against him, and praise offered
to him. The term "life" has become acceptable now, after the Enlightenment, because it has never been identified with any specific
religion. This term, "life," has come to describe that reality which
was earlier designated "God" or "the Creator."

Modern culture has practically eliminated concrete religious expressions, but cannot abolish those situations that remind human
beings that they are not lords over what happens. Nor can people
avoid the elemental attitudes of hope and fear. These attitudes are
especially strong when human life is beginning or is under threat—
such as birth, sickness, death, and situations related to these. Even
though the worship service is commonly neglected in our time, those
actions which are tied to the corresponding biological points (baptism, marriage, burial) continue to receive a measure of respect even
from secular people. The reason is that one never stops hoping,
fearing, sorrowing, or being grateful.

In those situations in which the individual is not in charge, and
no one else seems to be either, the fear-hope-gratitude impulse must
direct itself outward toward something that is neither seen nor
heard, toward "life." The post-Christian culture has not been able
to develop any liturgical forms for these inescapable human attitudes, which even in their atheistic formulation remain clearly
mythical and religious. This is the reason that the traditional Christian ceremonies must be used also by the skeptics. It is strange that
the church's theologically-trained representatives seldom see the
theological heart of this matter. The skeptics are preserving an elemental ingredient in the Creed, that is to say, in the church's own
confession.

What the skeptics are preserving is an important aspect of our
creation faith: the realization that life for the human is something
always given and always threatened. Translated into biblical language this implies that the Creator gives, generates, awakens to life;
and that he does this in opposition to that which damages, destroys,
and distorts life.

The New Testament is full of expressions for this belief in creation, expressions which have played a very subordinate role in the proclamation of the church in recent times. Yet the message of Jesus' support for life over against the threat of destruction has a much more central place than the message of his forgiveness in the face of guilt. There is the ability to see (over against blindness), the ability to hear (over against deafness), the ability to move (over against lameness), and the ability to speak (over against dumbness). In the end, God "awakens" Jesus out of the grave, after which the gospels offer new life to all (1 Cor. 4:15; 1 Peter 1:23-25). Despite the fact that the gospel pericopes for more than a thousand years past have been dominated by texts about Jesus as the giver of life, and as the healer, this side of the church's creed has left very little imprint on the church's prayers, hymns, and sermons.

The very center of the gospel—the crucifixion and the resurrection—clearly was interpreted in an anticipatory way by Jesus himself with the help of parallels from God's creativity in nature. Jesus is the grain of wheat which would have remained alone if he had not been willing to die (John 12:24). Now he bears instead "much fruit." The whole of eschatology is a teaching about how the Creator finally conquers—it is "grain-of-wheat eschatology." But this aspect of the belief in creation belongs to the third article.

Humanity Present in Everything (The Second Article)

In dogmatic formulations it is often said that God "has become" human. This could easily be understood in such a way that it would mean that he is not actually human—he temporarily became something opposite of what he is. In the fourth century, which was the great period of dogma construction and which was also a period strongly dominated by Greek philosophy, the idea of God becoming man was certainly regarded as logically absurd—it meant that God had become a corruptible body. It was felt that the gospel's all-embracing miracle should therefore be expressed in a logical contradiction.[1]

The presupposition is that anthropomorphic speech (which refers to God as a person), is an unreal and primitive way of speaking; it is an impossible language with which to give adequate expression to the divine attributes. A biblical person on the other hand, untainted by the fourth century and its philosophy, could undoubtedly assert that anthropomorphic speech is the only intelligent language about God available. To begin with a definition of "God" before saying anything about what God does, reveals not only a lack of understanding of the subject but also a lack of the capacity to understand.

In fact, God's humanity is present in everything that is said about God in the Bible. He wills, he repents and is troubled (Gen. 6:6), he becomes angry, he overlooks our mistakes (Isa. 43:25), he is faithful. When he is unfathomable he is so in the same sense as a great human being may be difficult to comprehend. We may live in the immediate presence of such a person and yet there will remain depths that we cannot penetrate. But we do not say that a person is unfathomable in the same sense that a text in an unknown language or a riddle may be unfathomable. If one comes to understand the language or the riddle it is no longer mysterious or unknown. But famous or important people may become all the more unfathomable the closer we come to them. When we seek to explain such people to others we can only relate event after event, and action after action. The same is true of the Bible; it tells about God. The texts speak about God in an anthropomorphic way: This is the way he is.

When, therefore, it says in the Creed that God has become man in Christ, it does not mean that God has become something foreign or contrary to himself. The statement must rather be understood in light of the word about "the image of God" in the creation account (Gen. 1:26f.). When God wanted to create beings who were like him, he created humans. Other created things serve the humans and maintain human life.

When the creation story, in its own language, says that day and night, earth and sea are given to the human and that something good is thereby happening, the statement does not differ in fact from our modern thesis that the human has "adapted" to the situation encountered in the world. Both propositions mean that the person is not lord, but that one has the possibility of living by virtue of what one receives *from without*. And when the story of the fall into sin, in its own language, portrays death as something which people draw down upon themselves through disobedience, this does not differ substantively from our modern thought concerning human behavior as the greatest threat to humanity's continued existence. Despite the fact that natural catastrophes also threaten us, the really frightening destruction comes from *within*, from the "heart" (cf. Mark 7:15-23).

In the person of Jesus something happens which could be called "the driving out of destruction," [2] or "the driving out of the destroying power." When God becomes a person he becomes a person "in the image of God" that is to say, in one who realizes the intention of creation (Col. 1:15-22). Therefore temptation is necessary.[3] The poisonous tides that have laid waste one's inner life can be driven back only by the one who himself stepped down into devastated humanity, the completely pure one who, standing in the midst of the polluted currents, allowed himself to be besmirched—Jesus on the cross. When Jesus remains unconquered, the "image of God" is realized. This binds together the creation story and the gospel.

What seems incongruous in Greek philosophic terms—that God has become human—in terms of the biblical perspective is not incongruous at all. The human is the image of God; this was the intention of creation. The destruction that takes place in the human heart spoils the person and, at the same time, frustrates God's own plan. When one who is tempted remains pure, then God's innermost will is revealed. Then, for the first time, true and untarnished humanity is revealed as well.

What is incongruous is that God himself wanted to go down into the destruction and risk being besmirched and put to death. This is the incomprehensible miracle. What is foreign and contrary to God is not the human body; that suits him very well. The human is present in all that God does; it has been present from the beginning, from the dawn of creation. But the enemy of the human body—death, destruction, the impurity of the heart—that is something that is foreign to God. But God must enter this foreign territory if he is to drive out that which destroys. The gospel says that this has happened in a definitive manner; that is why it is called "gospel"—good news!

Consequently, the gospel *narrates;* it tells about things that happened on a human plane—about soldiers who throw dice, about crowds that scoff. These are all outward circumstances that tempt him who hangs on the cross. Everything that happens is a test of his heart, and every response from him demonstrates that the heart is holding firm. He conquers that which destroys the image of God in us. We are therefore cleansed in and with his death on the cross. The Easter hymns of the earliest church fathers were hymns about the crucified.

The resurrection means that truly human life on earth is life for others. It has as a direct consequence that messengers are sent out to all people; it expresses itself in baptism and in the Lord's Supper, in ordinary dealings with other people, and finally in the resurrection of the dead. That is to say, it has as its consequence the decisive liberation of human beings from the destroying power that has hindered them from truly living. Thus, God continues also in the third article's redemptive activity to work in such a way that his humanity is present in everything.

Eternal Dominion the Aim in Everything (The Third Article)

That eternal dominion is the final goal of everything, including creation and the work of Jesus, is a relatively uncontested claim. It is the end-point of the third article, and thereby also the end-point of the Creed as whole. The two preceding theses (that everything from beginning to end deals with the work of creation, and that everything from beginning to end reveals the humanity of God) were more controversial.

The Bible uses the word "rule" or "to be king" in a manner which diverges from our usual practice. A king is one who finds himself in the midst of conflict but stands firm and does not yield. It is because he does not yield that he is king. Over against the one who rules, stands the power of the enemy. This is why the bedraggled champion on the cross can be a king. About Christ, it can be said that "he must reign until he has put all his enemies under his feet" (1 Cor. 15:25). We are disposed to reformulate this so that he must first fight and conquer the opposition, then he can rule in the undisturbed calm which follows victory.

This difference between Paul and ourselves may seem small, but it has important consequences in several different areas. In the first place, Paul includes the idea of opposition in his concept of salvation. This extends even to the absence of salvation—that is, to the situation in which one still waits for "him who is to come." In the second place, the elimination of the opposition, or the enemy, is the central feature of the goal the Creator is trying to reach. This implies that it is not the construction of a new order, or an eternal system of rules which is the goal, but rather the opposite and typically biblical goal of *freedom*. The goal is the creature's freedom to be one's self, to be a created being who thanks and praises God, whose life is a song of praise.

The aim in all that God does, even that which to our eyes does not seem to have the slightest hint of lordship or kingliness, is the striking down of the enemy who is hostile to creation and hostile to God. This is the victory God seeks. The gospel of John speaks about Jesus being "lifted up," and this expression is full of conscious double-meanings; it keeps before us the fact that Jesus becomes king at the same time that he is being lifted up on the cross, that is, in his humiliation (John 3:14, 8:28, and finally 12:32, where a direct clarification of the expression is given). Therefore also the Holy Spirit works in the Christian life through anxiety, sighing, and uncertainty (Rom. 8:26). Those who constantly bear witness to their victories and never to any unresolved difficulties are apparently far removed from the Spirit. Also, in the present, the kingly dominion is a bedraggled and imperiled dominion.

Such a concept as "the law" receives its particular coloration from this general setting. The law acknowledges God's will and is pure and holy (Rom. 7:12), but the point of the law is that it addresses those who need to hear the law. It is addressed to those who harbor opposition to God. That is why it does not seem natural to the biblical writings to describe eternal life in heaven as conformity with the law. Eternal life is liberation from God's enemy (which is also the enemy of creation). That is why, rather, eternal life is described as a song of praise, of which the book of Revelation gives many examples. The turmoil has ended forever—that is the basic note in everything that is said.

And this removal of the turmoil is the goal of everything that precedes eternal life. Paul is very clear in his terminology on this point. He rejects as a general rule every formulation that could be interpreted as pointing toward an imminent and eternal dominion of law. For instance, after he has counted up all the ethically good things that a Christian does (or should do), and when one would expect a positive statement about all these good acts as comprising obedience to God, comes this surprisingly negative twist: "*Against such there is no law*" (Gal. 5:23). The same peculiar twist can also take the following form, "Love does no wrong to a neighbor; therefor love is the fulfilling of the law" (Rom. 13:10). The image is this: One sees a law, an accuser, that stands up to say something—but is silenced by "the fruits of the Spirit." The law is silenced when it no longer encounters opposition. Therefore the law is silenced in heaven.

The three articles are thus three aspects of the whole. Everything is faith in the Creator, in Christ, in the Spirit. But we must note that regardless of which article we take as our starting point—the first, the second, or the third—in each case we come to something which is not directly named in the Creed: the opposition, the enemy, the destroying force, that which threatens life. It may not be strange that this receives no separate consideration in the Creed. To keep silent in this way about that which strikes down, not to give a separate section of the text to the description of the enemy, is characteristic of a song of praise which is what the Creed is. The three articles in the Creed thank God for his deeds, but they only presuppose the enemy, without devoting to the enemy any article of its own.

GOD'S ACTIVITY ENCOUNTERS OPPOSITION

In a contemporary analysis of the Christian faith, the opposition needs to be made a separate theme and given its own rubric. In many other modern views of life there is no conceptual language for talking about a permanent life-destroying force. On the theoretical side this leads to systems of thought in which the morally objectionable is attributed to lack of insight, lack of intelligence, etc. Among the masses one finds local variations of the ancient representations of the devil. Stalin, Hitler, or Nixon can serve as substitutes for the permanent destroyer of life which is active in all of us, collectively and individually. We seem to imply that if only this or that tyrant were done away with, there would be nothing seriously wrong anymore.

The ancient church fathers, who were not only competent exegetes but also sound psychologists, knew better. Original sin, for them, meant envy. They could imagine nothing less creative or more contrary to giving than envy. Compared to envy even killing someone is a relatively positive and innocent action! It may be that the one I kill is perpetrating evil and that I am protecting life. But to be envious, to see something good happen to another and to react negatively only because it did not happen to me—this is sheer destructiveness. It is displeasure in the presence of the one who gives, and therefore it is enmity against the Creator.

Envy is universally human; it is found in the hearts of all of us. It is already present in the small child, even before aggressiveness appears. That the destroying force rules from the very beginning of our lives, that this destructiveness is to be found in the source of everything human, and that it cannot be rooted out through any effort or decision of our own—this is expressed, according to the church fathers, through the biblical story of the serpent (Gen. 3:1-15; cf. Rev. 12:9; 20:2). Envy simply is there. That is a naked fact—like saying that life is there. But these two naked "givens," although they are alike in being original phenomena, are totally unlike in their structure. Envy corrodes and eats away at life. Envy cannot exist unless the good is already present.

Let us visualize two different types of people. On the one hand, imagine someone who continuously gives and shares—one might call that person a sovereign waster. On the other hand, imagine someone who is envious and self-centered—a miserly, joy-killing individual. This is the way the early church fathers pictured God and Satan.[4] Viewed in this way, it must be clear that the superiority in the struggle can never, even for a single moment, rest with anyone else than the one who gives. The one who is driven by envy is subordinated by the very nature of that envy. Such a person must wait for the good and then react negatively to it. One who is envious cannot independently create anything.

There are two things that are important for our understanding of the Creed. The first is that Christ, or the Son, stands entirely on the "giver side," or "the creator side." He forgives sins, he heals the sick, he establishes fellowship. His whole existence has as its reason for being to "make the earth be filled with joy," as Luther formulates it. The second is that among us humans, without exception, the web of envy remains until death. Our personal history (which in its negative aspects is recounted in Genesis inasmuch as Adam is each newborn child) is not located in the second article but in the third— "the forgiveness of sins, the resurrection of the body . . ." [5] These are the positive stations on the road to a liberated humanity. It is when the Spirit is spoken of that we are being talked about.

The opposition is presupposed as self-evident in both the article about Christ and the article about the Spirit. He who would save humankind must go down into the abyss. This is made clear by the participial forms: suffered, crucified, dead, buried. Those to be saved, sit bound in their prison. That is contained in the substantives: forgiveness of sins, resurrection from death.

What we have here called "the opposition" corrodes, eats away, and destroys, and thus in a sense "lives off" the created. Therefore the work of the Creator is always primary and the opposition is always secondary. In the first article—i.e., in the first divine action—there is only God, there is not yet any opposition. This is a remarkable fact. In the foremost Oriental creation myths, the world came to be as a result of the conflict between the creator God and the powers of chaos. But the Bible mentions no enemies of God at the beginning. There was only "darkness" and "the deep" (Gen. 1:2). For the biblical writers the nature of the enemy is that which destroys, namely envy. The enemy, therefore, cannot exist before the Creator.[6]

K. E. Løgstrup has attempted to clarify what this biblical view of life implies through a phenomenological analysis of the human situation. He reasons this way: If God is at work as Creator, and if the destroying power is the enemy of God everywhere in all human life, it should be possible to observe and to describe these two activities without using the terms "God" and "the devil."

What are traditionally called actions of the Creator, are by Løgstrup called "spontaneous expressions (or manifestations) of life." What are traditionally called actions of the devil, are described as "confining expressions (or manifestations) of life." The "spontane-

ous" expressions are sometimes called "sovereign" and the "confining" are sometimes said to be "locked-in."

The most important aspect of a spontaneous expression of life is
that it is given and definitive. Love, as an example of such spontaneous expressions, cannot be used for anything base or unloving. Love
wells up within the individual; it takes hold of the person—that is
all. If it is calculating, it disappears. If one tries to use it for some
unloving purpose, love is destroyed. The same thing applies to sincerity. A person cannot be 80% or 90% sincere. To the extent that
we make reservations, we are insincere. Spontaneous sincerity is
whole, decisive, and cannot be used for calculated ends.

The confining or locked-in expressions of life, on the other hand,
do not go out from the individual and are not fulfilled in human fellowship. Hate, mistrust, and envy are always unfulfilled. They are
like caged birds that fly up toward the grating above them, flap their
wings, and then fall back to the floor of the cage, always securely
locked in. Hate and envy are reactions to something which was there
before them; they are by nature secondary phenomena, parasites on
something stronger. While the spontaneous expressions of life create
something new and give the environment a new start and new possibilities for life, the confining, locked-in expressions of life are destructive. They lock up and destroy the new beginnings.

If one now reflects on the fact that everyone harbors envy, the seed
of destruction, within themselves, it is a real mystery that life continues. One would expect life simply to die out. There is no other
explanation for the continuation of life than those spontaneous expressions of life—love, giving, the willingness to die for the young
to whom we give birth. (The human is in this respect like other
created beings.) This is the background for Løgstrup's designation
of the spontaneous expressions of life as "sovereign." They are
threatened by destruction but they are not conquered. After each
onset of hatred, lovers smile at one another, children play, lives are
built up—they are sovereign.

A common attitude today is to be astonished at the evil in the
world and, in view of it, to doubt God's existence. Using Løgstrup's
analysis, one could instead argue that the sovereignty of the spontaneous expressions of life—their unconquerable character—is the
great miracle, and that in view of this inexplicable sovereignty there
is no other human attitude so natural and self-evident as faith
in God.

The early church, which stood closest to the events of the second
article, and which considered martyrdom to be a noble ending for
life, freely took nature's own phenomena as illustrations of the

crucifixion and the resurrection. The grain of wheat dies in the earth, but it triumphs in uninterrupted harvests; the pelican tears up its own breast with its beak and dies unconquered (sovereignly) when the young drink its blood. If one wishes to use Løgstrup's terminology, one can say that the phenomenon, Jesus, is an unheard of "spontaneous expression of life"—whole, decisive, sovereign, fulfilled, "the only completely healthy and harmonious human in history." [7]

Finally it must be emphasized that with respect to the opposition between the creative "givens" and the destroying forces, we cannot move beyond the realm of *faith*. This is true from the simplest everyday situation all the way to the gospel's most offensive message—the cross. At no point do we have access to any proof. False giving, that is giving with calculation (which in reality is taking rather than giving) might seem to all outward appearances, exactly like spontaneous and genuine giving. Even one without love can give one's body to be burned (1 Cor. 13:3).

THE HAZARD FOR DOCTRINE: THEORIZING

The lack of certainty, which results from a lack of evidence, has been the constant companion and tempter in the formation of Christian dogma. Much of the actual theological production in the history of the church consists of attempts to remedy this lack of certainty. That is why the original documents of faith continue to have such surprising freshness for each new generation. One side of this tendency to seek greater certainty can be described as *theorizing*.

There are two kinds of theorizing that call for our attention in this introduction. The first consists of putting the term "revelation" in the center. This term is found in the Bible but it is not the central concept under which everything else is placed. The other form of theorizing asserts that the formation of the biblical books guarantees that everything in the books is true.

These two approaches are often tied together. Both are characterized by a tendency to confine God's activity to a limited segment of history, and by an inclination toward nihilism in the evaluation of human life outside that limited piece of history. The divine contribution to human salvation is, in both cases, thought of in terms of *knowing*. In neither of these lines of thought would one have perceived that the grain of wheat in the earth, or the pelican with its young, are parallels to Christ. Exponents of these theories may accept similar parallels from nature as a part of the churchly tra-

dition, but the examples seem to them to be singularly irrelevant—
the pelican and the grain do not know what salvation is. These
unthinking creatures represent life, to be sure, even life from death.
But it is not life that we are concerned about, is it? Salvation is
knowledge—that is what is assumed.

Yes, to be sure, to "know" God, that is salvation or eternal life,
as is said in the gospel of John (17:3). But then we must remember
that the verb "know" in the biblical tradition can also be used in
a sexual sense. When a man has intercourse with his wife, then he
"knows" his wife (Gen. 4:1). And it doesn't matter that the grain
doesn't know very much when it falls to the ground, but in its dying
it represents more faith than the human is able to call forth; "If you
had faith as a grain of mustard seed, you could say . . . ." (Luke
17:6). In our European tradition, which is determined by the need
to theorize about matters, to have knowledge of God and to have
faith have been uncoupled from those acts where living beings in
their surrender and giving of themselves participate in God's work
as Creator.

For this reason we must in a preliminary way take a critical view
of theorizing. By doing so we will come closer to the basis of the
Creed, the biblical starting point. It will serve our purpose best to
begin with the dislocation in the concept of revelation, and then
take up the theory concerning biblical authority.

The View That the Concept of Revelation Is Dominant Is a Misconception

The biblical verb "reveal" means "unveil." The assumption is that
something has long existed but has been overshadowed or hidden.
What becomes visible, unveiled, and now fully observable, can be
different entities. Generally it is the plan of salvation (Titus 1:3;
Rom. 1:17; Col. 1:26), but it can also be wrath (Rom. 1:18), or the
justice in God's judgment (Rom. 2:5). The stereotyped formulation
that "God has revealed himself in Christ" is, on the other hand,
quite modern. It builds on the presupposition, which became increasingly common after the Enlightenment, that God's existence is im-
probable and without support in our existence. Out of a long line of
human existences which fail to make God's existence probable, one
human life is isolated and declared to be the only one that makes it
believable that God exists. That which does not appear to be plausible
in view of ordinary human life becomes plausible in the light of the
picture of Jesus.

It is a fact that the words "God's revelation in Christ" do not constitute the organizing principle in the New Testament, nor is it the principle that determines attitudes within the New Testament. It is also a fact that the sixteenth-century Reformation, in all its varied trends, ran its course without this term becoming a rubric for the designation of the gospel. In the light of this, we must conclude that the self-evident domination of this term in recent theology is connected with the fact that the entity "God" has generally become problematic. But this also means that the term "revelation" has been slanted in a manner which is entirely foreign both to the biblical texts and to the tripartite Creed. It assumes that within a limited and enclosed segment of history a knowledge of God has been given. All around that fragment there is emptiness—the absence of all knowledge of God.

There are two important differences between this way of thinking and the early church's view of life. First, that which God does in Christ is now thought of more theoretically than was the case in earlier times. One does not think any more that in the death and resurrection of Jesus God is lifting humanity out of death into life, out of bondage into freedom. Instead, the chief aspect has now become the contribution of supernatural knowledge from God to us by way of Christ. The other difference is that the view of ordinary human life is now more nihilistic than it was in the early church. One is born, eats, drinks, accepts the day and the night, but meets no God, only "life" as it is now called.

But whoever talks about what we can expect from life (or what life gives, etc.), is clearly speaking mythical language. Since the Enlightenment, the term "life" has come to cover a territory which in former times was called "God." When one nihilistically empties common human occurrences of all divine activity, and then confines God's revelatory contribution solely to Christ, one is following the same interpretation of existence as the Gnostics in the second century. *It was against this view of life that the Apostles' Creed with its three parts was constructed.* We can sum up Marcion's theology in this thesis "God has revealed himself in Christ and nowhere else." That the church fathers viewed this theology as a greater threat to faith than atheism, testifies to their good judgment.

Even now, in the twentieth century, this view of creation is fatal to faith. Very often in our everyday life, especially in times of testing, trust and confidence are arrayed against mistrust. This confidence is in reality faith in the Creator, but from the viewpoint of the narrow concept of revelation it cannot be interpreted as such. If a person rides out the storm without having had Jesus consciously in mind, this appears to be—from the viewpoint of this cramped concept of revelation—not something positive but rather as something one should be disturbed about. Faith in its fullness seems to be threatened by such happenings. When "faith in its fullness" is presented, it is presented as a package of statements which often collide with the human intellect.

The effect of this is that faith is put to death. Those strands of faith which were alive in the everyday situation, under attack from mistrust—that is from the destructive power—are not regarded as faith but are downgraded as "outward optimism" or something of the sort. But as a matter of fact, this web of faith, this elemental courage, is a form of life that is supported by the second article (about Christ) and by the third article (about the Spirit).

To bring an end to this theorizing and to return the Christian faith to the human situations where it is at home, may well be the most important task for contemporary theology.[8] The task cannot be accomplished without a conscious rehabilitation of the naive, anthropomorphic language which is faith's natural form of expression. Just as two lovers, even though they understand anatomy, can talk about the "heart" in a less than scientific manner, so faith has the right to use language which may be considered dubious from a scientific point of view.

It is in part the fault of scientific language in contemporary theology that the Christian faith finds it difficult to free itself from theorizing, even in practical matters and in worship. Any presentation of the Creed that did not include naive and anthropomorphic speech would be a flawed presentation.

The View That the Authority of Scripture Is Dominant Is a Misconception

Among the indispensable elements in the Christian faith is the conviction that God has concentrated his activity in certain times, persons, and places. Israel has a different position in God's plan than all other people—the person of Jesus is unique. These statements can, of course, be disputed without depriving us of our religion. But it would be difficult to apply the name "Christianity" to such a religion.

Such a conviction does not offer any greater offense to the intellect than does the thesis that the sun is the entirely unique source of our biological life on earth. But it is perceived as a greater offense. For one thing, all evidence is lacking (which is not the case with the sun). Furthermore, the thesis concerning the unique position of Israel and of Jesus negates a whole list of positive theses concerning our ability to save ourselves.

Since God's activity according to the Christian faith is concentrated in the Old and the New Testaments, these two books have come to have a central place in worship and instruction throughout Christian history. These two testaments bear witness concerning God's activity in Israel and through Jesus. Throughout the centuries, Christian worship has been based on texts from these two testaments. All other texts are secondary and subordinate.

Because one cannot now prove that these biblical texts deserve the central place which they have attained, there is an inclination to justify their distinctive role with *theories about how they came into existence.* Several different theories of verbal inspiration had been constructed to serve this purpose already in Old Testament times; there are traces of it also in the New Testament (2 Peter 1:21). In and of themselves these theories are no more offensive to the intellect than is faith in Jesus. If one believes (without proof) that God has acted through Jesus in a unique way, one can of course also believe that a certain holy book has come into existence in an entirely different manner from all other books.

But when one pushes forward the idea of the authority of the Bible and makes it the fundamental position, certain peculiar distortions occur. We confront here a variation of the concept of revelation discussed above and we meet again the same features as before.

In the first place, the way Scripture came into existence was never preached as gospel in the original Christian period (Christ was), and it never received a separate article in the Creed (as Christ did). In the second place, a person or an event can be unique in many different ways. A person can be the only one who liberates from slavery, the only one who heals the sick, etc. But the coming into existence of a book is unique in a specific way—that which is written in it is a unique revelation, a unique insight, a unique knowledge. When one concentrates on the book, the tendency to theorize is already given. In the third place, the kind of nihilism we observed before is strengthened by the emphasis on the book. The more empty I am, the more I prize the unique book.

It needs to be underscored that one can assert that something "saving" is unique without holding to this kind of emptiness with reference to one's self or other values. Even if healing is available at only one place for my sickness, I can prize highly the unique healer and at the same time hold in high regard the good health which I had before I became sick. The created being is good in itself; there-

34   INTRODUCTION

fore the healer who restores me to health is also good, uniquely good. When the revelation contained in a book stands at the center, on the other hand, the temptation is great to combine the uniqueness of the book with emptiness on the human side.

We know now through historical biblical research that the biblical writings came into existence in much the same way as did literature in general. The composition of various segments, variations in the textual traditions, contradictions between different parts of the text —all of this we have become accustomed to in the history of literature. In other words, if these texts witness at all about God, they witness to the fact that God has become *human*. That is what the Creed says about God.

Therefore, it is critical biblical research which has liberated the gospel. Sometimes people talk about this kind of research complainingly, as though we can live with it only because it speaks the truth. They seem to imply that it would actually have been easier to believe if we could have retained our theories of inspiration undisturbed. Among those who have seen the direct positive value of critical exegesis as a support for the purity of faith are Einar Billing (in Sweden before the First World War) and Gerhard Ebeling (on the continent after the Second World War). Both make the same point in their argumentation: the faith that is preserved when one sets aside biblical criticism is different from faith in *the gospel*.[9]

The historically-informed exegete leads us back to certain events, with Israel and Jesus at the center, and places us in the same situation as the earliest Christians. We are thus able to share their situation with them. The contemporary circumstances are also like the original in that several different interpretations of the event are possible and legitimate from a Christian point of view. The multiplicity of interpretations is not a problem for faith if it is the event itself on which faith lives (rather than some particular theory about it). But when it is the supernaturally produced Bible which is the object of faith, the multiplicity of interpretations must be suppressed.

The frequent attempts to eliminate the contradictions among the four Gospels are typical. None of these four writings has any other center than the death and resurrection of Christ. Everywhere it is presupposed that Christ—the one and only, the first-fruits—has gone through what no one else has gone through. Even a cursory reflection on the procedure involved in "proving" something, makes it clear that those events of which the narrative concerning Jesus consists cannot be the object of proof. Rather, it is a message aimed at a listener and requires a yes or a no.

If faith embraced the same central reality as this message (and which is also the center of the Creed), the question of the sequence of events in Jesus' life, and the question about the remaining discrepancies between the four Gospels would never have arisen. When one constantly returns to these discrepancies and wants to eliminate them through the most transparent efforts at harmonizing, this demonstrates that the object of one's faith is something other than that which the gospels and the Creed present. For those people the object of faith must clearly be a book—precisely the inerrancy found in a book.

But this is not a true picture of faith. It is a picture of a lawyer (the creature) who has undertaken to defend a client (the Creator). This is backwards. The roles are reversed. The creature is engaged in propping up God! But surely, it is not God who needs propping up.

The First Article
The Father

Creation and Law

Then Jacob asked him, "Tell me, I pray, your name." But he said, "Why is it that you ask my name?" And there he blessed him.

(Gen. 32:29)

You believe that God is one; you do well. Even the demons believe—and shudder.

(Jas. 2:19)

I

Creation

CREATION IS HAPPENING NOW

The question about Adam belongs to the controversies within biblical theology. The word is Hebrew and means "man." But unlike the Swedish language, the word cannot be found in the plural. It corresponds therefore most nearly to "humanity." In Swedish we have further complicated our understanding of the word "Adam" by making it a personal name and placing it in our calendar (Dec. 23 is the "name-day" for Adam). No Old Testament person is called "Adam," just as we do not baptize a child as "Man."

Adam becomes controversial for biblical theology because we lose something when we understand the account in Genesis as a story that is *only* about us. That the essential point of the biblical text is broader than that is entirely clear. But through the description of how Adam was created and fell, the narrator is also painting our present situation. He depicts our life as a life that is given to us, and in which the forces of destruction immediately take hold.

But still, one loses something essential when this event takes place only in each individual—each Adam who is now alive. Adam needs to be a person in the procession of the generations, just as Jesus is a person in the succession of the human family (cf. Rom. 5:12).

We will return to this problem later on. For the present we will content ourselves with something which is not controversial. The essential point in Genesis is: Adam is "we," "I." This point is underscored by a whole series of Old Testament texts in which it is implied that God is creating *now* in every birth, every emergence of life

(Job 10:9; 33:6; Ps. 104:30). In Amos and Isaiah there are a number of similar expressions. Luther is one of those who have most clearly understood this biblical emphasis. When in the Small Catechism he wants to set forth what "maker of heaven and earth" means, he points directly to the fact that he (Luther) *is himself alive*, with "all my limbs and senses, my reason and all the faculties of my mind."

To Live Is to Be in Relationship to God

The relationship to God which is given in existence does not mean salvation, because the individual is at the same time a prisoner of the forces of destruction. But the human activities which mark one's day-to-day existence are at the same time vehicles for God's creative activity, even though they are human and therefore imply human effort. When we humans survey our whole situation, including that which we have not gained through our own efforts but have *received* at birth and every day, then we stand at the very boundary of our existence, and therefore we also stand in the presence of God. What is added when one describes all of this in religious language is the word "God." But even without that word, we were already standing in the presence of God, without using God's name.

However the story of Jacob's wrestling at the ford of the Jabbok is to be understood (Gen. 32:22-32), it certainly means that one can wrestle with God without knowing his name, and one can be blessed by God without knowing the One who gives the blessing. Those speeches in the book of Acts addressed to the Gentiles (i.e., to persons who were not acquainted with Israel's texts) show the same direct anchoring of human existence in the Creator, in him "who gives to all men life and breath and everything" (Acts 17:25; also 14:15-17).

When Christians today speak of life as a gift, their statements are often quite different than was the case in earlier times, and a good deal less generous in acknowledging God's universal goodness. Paul even includes Christ and the gospel with which he has been sent out, as part of God's general benevolence. God has already given; now he would give even more. As human we are already a part of creation, whether we designate ourselves with the term "creation" or not. The best thing that we can do as a part of creation is to receive and to give to others, in fellowship with others, rejoicing in what has been given to us. It is possible that we can have such an attitude toward all that happens without specifically articulating in words or in feeling any awareness that we do in fact live in *God*.

Atheism in modern culture constitutes a hazard for the Christian congregation because the church's proclamation can so easily be distorted into a concern that the word "God" be articulated in every possible relationship. Some Christians resent that the atheist lives in the midst of God's blessings without acknowledging them. But to insist on the acknowledgment of God in every manifestation of life may mean that these events are deprived of their immediacy. God intends that such immediacy should exist between his human creation and himself, and it does exist between him and the rest of nature —the lilies of the field, the birds of the air. These are examples of the right attitude toward life in the Sermon on the Mount (Matt. 6:26-28). It is in this sense of immediacy that we humans should live; it is thus that we follow the Creator's will.

The limitations the church has placed on God's activity, and the grudging attitude it has taken toward what is universally human has been unchallenged so long that among many moderns the very word "God" awakens an uneasiness. They expect that anyone who appeals to this word intends to tighten the screws on ongoing human activity, to deprive human life of some of its freedom. But the first article of the Creed turns upside down our idea about God wanting to be "acknowledged." It is not primarily a matter of those outside the Christian congregation allowing a place for the word "God" with reference to their expressions of life as often as possible. Instead, the primary concern is that the congregation that knows God in the Creed recognize that *God is larger than the congregation* —that it recognize God's presence at those points in human life where the church is not.[1]

That is the way the Creed functioned in the beginning. This is especially true as far as The Apostles' Creed is concerned. The Gnostics who denied creation, were not outside the congregations but ravaged them from within. (Many claim that the Gnostics in the second century constituted the majority in the church.) In this sense, the construction of the confession of faith was a critique of the church. Paradoxically, it cleared out of the church many who spoke very positively about Jesus—"Jesus only." We are in a similar position today, in the twentieth century. The first article must be directed critically against religious people, people active in our various communions. The point which must be made is that God gives gifts both in nature and through the work of others outside of Christ's congregation, and these gifts come without the instrument of God knowing that it is God's instrument!

Creation faith implies a positive evaluation of what in many religions is evaluated negatively: the material, the body, striving to maintain the outward life. This is especially true of Indian religions. For Buddha, "the thirst for life" is evil; extinguishing it and gaining freedom from karma, "the chain of deeds," is salvation. In sharp contrast, the Bible is filled with joy over human activity. This reflects the conviction that God is active both in the creation of the world and in the events of history (such as the liberation out of Egypt and out of Babylon). The contrast between Christianity and the world view of the Greek philosophers is equally marked. For the latter, the world of senses and of change is lower in the scale than true Being. According to the Christian faith, the Creator is at work precisely in change.

The dissimilarity over against Marxism is just as striking. Marx has certainly turned many biblical features to his own account, by way of the secular Jewish tradition. But for Marx, the individual as worker is the creator; there is no Creator over the worker. This position has two consequences: a very dark view of the situation in which the working class is exploited by the self-interest of private capitalism, and a very bright view of the situation in which the exploitation has been broken through revolution.

The Christian faith proceeds from belief in a sovereign Creator who upholds the world in spite of the destructive forces at work in it, and who compels selfishness to be selfish under conditions that yield mutual service. Giving is such a sovereign fact about existence that the egotist cannot find effective ways of being self-centered without accepting a model which is shaped by giving. The egotist must, for instance, provide goods and services other people need. The egotist does not, of course, become any better on that account, but remains in the position of a subordinate. It is the Giver who determines the action of the egotist and who retains that dominion even in the midst of the ongoing destruction. This will continue to be the case, since we will never reach a point where the forces of destruction are completely overcome within the bounds of history and social development.

Hope Is Prayer

To hope for something is to be stretching toward what one has not yet reached. Hope implies that one believes that the course of events in the future will bring that for which one hopes.

Prayer is regarded as something quite different. It is assumed that certain representations about God are to be found in the psyche of the pray-er, and that when one prays, words and sentences are addressed to God. Unless these are present, there can be no prayer.

In other respects prayer can have the same factual content as hope. It is directed forward to something which is not yet achieved, and it implies an expectation and a desire that the future might give that for which one prays. The liturgical shrinkage of prayer so that it consists of just those limited activities described above implies that prayer must somehow become visible; one looks for external signs that it is taking place. One factor which belongs to prayer according to Jesus' teaching, namely, the complete confidence that prayers will be heard (Matt. 21:22), can easily be stifled when it is felt that prayer has to be visible.

When one hopes in a general way, without expecting help from any particular person, one may say, "In some way it will happen, I am sure of it"—then the person who hopes is surveying the whole situation without seeing any way out of it. One is then standing at the boundary of one's own existence, and therefore really standing before God. This hope is prayer, even when the person does not call it prayer. It is indeed possible that if we have always had prayer liturgically limited to certain circumscribed acts, we may find ourselves with a split in our psyche: on the one hand we are inspired by hope, confidence, and trust in the future, and on the other hand, we automatically recite prayers as a ritual because we want to "keep our prayer life in order." Such people probably pray most intensely when they are not reciting prayers.

Here also the gospel picture of Jesus as the healer is illuminating. There is no special religious content in those appeals that come to Jesus—Give me my sight! Let me be well! These appeals could have been directed to people other than Jesus. They are wholly anchored in the need of the one who cries out. And yet, in no other texts are we so often told that Jesus "finds faith" in people. Faith is grounded in the purely human existence of the one who prays, and in one's openness toward the future (Mark 9:23f.; 5:34, 36; 2:5; Matt. 8:10; 15:28). Faith is not dependent on the pray-er's having participated in the revelation to Israel or in the apostle's instruction. On the contrary, the Gentiles are examples for the people of God in this form of "faith."

The two stories about the Canaanite woman and the Roman officer witness to this especially (Matt. 15:21, cf. 8:5-13). These two texts are also illuminating in that they show that "love to the neighbor" is independent of any theoretical insight into the biblical revelation. Both of these Gentiles come to Jesus with the purpose of finding health and healing for someone other than themselves—the officer for his servant, the woman for her daughter. The feeling of solidarity with those in need is something which is given in human existence as such. Mercy is, to use the language of Løgstrup, a "spontaneous expression of life" which takes possession of a person. That person has to make an effort to shake it off (something which both Gentiles and Christians sometimes succeed in doing, the former without revelation, the latter in spite of it).

Hope and openness toward the future has become a main theme in our time, in a new and surprising way, especially in the dialogues between Marxists and Christians. Almost always it is accompanied by a strong criticism of the belief in creation. Hope reaches forward toward something entirely new, which has not the slightest anchorage in the past.[2] But it remains a fact that when people hope, they feel that they have lost something which they need to get back. Hoping includes a memory of wholeness and of lost roots. Therefore it is typical that so many of the accounts of Jesus as Savior in the gospels are about sick people who received their health again—people who in their appeal for help already knew what they were lacking.

Why is it that modern theology is afraid to talk about our origin in creation, and about the need to restore a damaged creation? Presumably because the terms "creation" and "nature" have long since been filled with unbiblical content. Nature is understood to be the completed product of a finished act of creation, an established and unchangeable "order." God is thought of as having been alone at the beginning, but he is alone no longer. To return to the pure source would in that case be to return to motionlessness—to the death of the status quo. The well-documented predilection of church organizations for static communities seems to be fully grounded in the belief in creation. If one wants instead to have openness toward the future, one flies away from the vocabulary of the first article into "the theology of hope."

Hope itself becomes thereby—paradoxically enough—nihilistic, without content, utopian. In addition, one loses the possibility of interpreting the good actions of persons outside the Christian congregation from the point in the Creed where they actually allow themselves to be interpreted, namely, creation faith.

Two things are important when we speak of faith in the Creator. The first is that God's creation cannot be a finished and completed product, because God is creating *now*. To talk about creation as finished is inconsistent with talking about the *living* God. The second thing is that God's creation cannot be a finished and completed product because God's work is being destroyed. The fact of destruction implies that even what is good can be used in such a way that evil will result. Consider, for example, God's good gift of intelligence; it would not be easy to find something that has brought about as much damage as intelligence. That is why the Creator must "constantly make new."

What we mean by "destruction" now requires its own analysis.

DESTRUCTION IS HAPPENING NOW

According to the Creed, God's most sovereign, free, independent, act of "new creation" is Christ's death and resurrection. One can see how enduring is the role of evil in existence if one contemplates the evil which remains unconquered there. In the account of Good Friday and Easter, Peter's denial represents the possibility that God can bring back the lost person. Judas Iscariot, "the man of perdition" (John 17:12), shows that there is room for the destructive forces to work even in the definitive salvation-deed. Also in the future, at the eschatological fulfillment, there will be a "man of perdition" (2 Thess. 2:3) working still (the same Greek expression is used in both cases.) [3]

This Destruction Cannot Be Terminated During the Course of History

Perhaps no biblical idea is as foreign to our cultural climate as the thought of permanent and invincible evil. This may be true in part because of the influence from world views and world religions in which evil is relatively trivialized, or is localized in concrete forms of power (as in the case in Platonism, Indian Religion, and Marxism). But such influence is not the only source of our feeling of strangeness at the thought of never-ending evil. Many other interesting and captivating elements in these religions pass us by without exercising any notable influence upon us—at least they do not take root in our culture.

If we were to take seriously the thought that destruction of life will persist regardless of what we do, we might despair, and cripple both ourselves and our society. Moreover, we have an inner need, today as always, to place the evil outside of ourselves, among "the others." And it is easier today than ever before to find someone else to blame—with competition, special interest groups, etc. Finally, much so-called Christian preaching has watered down the concept of sin and has turned evil into individual qualities that can be worked off if the person is serious enough to do it. Even those who acknowledge that there is something permanently evil in the world are reluctant to identify it with what Christians used to call "sin."

All of these factors, and several others, work together to make us allergic to the very idea of an invincible and permanent destructive force at work in all that we do. It is significant, for instance, how we explain asocial attitudes in children and youth. Parents and the grown-up culture are regarded as the causes, and the explanation, for their unfortunate behavior. To be fair, this should lead to excusing the parents, since they too were the victims of a harmful milieu, which in its turn was affected by an even earlier generation's mishandling of its youth, and so on back to the beginning. But for some reason we do not argue that way; we stop with the misbehavior of the children now living because we believe that we can break the chain through *social measures*.

The next generation must not have this unwholesome and adverse starting point which drives them toward asocial activity. We do not want to have to "understand" others forever, generation after generation. Instead, we want to change the conditions under which future persons begin their life's journey. But the Bible has a different point of view. It says that we are all "in Adam." I am more than myself. In me all past generations are at work; I take over the stored-up destructiveness of the race before I make any decision with regard to my own activity. I cannot break that chain through any measure that I may devise.

Here is the point at which it becomes very clear that if one just identifies Adam with each existing person something essential is lost. There is a kind of nihilism at this point in modern theology. Everything that is past is telescoped into the present—into ourselves. "Adam" is just my own old self, which I leave behind in the act of decision. "Christ" is in the same way my own true self, as I press forward in the act of decision. It is typical of contemporary existentialist theology that if someone raises the question whether Jesus ever existed, it is apt to be regarded as an uninteresting problem. Jesus does not need to have existed. Adam doesn't need to have existed. I exist, standing at the point of choosing between the old and the new, that is all.

Oscar Cullmann built up his whole scholarly production against this sort of existentialism. Everyone who "rides a thesis" runs a risk, and so does Cullmann. He has the contrary tendency to spread the biblical facts out along a time-line, separated from us and with no direct function in our own existence. It is characteristic that he has most energetically asserted that Adam represents an "origin-event" in history, and not just a condition in ourselves.[4] That Adam means "I" and that Adam is "another than I," these are two interpretations of the creation story which must stand alongside one another. One cannot claim that one or the other is "wrong."

In what follows we will meet examples of pluralism in the interpretation of the Christian faith. On the point where we are now focusing our attention—the inescapability of evil—the parallel between evil and death is revealing. The cleavage between what is said by the biblical texts and by our contemporary culture is even clearer. How can it be that we keep on with the care of the sick, with operations and medicine, in spite of the fact that we *know* that every individual we care for is going to die? This insight does not cripple us so that we cannot act. What we gain is at best a few years or months of life, and we consider that something to be proud of.

Just as it seems self-evident that we should value health, even though it is the vestibule into "death's waiting-room," so Christian faith looks upon goodness and mercy as self-evidently good in the midst of ineradicable destruction where hate and envy reign, and will continue to reign.

Indeed, the parallel between life and goodness is even more deeply grounded. The life which we take such good care of is a gift. It is *given* to the one who lives, and to one's dependents and neighbors. Because it is a gift, one can advise people to keep it strong and to heal it when it is sick. Such an admonition does not imply that we can create life. Neither are the biblical exhortations to love, mercy, and perseverance indications that these manifestations of life come about through our own decisions and initiatives. They are gifts; they empower us to act in situations of need. That is what is morally deepest in human life and comes *before* anything and everything moral. These basic expressions of life do not appear because we exhort people to have them; what we can be exhorted to do is to make room for them and regard them as higher and of greater worth than all other values.

In Destruction One Perceives What Creation Is

Since goodness is given in the same way that life is given, the good, like life, can be perceived. We do not primarily effect the good through acts of the will. Rather, we find it already realized in the sort of community feeling and fellowship that comes into existence when no one has made a conscious decision to bring it about. That is why situations of need are productive; they bring about more spontaneous goodness than mere undisturbed existing is able to call forth. Every need that exists is a call for help. This call awakens someone else and prompts that person to action. The one who so acts

may indeed have been reflecting on an "ethical problem," but even
so, that has relatively little to do with one's acting.

What accounts for life enduring over against death is not the
action which is driven by our reflection and decision, that is, by our
morality. What sustains human life is rather the action from which
we cannot withdraw ourselves, what Løgstrup calls "spontaneous
expressions of life" (which in the Creed are acknowledged and
praised as actions of the Creator). We are aware of the good, and
are surprised at it because evil is present, just as life is perceived
as a gift and received with gratitude because death threatens. No
one is so aware of one's biological life as the convalescent. Also, no
one has so clear a picture of *reality* as the convalescent. One might
say that the convalescent has been given birth back again.

The same is true of goodness. We become aware of goodness in
the midst of the destructive forces in the world. In a world characterized by intrigue and power, even the smallest movement of a hand
in thoughtfulness toward another, a smile which does not have some
gain in view but simply streams forth without any special meaning—
all of these can seem like miracles. And that they are. No person can
on one's own initiative produce such a miracle. If it is found at all,
it exists as a gift. And its character as gift—just as its character as
goodness—is understood because it is surrounded by destroying
powers. No one is so sure of what goodness is as the one who has
been surrounded by hypocrisy. Such a person tastes the spontaneously good with the convalescent's renewed sensitivity.

It follows that we could not understand Jesus apart from the conflicts and the crucifixion. The notion that the Sermon on the Mount,
with its high ethical imperatives, could be the foundation for human
fellowship is a typical twentieth century idea, which grew up in a
culture that did not want to think that destruction was something
permanent and ineradicable. But Jesus was immersed in conflicts,
conflicts that resulted in his crucifixion. This Jesus continues to live
and to address us. If he had only delivered the Sermon on the Mount
and nothing more, he would have soon been forgotten.[5]

But this does not mean that the legal requirement that we show
consideration to our neighbor is evil. That would constitute a sort
of theological anarchy which, though it has some antecedents in the
"enthusiast" movements in church history, has no support in the
New Testament. On the contrary, in the New Testament a positive
evaluation is given to respect for others, even when it is coerced by
the sword (Rom. 13:4). But such legally-imposed actions do not
belong primarily under the rubric of Creation. They do not have the
effect of causing life to come into existence.

The law always presupposes that life already exists, and that the problem is how to protect it. All law—without reference to the radicality of the ideology out of which it comes—is unproductive and conservative; it is always secondary. Therefore, also, it is to come to an end, it does not rule "in heaven." The law's final act is the "last judgment"—with that it has coerced long enough and is finished.

But to regard law and commandment as the Christian congregation's primary ethical contribution to society would be to turn upside down the relation between creation and law. This kind of moralism is understandable only as a consequence of the disappearance of belief in creation. The most important ethical contribution of the Christian congregation does not lie in the area of appeals to action but in the area of the interpretation of life. The church should be able to help people to be aware, to discern. Through the first article of the Creed, the congregation interprets what we are calling "the spontaneous expressions of life" as actions of the Creator. They are actions which bring life to birth and keep it healthy in advance of morality and independently of it. Moreover, in its faith in Christ as the renewer of life at the point where life seems most destructive, the Christian congregation contributes a positive interpretation of death, even such a death as seems meaningless.

Neither faith in the Creator nor faith in Christ can primarily take the form of commandments, imperatives, and appeals. To believe is to be able to interpret what happens. And therein lies an access into ethical insights of great dimensions, especially in a time when people do not want to accept the fact that destruction is permanent and ineradicable.

To Find Meaning Is to Interpret Death

To interpret something in faith as God's action implies that one accepts that event as good. This means that there is some point of view from which events can be understood to be beneficial and to promote life. Faith in creation is faith in God as the life-giving God. The boundary at which this faith encounters its greatest obstacle is death. The risk in every interpretation of death as something good lies in egocentricity.

This egocentricity does not need to express itself in any obvious form—it can be well camouflaged. The obvious form explains the death of the individual as a direct passage into the blessedness of heaven. Eschatology is surely the place where the egocentricity of individual believers has been able to celebrate its greatest and most undisturbed triumphs. This deviation depends in part on the shameless egocentricity of piety as expressed in prayers and hymns. Moreover, very few recent theologians have reflected on the views of eternal life. Therefore the inherited tradition of old prayers and hymns has been allowed to bloom, all alone in the important field of eschatology. The task of developing prayers and hymns that include expressions of hope concerning a life after death that are not self-centered remains to be done.

But as a rule egocentricity is camouflaged. If I die for my children, or my country, or my social class, or something similar, what God is supposed to be affirming through my death is my own evaluation of those causes for which I die. It is precisely what *I* want which is being furthered by my death. When God benefits someone he benefits only those whom *I* have chosen. But if the New Testament were to be the basis for our interpretation of death, this egocentricity would be highly offensive. It may be that in the Western world we will finally discover that we have no explanation for death, which means that death will have no meaning.[6]

In view of all the possible interpretations, we can turn the question around. We can ask: Is not perseverance in the face of meaningless death also a "spontaneous manifestation of life" and a gift of the same sort as mercy, love, and uprightness? To endure meaningless death is a gift the person receives when such death comes. Many who are not Christian receive this gift, and—even more remarkable—many who are in anguish over the thought of their own death also receive it.

Here it should be noted that the cross, in all its meaninglessness, is the basis for the interpretation of our own meaningless death. In those passages in the New Testament that speak of Jesus' anguish in the presence of death, the point is not that he died for some goal he had decided on by himself (Mark 14:36; Heb. 5:7). A specific and determinative word keeps recurring, the word *obedience* (Heb. 5:8; Phil. 2:8). To accept something as necessary—not as good or meaningful from my own point of view but simply as necessary—that is obedience.

The French author Simone Weil, who engaged in lengthy and intensive reflection on physical labor and on death, thought that both of these burdens are misfortunes laid upon us by God. The greatest purity of spirit, the highest level of fulfillment, in the face of these burdens, consists simply in the obedience which says, "This is something I must accept." So Christ did in the crucifixion.[7] He did not know where it would lead but he was obedient. Without Jesus' anguish in Gethsemane the cross would have been less gospel. With a preconceived plan for victory by way of Golgotha, the cross would have been less gospel. As the point at which Jesus accepted meaning-lessness, the cross is pure gospel.

This is true because loss is meaningful for the Christian faith if it is the same loss that Jesus experienced. To take the loss, to accept meaningless work and meaningless death obediently, this is to be "in God." This is the form of life for the grain of wheat; its mean-ing consists in the fact that it falls into the ground and dies (John 12:24); it is thus that the grain of wheat obeys. The resurrection, or the fruit beyond death, is not thought about in advance by the grain of wheat, nor does it accrue to the benefit of the decomposed grain of wheat (as the egotistically calculated gain does). Definite consequences for eschatology follow from this, which we will come back to in our last chapter about eternal life.

If our resurrection is with Christ (Rom. 6:5; 1 Cor. 15:22), then eternal life cannot be something that we own for ourselves. If we live after death, we live thereafter for others. The positive function that the departed has on those who remain is a part of the dead per-son's eternal life here on earth. In earlier times one viewed the worship service as a fellowship in which the departed generation "in heaven" partook along with those who still had their final install-ment of obedience ahead of them. And all of them sang praises in the worship service to him who was perfect inasmuch as he had endured the most meaningless form of death, the cross. The whole understanding of the church as Christ's body is lost if the church is not seen as now living in heaven through its praise, and at the same time that it is on earth, and that here on earth it is called to be like Christ precisely in its acceptance, its obedience, an obedience in the face of apparent meaninglessness.

To state it most pointedly: nothing is so filled with unbelief as the attempt to explain what the church is good for in terms of our profit and loss categories. All of these explanations—social, ethical, political, therapeutic—rob the church of its true role, which is believ-ing and obeying in the face of the meaningless. The church is, like Christ, both death and resurrection. That part of the church one sees with the eye, is that part which, like the visible part of Christ, ends in death.[8]

But death is not "good for something." It cannot be explained. Death is something which is laid upon us—it is necessary. One can only interpret death by falling into it, as the grain of wheat, as Christ, or as the departed have fallen into it. Death is the side of God's creative action which is turned toward destruction, toward the destroying powers; we can never understand or explain why destruc-tion is allowed to remain.

HUMAN BEINGS AND THEIR ENVIRONMENT

In the creation story the human is not described as alone. The human creature is surrounded by night and day, sea and land, animals and trees and, most important of all, from the beginning the human is already two—man and woman. None of those entities mentioned in the creation story has ceased to exist. Every person on earth lives today in exactly the same surroundings.

In recent times much has been made of one special point in the story, the human being as lord over nature. As long as modern technology was still perceived to be something good, hardly anyone argued that it had its roots in Genesis. After the discovery of the pollution of the environment, many more have asserted that the now damaging technology could never have developed if it hadn't been for the biblical words. This judgment about the creation story reflects a distorted view on the part of the judges.

Let us analyze the different parts of the human environment separately. In the environment are found certain conditions over which the human is not lord, such as night and day. But the human is lord over the animals, trees, etc. All that has here been placed under human lordship has in all cultures been subordinated to human jurisdiction. Moreover, current proposals for the improvement of the environment assume that humans could manage more cleverly than they have up to this point. This implies that we think that we could change our attitude toward this part of our environment and thereby improve our situation. In fact, then, we do view ourselves as lords in those instances where the creation story identifies us as lords. In contrast, the animals are not able to bring order into environmental problems by undertaking any measures that affect humans.

In looking at these various factors in the human environment separately, we will begin with that part of nature which we cannot manage—day and night, light and darkness, sea and land.

The Human Is a Part of the Created

The creation story presupposes a primitive view of the world. Bodies of water and darkness are understood to imply danger and the threat of death; light and dry ground mean life and rescue. The firmament which "separates the waters from the waters" (Gen. 1:6) is a vaulted roof above us. It prevents the masses of water above from falling and drowning life on earth. The light and the firmament protect human life, *along with* animal and vegetable life. This is the case also in the story of the flood (Gen. 6:13-8:22) where it is strongly emphasized that salvation from the masses of water applies to "every living thing of all flesh" (Gen. 6:19), and where the green leaf in the dove's beak is the sign that God has kept his promise (Gen. 8:11). The same imagery of how the human and the creation in general hang together appears in the Psalms, in Job, and in Deutero-Isaiah.

These texts do not convey the typical Western idea of humans as standing outside of nature in general. The biblical texts would have to be combined with something totally different to yield such a result. But this in fact happened and one does not need to seek far for what that different ingredient was. Greek philosophy set spirit and matter against one another. It allows the uniqueness of the human being to consist in the fact that spirit (reason) governs the sensual, material part (the body), and can even set itself free from bondage to the human body. But the Old Testament gathers together humans and animals into one unity and calls it "all flesh." This would have been an impossibility for Plato or Aristotle, or for Greek philosophy in general.

In Europe, and later in America, the combining of Greek and biblical views has been quite evident. These countries have emphasized the notion of dominion which in turn has given rise to technology and industrialization, and finally to environmental destruction on a global scale. Nowhere in the civilization of these countries have people really felt at home in the biblical picture of the world with its deep sense of unity between the human, the animal, and the vegetative. There, in the biblical view, all are fed by the same Creator— the trees (Ps. 104:16), the animals of the forest (104:20-22), people (104:14f., 23). All are mingled together without the ranking which puts humans at the top as is typical in our culture.

To this general biblical picture we must add some other strands from Genesis. For instance, there is the fact that Adam means "man." Everything that is said about Adam constitutes a description of our present human life. This is true not only of the story of creation but, equally, of the story of disobedience and the consequences of disobedience (Gen. 3:1-19). "You are dust and to dust you shall return" (Gen. 3:19). With variations in language this word has been included in most burial rites. Hardly any word or expression spoken at a funeral more strongly articulates the recognition that humans *are* indeed part of the continuum of nature (see also Gen. 3:23).[9] It would be more than a little strange if the biblical literature, in view of such passages as these, would need to bear major responsibility for the fact that modern technicians and industrial

magnates feel elevated over nature, and in their conduct freed
from it.

To this we must now add the two biblical stories about technology
—about buildings planned and carried through, what people can do
that animals cannot do. For in these ancient texts there are actually
two stories about technique, both of them naive and mythical in
form but very different in purpose and message. The one is the story
about the ark (Gen. 6:14-8:19), the other the story about the tower
of Babel (Gen. 11:1-9). The same human capacity is being exercised
in both cases. But the ark is a technical project to save all that is
living from the destruction of the flood. The tower is a building that
grows out of egotism. It has the single purpose of making the builder
and his helpers famous: "Let us make a name for ourselves" (Gen.
11:4). The ark gives life to creation; the tower brings death.

This is a good critique of intelligence, and provides valuable advice
to the technically competent. The Bible supplies this critique and this
advice in the form of a story about human beings and God. For the
biblical writers the epic form and the anthropomorphic language is
the highest form of expression; for them an analysis followed by
evaluation would have seemed trite.

But we must point out two other important observations. First,
the critical attitude toward intelligence found in the biblical texts
would hardly be thinkable in a culture stamped by Greek philosophy
with its confidence in the goodness of reason. Second, in spite of this
lack of criticism of reason, there did not arise in Greece any revolutionary change in the realm of nature. Homes, external ways of
doing things, and tools remained unchanged throughout antiquity.
It was only when Greek philosophy mingled with biblical ideas that
the Western world with its technology came to be.

The Greeks held that the spirit, or reason, should govern the
instincts of the lowly body. But both the higher (that which governs) and the lower (that which is governed) were found within
the person; they were two parts of the divided human. Genesis, on
the other hand, views the person as whole and undivided, good both
as to body and spirit when obedient to the Creator, evil both as to
body and spirit when disobedient. In obedience the person is God's
instrument in his creation. The created world has been given to
humans as a field in which to work (Gen. 1:26-30). The Israelites
work with their own hands and do not leave all the physical labor to
slaves. On the other hand, the Israelites do not pursue some purely
inner activity in order that they might become individuals, in isolation from other people, animals, and inanimate objects.

Human Dominion

To be a part of something and at the same time to be lord over it may seem logically irreconcilable. However, this is, in fact, how many communities are built. It is also the way the body is constructed (the brain directs and is at the same time a part of what it directs). What is important in Genesis is that the context of human dominion lies outside the individual; the person is principally directed outward (cf. Ps. 8:4-10). Moreover, human dominion is set within a relationship in which the individual is *not* lord—i.e., within God's relationship to all that he has created. Humanity is something God has in his hand when he deals with those objects and creatures that are placed under human beings. We used to say that a human being is a governor or deputy or steward.

When this outward-directed person moves into the world, he moves out into something that is created by God. This is the biblical view. If we wish to describe the Old Testament contribution to our modern understanding of the world, we must distinguish it both from Greek philosophy and from the folk religions of Israel's neighbors. Despite the Greek philosophers, it is not possible to look down on creation as something "lower"; neither is it possible, despite the neighboring religions, to entertain religious awe for something on earth. The world is something good; it belongs to God and it is something in which the human can move about freely and without fear.[10]

One would expect that this attitude would be able to break down the fear of nature which is deeply rooted in older cultures, and bring into existence a kind of human sovereignty over against all that happens in the world, a sovereignty combined with service. One would especially expect such a sovereignty and such a caring attitude toward the environment to grow out of the biblical message—that is, the message of the Old Testament together with the story of Jesus. Jesus was the healer; and he was executed. Following him means to protect the weak and calmly take the ultimate rebuff. Neither of these paths lead to technological terror nor to the destruction of the environment. In short, it is difficult to see how the idea of dominion in Genesis, with the development which takes place in the New Testament, could be responsible for our current problems.

But if, on the other hand, one combines the idea of dominion in Genesis (over objects, vegetation, and animals) with the Greek idea of dominion which reason or spirit is to exercise over the physical and "lower" parts of human beings, the dominion that results is without limits. The spirit in the human being is divine; it cannot be evil. To state it more simply, it can never rule the lower too com-

pletely. From this point of view, stories such as the tower of Babel
appear to be sheer naiveté. One must give human dominion free
reign without restraint; one must give human reason complete freedom with respect to everything that exists. Here lies the unbiblical
feature—that human beings stand outside of nature. We are no
longer "of dust" (Gen. 3:19).

This combination—a bit of the Old Testament view of life plus a
bit of Greek philosophy—is disintegrating in the twentieth century.
The biblical content is being released from its association with Greek
philosophy, but at the same time it is in danger of losing any possibility of influencing social planning. There are free groups of Christian people living together according to the biblical word. These are
characterized by solidarity across national and cultural boundaries.
We need to ask what having "dominion" means in this new setting.

What the human was originally freed from through the belief in
creation was an unproductive respect for the environment. Gods
were formerly found in rivers, floods, and storms. Then suddenly
everything became powerless, robbed of the capacity to frighten
people. Is there anything before which the modern person feels an
unproductive and crippling respect? "Unproductive" and "crippling"
can be defined from the biblical witness (from the creation texts
plus the story of Jesus). According to the biblical witness everything
that hinders a person from serving others is unproductive and crippling, and consequently must be overcome by faith in God.

We should first take note of the fact that today in many places in
Asia and Africa faith has the same effect as it did when Genesis
was written. The belief in "powers" dies only when faith comes.
But after these powers are dead one observes in these countries
parallels to the development in the Western world. Around us, too,
are comparable powers, stripped of any explicit religious dignity,
confronting the individual as social and economic patterns to which
we are to conform. These patterns are clothed with esteem or status,
so that the nonconformists invite contempt. The view that we should
receive our livelihood and no more, and that the measure of existence
is to be found in our relationship to our environment and not in what
we possess, does not fit into any contemporary pattern. An individual
with such ideas can be regarded as weak (in terms of a competitive
pattern) or as naive (in terms of a revolutionary pattern).

To live according to these competitive and revolutionary patterns
is to be burdened by what faith regards as unproductive and crippling. These patterns are the contemporary counterparts of Baal and
Astarte; they hinder one from living freely in God's creation. Both

of them—the competitive pattern as well as the revolutionary pattern—are materialistic, they are built around the worship of things.

It is not the case that the person's free development in community is favored in one part of the world and repressed in another. Rather, it is the case that the individual is repressed in contemporary culture, both East and West. The cause is everywhere the same—the dominion of the machinery of production, and the viewing of people as a part of the apparatus of production. The attempt to justify such a view of life by asserting that its values can be the basis for a decent concern for all the people of the earth, is absurd. On the contrary, this deification of production can only lead to military build-ups, explosions, and attendant catastrophes for the people of the earth. Threats of such catastrophes are uttered constantly; indeed, such threats are an integral and normal ingredient of the military competition between the superpowers.[11]

When Christian people today respect ideologies of this type, they are *not* exercising their dominion. It would be asking too much to expect the churches to achieve a victory over such ideologies. Israel could not wipe out the fertility cults in the Orient. But every Israelite could stop worshiping Baal and Astarte—this was each individual's "dominion." In the same way today, dominion consists primarily in freeing oneself from the ideologies which have the production apparatus at their center, and which rule as "powers" in today's society. Such a dominion does not lead to destruction, but it does lead to freedom from fear among many people.

Man and Woman

Karl Barth's observation that "man" in the creation story is the equivalent of "man and woman" is one of the most original features of his theology (Gen. 1:27). Man is not only male, which in the then current culture would have seemed natural. A complete man is not one specimen but two. A complete man, then, is an elemental form of fellowship. Much criticism has been directed toward Barth's exposition of the creation story, and rightly so. Among other things, it is not reasonable to make the relation between man and woman into a reflection of Christology (a favorite pattern of thought in Barth). But it cannot be denied that Barth has pointed to something essential; in a civilization that was grotesquely masculine, Genesis allows man and woman together to represent humanity.

Not only that, right after the account of the creation of man and woman there follows in Genesis the word about dominion. And the text is entirely clear: it is man and woman, *together,* who are in-

stalled as God's deputies on earth (Gen. 1:28). In this placing of
man and woman side by side there comes to the fore that high ap-
praisal of marriage, family, the treasure which children represented, and the positive attitude toward bodily existence in general that was characteristic of ancient Israel and later of Judaism.
In modified form it is to be found also in Islam. For Indian religion and Greek speculation it is, on the other hand, completely
foreign. Practice, however, seldom conformed to this principle of
equity in the creation story. In fact, the man dominated and the
woman found her place at the periphery.

But what is most important in our context is not the equality of
man and woman. It is rather the realization that other people are a
part of every person's environment. One cannot think "man"
without thinking of him in relation to another people.[12] Humanity is human community. Already in creation the human is disposed toward fellowship with others; we become aware of this when
we are totally alone. Then we cease to be a whole person. For God
has in creation laid upon each human being the necessity of becoming part of a fellowship with other humans in order to derive life
from the surrounding nature.

This is the reason that love and mercy, as "spontaneous expressions of life" are given with human existence. If we destroy them
we destroy ourselves. That which in the previous section we called
dominion, which manifests itself in the freedom of a person to
move among things without awe and without worship, this is a
presupposition of all free activity among persons. We can give to
another and rejoice over what another owns, only if we do not live
under the dominion of things, do not worship them, and do not
cling to them.

Stinginess is born out of fear. It expresses itself in the convulsive
grasping after things and this constitutes idolatry, which in turn
constitutes a direct closing off of oneself from others, and a slow
suffocation in a cramped, closed-in life. Stinginess represents a
perverted relationship to God, to material things, to other people,
and to ourselves. These are all basically one; we are talking about
destruction occurring in all of these directions. It is only that different aspects of human destruction become visible from different
points of view.

The wonderful thing is that no such destructive process can nullify the spontaneous manifestations of life. In the midst of the destruction the child emerges—not only the child who has not yet
attained the age of the grown-up, but the child within the grown-
up as shown in the need for contact, for play, for laughter, for re-

sponse from another, the expression of sovereign freedom from the world of things. To play with things like a child is healthy; that is something the greedy can never do with money. Neither can the heathen do that with the idols they worship in nature. It is significant that it is covetousness which is called idolatry in the New Testament (Col. 3:5; also Eph. 5:5).

Where spontaneous giving and spontaneous fellowship are repressed, the Creator must bring about consideration for others by coercion. This is the function of law—to compel people to do the good which they do not voluntarily want to do.

Lord, my God and Father! You know me completely. You know what I can do, and you know where the limit of my ability is. Give me the joy of having a job that will make use of all the good with which you have endowed me. Grant me the encouragement I need if I am to carry out that which you want to accomplish through me. Give me self-confidence, so that I can work together with others and so that I will not be crippled by changes.

Help me to accept life's inescapable variability, as I accept sunshine and rain, day and night. Let me accept calmly the experience that I am not the center of the world; that I am only one of many, one of the thousands of grains of wheat that fall into the ground and die. You only know when the time of harvest comes. Let my task then have been accomplished. O God, bless me so that my life bears fruit. To you be glory eternally.

II

The Law

God acts through the law in two different ways—he compels and he accuses. In both cases God wills the good over against the evil. What is characteristic for the work of the law is that through it evil is opposed and the good is promoted even if the individual does not freely will the good. The individual remains God's creation nonetheless. This becomes clear when we realize that, in spite of resistance, a person cannot refrain from spontaneously, and unwillingly, being drawn toward others in love and trust. The compulsion of the law therefore never implies total coercion. There remains in us enough insight into what a free person should be that we both acknowledge that our lack of freedom involves guilt, and that our true freedom lies in the gospel's picture of Jesus.

GOD COMPELS

In what follows we will consciously hold together two things which at first sight seem to be separate—the law which in the biblical writings is often spoken of in the singular, and the laws which are valid in worldly societies. The connecting link between the law in the singular and the laws in the plural is the "other," or the neighbor. The Bible summarizes the law several times as love to the neighbor, and the laws in the community can in turn be regarded as statements of obligation owed by us to our neighbors.

The Bible and Our Neighbor

In the New Testament the whole law is often summarized in the single commandment: "You shall love your neighbor as yourself"

58

(Matt. 19:19; 22:39; Rom. 13:9; Gal. 5:14; Jas. 2:8). This commandment of love toward the neighbor is not unique to the proclamation of Jesus but has parallels also outside of Christianity. However, the fact that the commandment is found does not mean that perfect obedience is also found. Paul, who says that the Gentiles "do by nature what the law requires" and thus "are a law unto themselves" (Rom. 2:14), has never said that the Gentiles are therefore without fault. On the contrary, there are whole columns of utterances about the Gentiles which give a very dark picture of the moral situation in the Roman imperium outside of Israel (Rom. 1:18-32). Some of these statements are to be found in close proximity to the expressions about the law noted above.[1]

This coincides with our general observation that the presence of laws is often coupled with the presence of violations against the law. This may suggest something about human nature, but we are not here interested in making a judgment about human goodness, or the lack of it. We know already from our earlier analysis of creation that what we have called the "sovereign expressions of life" (which support life) become visible precisely because of the destroying powers (which lay waste to life). We also know that these two opposing phenomena exist side by side, not only in society but even in the same individual. But what is of particular interest to us here is the role of the neighbor. The Bible places the neighbor in a key position. His need is God's own call to us. It is a call that requires action on our part—in other words, a command, or a law.

What we have now said implies three things, each of which is closely interwoven with the other two. The first is that it becomes unreasonable to expect to derive a specific Christian ethos from the Bible which will contain patterns for contemporary action toward the neighbor. It is to the needs of the neighbor that we must respond, and these needs cannot be anticipated in detail in the Bible. The second thing is that our neighbors, like ourselves, combine both good and destructive desires. Therefore the neighbor's cry to us may include something we must decisively stand against. We must sift and separate that which supports life from that which despoils life, even though we always run the risk of making wrong judgments. The third thing is that we always swing back and forth between responding to external compulsion to perform a certain action and a kind of free spontaneity which has often already acted before any reflection about it has begun. Conscience is not so much a guide as it is something which judges an action which I have already, perhaps in haste, carried out.

The biggest complication for us in responding to the needs of our neighbors lies in their vast numbers, and in the varying degrees of need among them. The most common way of dealing unfairly with others does not consist in an intentional act of ill-will against them, but in neglecting their needs. That is why the harshest judgment over actions pronounced anywhere in the New Testament is the exposure in the final judgment of what has *not* been done (Matt. 25:45). The following two examples should put an end to the idea that the ethical contribution of Christianity consists of the proclamation by Christ of a new law that was unknown until he came.

The first example relates to the Pharisees. They were well aware of the commandment to love the neighbor. No one at that time needed to get that commandment from Jesus; the rich young man knew it by heart in advance of his conversation with Jesus (Matt. 19:20). Nonetheless, it was Jesus' view that the prevailing legal piety of the Pharisees set aside their own commandment. They shut out certain categories of people from the fellowship; indeed, they most particularly shut out all those who most needed fellowship, and who also, in Jesus' view, stood closest to the kingdom of God (Mark 2:15-17). The commandment to love, which they espoused, did not help the law-informed Pharisees to discover their neighbor.

In the second example, the relations within the Christian congregation after the death of Jesus show the same characteristics we have noted among the Pharisees. In these churches there is not only the command to love the neighbor, but also the illustration of how that command looks when realized in Jesus. In spite of this there is the same kind of neglect in Corinth as there was in Israel. The fellowship comes to be closed, and it is just the poor and the hungry who are closed out, those who need the fellowship the most (1 Cor. 11:20-22). Not even Christ, painted before the eyes of the assembled congregation, could enable them to understand who their neighbor really was.

That is why the law in the sense of *compulsion* is needed. To be sure, isolated texts from the biblical writings and later doctrinal statements taken out of context, have sometimes been interpreted to teach that law and compulsion apply only to those outside of Christ's congregation (who do not honestly believe); while in contrast, the Christian spontaneously, without law and without compulsion, keeps the commandments in complete and undisturbed freedom. The same has been claimed for certain Reformation documents. But this is a mistaken interpretation, both as concerns the Bible and the Reformation. Such antinomian trends are to be found in church history but they lie outside Christianity's main stream. God's compelling law remains—that is generally accepted Christian doctrine. God's compelling law must exist if our neighbors are to get what belongs to them.[2]

Legislation Constitutes Our Neighbor's Demand-Note Against Us

We Christians are tempted to choose who is to be our neighbor (while pushing others aside). In this the Christian is like anyone else. It is then left to secular society to take care of those who are not chosen. It is largely because the law requires us to care for those we do not choose that it is thought of as compulsion. Those paragraphs that contain the enacted laws constitute the neglected person's demand-notes against us. When the laws are such that they actually protect those who are set aside and not voluntarily chosen, then it is correct to say that they are expressions of God's law. This is not always the case. The laws which are in fact enacted in a given society may profit quite other groups than those who are left out by our choices. When this is the case, they may in fact be promoting thievery rather than service to others.

It is important that laws can be changed, for this makes it possible to create something new in the interests of the neighbor. We have earlier commented on how God continuously creates through what we have called, in dependence on Løgstrup, the sovereign and spontaneous expressions of life. But God's creative action is not limited to these activities; he also creates something new and wholesome even in the hard, impersonal enactment of law, even in the midst of the compulsion it involves.

All people carry within themselves the risk that they will become victims of their own confining or locked-in manifestations of life, to refer again to Løgstrup's terminology for what may otherwise be called sin, or actions of the devil. Since this is the case, that form of society is best in which the largest possible number of persons can vote and thereby remind other citizens of what is most reasonable for all. This is why democracy has an advantage from the point of view of the interest of all the citizens. All have power, but each individual has very little power that he can abuse. In those forms of government in which an individual or an elite group rule, even an occasional deviation among these few can have devastating consequences for many citizens.

However, the democratic style is inadequate in at least one respect —it assumes a specific and confined location of the need. It presupposes that the need exists in the country where the democratic voting is taking place, and that the problem to be dealt with is a just division of the resources available among a country's citizens. To be sure, this is an important and enduring problem. Technical development, industrialization, the movement of populations and the difficulties that attend these developments, continually bring up new needs when the old ones have been met. Therefore, the reasonable division of resources within a country is a problem still to be resolved. As long as such a situation prevails, democracies are relatively free of problems from an ethical point of view.

But it is entirely possible that a situation can arise in a democracy where this is no longer the case. It can happen, for instance, that the boundary between poverty and affluence does not run within a country, between different social classes within a nation, but instead between poor and rich countries. Then the problem of distribution may simply be covered up as the democratic voting focuses attention inward on the country itself; then an unexpected and restyled nationalism can take over, even without any of the classical symbols of the fatherland having been invoked, and this will happen at the expense of those in need. A poor person in Uganda or the Sudan cannot expect that a just distribution of economic resources will follow from a democratically determined decision in the Swedish parliament. Neither can a poor person anticipate a reasonable distribution of resources to result from democratic decisions within the African states themselves, because the resources that need to be distributed are not located within the African state.

This does constitute an ethical problem which has become a major question for the whole of Christendom in the latter part of the twentieth century. The reason this problem has become acute just now is quite simple. The epoch of colonialism ended in principle after the Second World War, and independent African and Asian states began to be set up on a grand scale. Then it quickly became clear that political independence for the new nation was a chimera as long as it lacked economic independence. It soon also became clear that economic independence for them could not be won without some corresponding economic injury to European and American interests. The opposition between the South and the North has more and more tended to dissolve the opposition between the East and the West.

It is logical to think of the legislative enactments of a country as statements of account owed—statements submitted by those in need to the owners of property and the strong. But when the account is owed by the rich nations to the poor nations, by the North to the South, it is difficult for the bills submitted by the countries in the

southern hemisphere to get delivered to the countries in the north-
ern hemisphere—that is, to become enacted into legislation binding
upon them. Even though East and West are governed by separate
and different economic systems, they have shown very similar attitudes when confronted by this threat from the south. They have
both defended what is theirs against such a threat. Church bodies
will have a pioneering task facing them if they will be able to apply
a biblical view of God's law to the laws of society. International
ecumenical organizations have for several years directed attention
to the problems of Africa and Asia.

A nation's legislation does not, however, consist solely in measures
aimed at the distribution of economic resources, although questions
of this sort mark the election campaigns of democratic states to an
increasing degree. All of the statutes that govern working arrange-
ments, training, the care of the sick, the enjoyment of the environment—this whole collection of laws constitutes a series of pressures
on all the inhabitants of a country to so act that others will benefit
from their actions. Therefore all laws must be subject to change.
The destroying forces constantly assume new forms and must be
met by new and revised laws.

No Law Is Eternal

When someone today refers to law, almost all who hear the term
associate it with a situation in which there is no change—the
status quo. But in the sixteenth century when one heard the word
"law" one would rather have thought of "movement." It would
have suggested the disintegration of European unity, the establishment of new and free secular states, and continuing new developments in virtually all areas. Luther says specifically about the law
that it must "accommodate itself to the situation"; and about love
he says that it is the sovereign "master of all laws." If one were to
use language as Luther did, one would not identify law with the
status quo, but rather set the status quo and law against one
another. For laws to him represented movement in society.

There are several reasons why law in our mind is associated with
rigidity and constancy, rather than with change. The doctrine of
creation which was dominant in Europe a generation ago, especially
in Germany, proceeded from a premise which Luther consistently
rejected—the premise that God's creating action took place "in the
beginning" and that consequently God had once been Creator but
now was something else (i.e., Savior). Because of his activity at

the beginning we have received certain fixed ordinances (orders of
creation) that make any further creative work of God unnecessary.
Luther, by contrast, makes his view clear in the Small Catechism.
When he is going to explain what "heaven and earth" in the first
article mean, he does not once mention either the word "heaven" or
the word "earth," but says instead: "God has created *me* . . ." Each
birth is an act of creation. God creates now.

A comparable development away from the idea of movement has
taken place in Roman Catholic theology. Just as confessional Lutheranism, especially after the Enlightenment, felt compelled to
assert the value of the establishment first against the influence of
the French Revolution and later against Marx, so the church of
Rome found itself in opposition to the entire movement which
characterized the society of the nineteenth century. The concept
of natural law was consequently interpreted in much the same manner by Roman Catholic theologians as orders of creation on the
Protestant side—the right of ownership is asserted and reasonable
land reforms are rejected. The interpretation favored the status
quo, and promoted quiescence as the ideal.

This tendency toward supporting the status quo, along both
Protestant and Catholic lines, seems now to be finally breaking
down. This may be due in part to the fact that the doctrine of creation has again begun to be interpreted in a more plausible manner,
and in part to the fact that criticism has been directed toward the
church's conservative view of natural law. The latter observation
relates especially to sexual ethics, where various Catholic theologians have rejected the right of the church to preempt the decisions
of individuals that are not bound by law.[3] Seen in a larger perspective, this shift implies two things. The first is that law is
joined much more closely with "creation," and most especially with
"new creation." The second is that law has become a shifting rather
than a rigid and fixed reality.

It is then also clear that no law is eternal. God's law is God's
precisely because it is changeable. If it were unchangeable it could
not be God's law because it would then put an end to the proposition
that God is the Creator *now*. God undertakes constantly new actions,
and destruction appears in constantly new forms. The old law, the
law that is in force, is a marvelous instrument for the egotist to use
in accomplishing his ends. If people are clever enough and hunt long
enough, they will be able to take advantage of the law for themselves (i.e., deprive others of their rights). When the God of the
Decalogue creates, he exposes the hidden, "tidy" thefts and mur-
ders; he sets up new barriers against cunning and, with the help

of law, gives freedom to the oppressed. But that law of God which is then positively established for the benefit of the needy also comes to be used by the forces of destruction; it, too, must be reconsidered and tested on the basis of neighborly love.

If the statement, "no law is eternal," only had this content it would be banal. It becomes controversial when it is taken to mean that the law is *not* the instrument God uses to offer eternal life. One of the lasting effects of the Platonic teaching of the two worlds —one spiritual and one material—has been the tendency to regard the natural law, which functions on earth, as a reflection of the eternal, fixed, and unchangeable law. It is very difficult to find biblical support for such a view. In the Bible the law is a divine work that is carried out with people who do not freely choose what God wants. Therefore, when eternal life is described, other terms are used than those which are associated with law—words like "freedom," "salvation," "praise." The thought that eternal life should consist of the subordination of the human under an eternal law is entirely foreign to the Bible.

Now this does not imply, of course, that what the law requires may be abandoned when we respond in freedom and with praise. Quite the contrary. The law requires something which if it were realized, would put an end to the law!

The law requires a free expression of life and therefore—paradoxical as it may seem—it requires its own disappearance. Those biblical expositors who have rejected the doctrine of "the third use of the law" (i.e., the law as a guide for life) emphasize the idea of a free expression of life in which compulsion plays no role whatsoever. Those who accept the third use of the law are uneasy about the heedless and egotistic freedom which could follow if statements about freedom from the law were included in a system of Christian doctrine.

What offended people about Jesus' appearance and proclamation derived primarily from the fact that he seemed to lack this uneasiness. His sermon in the Nazareth synagogue (Luke 4:16-21) implied a sharp conflict not only with Judaism's interpretation of the Old Testament law but with that law itself. The gospel of Jesus nullifies the judgment which God's own law pronounces over the sinner.[4] Therefore, those expositors of the Bible who recognize a conflict between law and gospel are more in accord with the premises on which earliest Christianity was built than are the harmonizing expositors. It is not the law which is the goal to be achieved—it is freedom from law, freedom and praise.

GOD ACCUSES

To represent the law as an accuser seems self-evident to one who thinks that the law is *not* eternal. The law is understood to have a function up to a certain point; then the opposite of law, the gospel, takes over. If one thinks, on the other hand, that the goal of everything is one's willing and obedient incorporation under an eternal law, then the accusing function of the law is softened, and the law becomes a friend, as it was in ancient Israel (Ps. 119 is typical).

Using traditional technical language one can express the different attitudes of the various Christian communions toward law in the following manner:

Where obedient subordination under law is understood to be the desired result of God's action, the "third use of the law" becomes its most important use. Where the law is understood in terms of its accusing and judging function, the "second use of the law" (i.e., show us our sinfulness) becomes the most important. Two typical features are always combined with this second understanding of the law: there is an accent on the requirement that we act freely (without coercion), and there is an accent on the capacity of the gospel to work ethical renewal and create freedom, without law, and in joy.

Calvin endorses the third use of the law, while Luther advocates the impossibility of law and the freedom of the gospel. Both have their off-shoots in the secular world. Kant's dream of a republic governed by respect for the law parallels Calvin, while the Marxist dream of the classless society with its carefree optimism resembles Luther's eschatology.

Memories and the Irreparable

Guilt is never abstract, certainly not before God. Much Christian proclamation concerning sin and guilt is ineffective because it is not specific enough. We readily acknowledge that our whole self is sinful. But we turn right around and become outraged at some minuscule personal affront. One who is genuinely conscious of guilt does not behave in this way. A genuine feeling of guilt is tied to concrete actions which I myself have done or failed to do.

In an introductory manner, we have already talked about *humanity* as a permanent side of God's nature, according to the Creed. In the parable of the final judgment (Matt. 25:31-46), the point is that whatever people may have done or left undone, they have met God in their contacts with other people. It may be that one who claims to be an atheist but considers the encounters with other people to be decisive for one's existence, stands closer to biblical faith in God than does one who lightly and freely affirms the dogmas, but claims that God is entirely "transcendent." Before a purely transcendent God it would not be possible to feel the guilt about which the New Testament speaks.

Human existence has a boundary—it ceases to be at a certain point. If I stand at this boundary, without the possibility of making amends for a fault I have committed, and if I assume the guilt for this fault, then I really stand in the presence of God. And I stand there silently, without sanctimoniousness, that is, with mouth stopped (Rom. 3:19). This boundary for my life forms a part of a universal boundary for all human life. When the Bible speaks of this boundary its tone is commonplace. There are no speculations about such frequently debated problems as whether we can attain knowledge of everything or whether there is some boundary for our knowledge, etc. The boundary is the most simple imaginable— we shall die. "All flesh is grass" (Isa. 40:6).

Therefore the memories of our encounters with people, especially as we get older, are confrontations with the boundary. One does not need to be old to stand in such a total and life-encompassing confrontation. The hedonism of the Enlightenment philosophers implied that we could subtract from the total of our misfortune those results of good fortune that we had achieved on our own and so come to an acceptable final balance. Dostoyevsky's comment about the suffering of the child—which, even if it is the suffering of only one child, can never be balanced off by the fact that thousands experience well-being—reflects much more surely not only the view of the New Testament but also the everyday experience of what guilt is. My whole existence can be tied up in my relation to just one other person. And it is precisely in this relationship, not alongside it, that my existence is related to God.

From the human point of view, this relationship to God through another individual is the same mysterious fact as the incarnation. God's becoming human must be seen from above. God encounters everyone in one single human existence—Jesus. In my relationship to an individual person, a child, a sick person, or someone who has been wronged, I am inescapably in fellowship with God. Therefore it is nonsense to say to a person who is suffering from guilt on account of certain actions against someone now departed, that this person must make reparation for this guilt by doing good to others. Those actions which this person performs toward others may indeed be good for them. But these beneficial actions have nothing to do

with the person's guilt. Memory continues to speak about that which
is irreparable.

These elemental experiences which all persons have and which are
seldom articulated in religious form, actually have to do with the
"second use of the law"—God's accusing voice. Traditionally, it is
also regarded as a function of the law that it "drives to Christ,"
or is a tutor to bring us to Christ (Gal. 3:24). This, too, is a proposition well anchored in everyday experience. When the proclamation
of Jesus as the crucified one is effective in the listener, two experiences are involved: 1) the experience of Jesus as the "genuine"
person, as one who does not corrupt the lives of others, as the kind
of person everyone ought to be; 2) the experience of Jesus' attitude
toward sinners, toward those who have squandered their possibilities. To experience these two effects of the proclamation as one listens is to be "driven by the law"—it is to know the meaning of
guilt (Rom. 3:20).

To use the traditional expression, "God's forgiveness," as a solu-
tion to the problem of sin, is regarded by most people as simply
mouthing a pious phrase. The failure to appreciate this clear New
Testament assertion—which is also the central assertion in the
early missionary proclamation (Acts 10:43)—is the greatest of all
the changes that have occurred from the earliest period until now.
Intellectual problems arising in connection with the miracles are
less modern than is often supposed. Doubt about Christ's resurrection was found even in the circle of the disciples and was included,
surprisingly enough, in the evangelist's report of the situation that
existed after Easter (cf. John 20:25, and especially Matt. 28:17).
But the doubters believed in forgiveness!

We will be able to see more easily the loss of substance that has
been suffered by modern Christianity if we consider again the
parallel from the biological sphere (the contrast between life and
death), and compare it with what one could call "the guilt sphere"
(the contrast between forgiveness and self-accusation). If one has
feared a severe illness—hence has regarded oneself as biologically
irreparable—the good news the physician brings is the renewal of
the person as a functioning being. No moralistic exhortations, appeals, or proclamations are needed. One is simply made active
through the assurance that one is healthy. Such good news is the
gospel—the word "gospel" means precisely good news. But in modern Christianity it is often thought that this good news does not
accomplish anything. The church must instead begin to pour it on
with morality, politics, and manifestos in order to motivate the
person to act ethically.

The consequence is that nearly all church bodies seem to be working under stress, while those few who are fortunate enough to avoid stress are unfortunate enough to appear careless and indolent. To act in freedom on the basis of the gospel is uncommon in contemporary Christianity. But if we are to give an account of that Christianity which takes its origin from the Creed, then we must assert that unconditional forgiveness—forgiveness even of the irresponsible—is a typically Christian element in the gospel, and beyond that, an element which distinguishes Christian faith from all other forms of faith.[5] When this point is allowed to weaken, Christianity becomes very much like enlightened, liberal Judaism.

Classical Christianity would say two things to the person who is plagued with memories of the irreparable. The first is that guilt before God is blotted out by the gospel. The other is that an individual's guilt toward someone that the individual can no longer get in touch with (one dead, or one living far away) is humanly irreparable—but God is the God of all people, even the dead. We must accept the fact that we cannot heal the irreparable by ourselves. The Creator's possibility of turning evil into good (Gen. 50:20) can never be transmuted into human possibilities. God remains the one who finally conquers destruction, and he does it in a human misdeed which defies all comparison—the crucifixion. The cross is a good example of God's way of creating.

The Conscience

Conscience is seldom mentioned in the New Testament but the few references are very instructive. For the most part they are shockingly negative. Conscience can become good only by virtue of Christ's resurrection (1 Peter 3:21), not because of its own initiative. The most that can be expected of conscience is that it cease to accuse us after a good act has been performed; it cannot be expected to give us guidance in advance. When conscience judges an action to be evil it may be functioning as a "weak" conscience—that is, a conscience not yet freed through the gospel—in the same way as individuals "under the law" are burdened with guilt (see 1 Cor. 8:7-12; Rom. 3:19-21; also Rom. 13:3-5). That is why conscience needs to be "cleansed" (Heb. 10:22). Even in that famous passage about "the Gentiles who have not the law" (Rom. 2:14) the primary role of conscience is clearly to accuse; the "excusing" of an action is an alternative mentioned in the second place (2:15).

The negative accent seems also to be consistent with human experience; the Socratic inner voice was a warning voice, not positive guidance. C. A. Pierce studied the New Testament references and found that the function of conscience is coupled with God's judgment. Conscience speaks about deeds already done, and it constitutes a foretaste of rehearsal of the final judgment. If a person listens to the voice of conscience and comes under its judgment, God's final judgment already *happens*. If the person does not listen—that is, if the judgment is not allowed to engulf the person—the judgment remains, and waits. When conscience is allowed to judge, it exercises a sanitizing function; therefore guilt belongs to health. It is health in its negative form.[6]

The negative character of conscience must not be allowed to overshadow a surprisingly positive characteristic—its universality. In principle, conscience acts the same in all people. Pierce asserts that Paul is convinced that a natural law is at work in all people. The argument that this universal natural law means too many different things in different situtions clearly misses the point of the New Testament line of thought. The fact that conscience in one culture may condemn me because I have been too obedient, and in another culture may condemn me because I have not been obedient enough need not be an argument against the concept of a natural law.

The point in both cases is the same: I am judged by conscience because I have not benefited others. We can obviously have different interpretations of what benefits others. But that I should act so that others are benefited is something that conscience asserts across cultural boundaries. Surely this is remarkable enough. If conscience were an empty form which could accommodate any arbitrary norms whatever, it should be able to reject those actions of mine that are *not* egotistically motivated; it should be able to declare that only selfishness is good. However, conscience never behaves this way—not according to the New Testament, not according to Socrates, not according to Buddha, and not according to Marx.

What is universal about conscience then is that it condemns actions which do not benefit others. What on the other hand is specifically Christian and has no counterpart elsewhere is the following:

1) Christianity is alone in being able to hold fast to a judgment that applies to the whole person. Everywhere else we encounter the thought that there are some qualities or attitudes that are good, or potentially good. They are difficult to achieve, but are still possible. The judgment of the total person is obviously the negative si: ‘f the Christian faith's conviction about God's gracious intervention. Where judgment rules, forgiveness rules also. Where death rules, there resurrection rules also. Neither forgiveness nor resurrection can be derived from human qualities. Both have the character of mir-

acle. Both are characteristically mentioned together in the third article of the Creed—"the forgiveness of sins, the resurrection of the body, and the life everlasting."

2) Christianity is also alone in its assertion that the meaning of all human life has already been realized. Everywhere else people are striving toward a goal not yet attained—the messianic kingdom on earth, the classless society, nirvana, genuine existence, etc. Christian faith is offensive because it asserts that no idealized picture of human nature, no showing of will, no asceticism or decision, can bring about a result which improves upon what has already been attained, and—mark this well—attained in one who was executed and beaten, one who was thirsty, one who, to the very last drop of blood, was "given for many"—and who *thereby* was made perfect. Before this one alone the law is dumb, every accusation is silenced. It is this one who will judge all others. Every person now living must yield in his presence.

On these two points Christianity is unique, and in a certain sense it can be said to be intolerant. It is however a question of being intolerant and being conscious of uniqueness under human conditions that are universal. Before proceeding further it is time to bring together what has previously been said about God's compelling and accusing activity through the law.

The Christian faith includes a concession that all people—even those who believe in Christ—are arbitrary in their choice of whom they will regard as their neighbor. There are consequently people who are deserving of concern but who are neglected. Their needs become relevant to all through what we have earlier called the demand-notes which are directed to the surrounding society. Therefore a society's legal enactments, since they demand that concern be shown for all, are God's work. They are means by which the Creator drives people to serve one another. No greater love for those in need can anywhere be found than in the readiness of church members to subordinate themselves to the public law, in order that actual service toward the neighbor, which the law intends, might become a reality. This implies that Christian people, with their unique faith in the One God, live intermingled with others, and that they are pressured by God to carry out the same actions as everyone else.

The Christian faith also includes the acknowledgement that God has full right to accuse all people, even those who believe in Christ. To say that God both compels and accuses does not mean that he compels first and accuses afterwards. If we believe in Christ therefore, have constantly before us the servant image, we cannot be aware of being *compelled* to serve without at the same time being aware that we are *accused*. The accusation is this: You should be willing, but you are unwilling. Inasmuch as they stand under this accusation, Christians stand on the same plane as all other people on earth. It is only before secular judgment seats that there are differences among people; before God, all are alike.

What we have now said about the Christian standing on the same plane as all others is further strengthened by faith in Christ— that is, by that feature of Christianity which is uniquely Christian. We need only look to the synoptic gospels as they report the scenes around Golgotha, with a sure instinct for what is the universally new and creative element in the crucifixion. All are alike—the apostles who betrayed, the soldiers who divided up the garments, the malefactors on the side-crosses—all are on the same plane; none has any other possibility than to accept forgiveness. It is impossible to begin talking about qualitative differences among people in the presence of the cross.

CARICATURES AND IMAGES

This segment of our presentation looks toward the second article about Christ, the Son. To indicate the threshold character of this segment we will use a series of metaphors, all having to do with pictures, in the three sub-sections. Some pictures are caricatures, but even in these the original is in some way reproduced. There are four points, related to this, which are of special importance and are here stated in a summary fashion.

1. Human beings are created in God's image. In our spontaneous expressions of life—which we do not control but which empower us—there is expressed both that which gives life its meaning, and also that which is constantly lost in the destruction that is encountered in the world.

2. We feel guilt when having been overcome by the destructive forces we also draw others down with us. This guilt is in negative form an image of what we ought to be; we view ourselves against the intention of God in creation and recognize that we have become distorted.

3. We are aware of being under compulsion to serve others, even though we do not feel love toward them. The works of the law (which result) are only imitations of spontaneous goodness, imitations which never succeed in reproducing the original.

4. Jesus is the complete, undamaged human, down in the midst of the destruction—he is "God's image," that which all humans were intended to be.

Guilt Is a Negative Imprint

Guilt results when we see how something ought to be but is not. We cannot feel guilt without having an idea of how we ourselves ought to be; it is only against that background that we can see our own deviation as something evil.

But just as the actual laws of a society can cover up what is wrong and give it the appearance of right, so also a person's feelings of guilt can veil one's actual guilt. The existing laws may not take care of what is actually wrong in society, and consequently need to be changed. In much the same way, an individual's feelings of guilt can give the appearance that a person is engaged in a genuine self-examination and is moving out of a destructive attitude, while the actual situation may be the opposite. Our guilt feelings may be a flight away from the real cause of our turmoil—a confrontation with ourselves which we are not able to bring about.

This does not mean that we should be able to avoid guilt completely. When old laws are rescinded it is not in order that we may have lawlessness instead. All societies that function are, without exception, built on law. A person who is without consciousness of guilt, a person who never feels that correction and regret have any place in human life, that person lacks an identity. "We are *no one* in guiltlessness," says Løgstrup. In the denial of guilt we overlook the fact that we do really live at the expense of other people in our very will to live and in our efforts to expand our existence. To live at all is to live in debt to others.[7] If we deny this fact we could destroy ourselves, for we need others just as they need us.

We mentioned earlier that the greatest difference between ancient and modern Christianity lies in the view that forgiveness has recently become "ethically impotent." Church bodies are undoubtedly conditioned by the prevailing culture that tends to ignore any suggestion of guilt. Everything that we receive and accept from without is thought to be our right. We don't need to thank anyone for the good that comes to us. That would demean the value that every person can properly claim. The old paternalistic attitude of doing good to those in less favorable circumstance has been succeeded by welfare based on taxpayers' money, collected and distributed as impersonally as possible. No one needs to feel that one has received a gift. A society so ordered tends to eliminate guilt and to deny its value for our human existence.

Other sectors of society display similar features. If we harm someone intentionally, it is evidence that we are "maladjusted." This can always be explained in terms of our earlier environment and

unfortunate childhood experiences. That is to say, one can understand a person's unacceptable behavior in the same way that one can
understand why a plant or a piece of land yields a poor harvest.
The land, the plant, the person are all objects which can be made
better. None of them have guilt.

When church bodies follow this pattern, they cease putting forgiveness at the center. Instead they preach "changing the structure
of society," that is, changing something which is an object, and
which ought to be viewed as an object. But this is not the case with
the person. We live because of the services others perform for us,
and therefore, regardless of how much we pay in taxes, we cannot
withdraw from these basic conditions of our existence. We continue to be ruled by what we have previously called "memories of
the irreparable," and we can find no help except from the psychia-
trist. The situation is made worse by the fact that if the Christian
proclamation is not socially "progressive" and does not busy itself
talking about "structures," it is often individualistic and traditional
and concerns itself with false concepts of guilt. Sin consists of
neglect of prayer time, carelessness about church attendance, etc.

Genuine guilt, which is anchored in our very existence, arises
from the fact that none of us lives without having received and
benefited from the self-denial of others. We cannot look into our own
life without realizing that each of us is called to be a person from
whom someone else draws the courage to live. Meaninglessness results when we fail to answer this call and instead burden and spoil
other lives. This sense of meaninglessness is the experience of guilt
in an unarticulated form. It is the claim made by those natural
expressions of life which belong to one's health but which have been
lost. Guilt is, therefore, health in a negative form.[8] Formulated bib-
lically, God's image is seeking to come to expression but is encountering opposition.

That Which Is Forced Is an Imitation

With this we have come back to the law which compels. God requires that certain external acts be done. The point in the "first use
of the law" is this: if we do not love our neighbor, we must be
coerced to act outwardly as though we do. A piece of bread is just
as nourishing for the hungry when it is given unwillingly as when
it is given in love.

Among pietists, deeds done under constraint were viewed as
evil, as hypocritical. This is because interest in the first use of the
law was very weak in Pietism. A favorite image for the pietistic

preacher was a tree on which apples were hung. But the only acceptable apples were those that grew naturally on the tree. There is, of course, a biblical saying concerning good fruit from a good tree (cf. Matt. 7:17). But the contrast is between the good tree with the good fruit and the poor tree with the poor fruit (Matt. 7:16, 18). According to Jesus, if an apple is good it is good, even if it hangs on a tree as an ornament without any vitality of its own.

When the law constrains or compels us to some action, it is not seeking to make us good. The law is a part of God's *creative* work. It aims, quite simply, at producing good exterior products, just as God does when he creates clothes, food, house, and home. Nowhere in the world are workers jubilantly happy all the time. God prefers willing co-workers, but when he does not find any he takes unwilling ones.

There are three things to be said about these deeds which are carried out under some measure of compulsion: 1) they are just as useful to others as are those services that are freely given; 2) they are risky for the one who does them only when one imagines that they are signs of one's private goodness; 3) they constitute accusations against the doer's own heart. It is appropriate now to look at each of these points by itself.

The first thing to be said is that modern Christianity, in comparison with older, classical Christianity, is egocentrically religious. The preaching constantly comes back to an examination of the Christian's motives for action; the sermon offers instruction on "how one becomes a Christian." When such instruction becomes dominant, it necessarily becomes egocentric. What really needs to be said about works according to classical Christian faith is simply that the chief place in our everyday work must be given to turning out good external products, and that this is just what God wants us to do.

The goodness in a deed is its usefulness to others. From the point of view of the deed itself it is a matter of indifference whether it is performed by the church or by a non-Christian group. There is no good to be found on earth, regardless of who carries it out, which is not worked by the Creator.

If one leaves this egocentricity where everything has to do with the soul's inner development, and goes instead over to the political preaching about "structures" in society, one continues to be bound by egocentric inclinations—at least this is the case if one feels it is necessary to cash in on social and political improvements for the benefit of the church's account. For instance, if one feels compelled to say: "This comes from Christianity," or "Here the church has made its contribution," one sounds like a politician during an election campaign. For the Christian congregation such talk is foreign.

One may compare the way contemporary groups who have become convinced of the early end of the world conduct themselves with the conduct of the ancient Christian congregations in Corinth, Ephesus, Philippi, etc. Those old congregations stand out as miracles of sober faithfulness to their ordinary, everyday work. Today such groups often give up their jobs and homes in order to await the last day on some chosen spot. The early Christians were diligent in their everyday work, in order that they might "earn their own living"—surely the most prosaic formulation of the motive for work which can be thought of—and in order that they might "be able to give to those in need" (1 Thess. 4:11; 2 Thess. 3:12; Eph. 4:28). The New Testament gives no account of improvements in the Roman empire as a result of contributions made by Christians. It is a reflection of the way modern Christianity has been distorted that this inner ethical strength demonstrated through everyday work has come to be regarded as a weakness. One must affect the social structure rather than just work within it.

The verdict of the Reformation is even more clear. Luther had struggled to find a gracious God, and his concern was that the *gospel* might be clearly and purely preached everywhere. But when he explained the Ten Commandments in the Small Catechism it is the *law* he was giving instructions about. From the Fourth Commandment on, the concern is always with the relationship to the neighbor— seven commandments in a row. What is remarkable is the completely "unreligious" relationship to the neighbor which is the mark of these explanations. Obey your parents, help those in danger, honor your true mate, support and protect other people's sources of livelihood, be solicitous about the good reputation of others, see to it that your neighbors are not robbed, attempt to get employees to stay with their jobs instead of enticing them away with higher wages. This is the shockingly trivial list of works!

Not once does Luther say that we are obligated to try to make our neighbor a Christian. Not once does he say that we should try to make our neighbor morally better. Such activities are not included in the deeds the law requires.

For the person who is doing the acting the trivial nature of the deeds to be done is the best protection against the danger that attends all legal righteousness—the notion that the works of the law are evidences of the doer's goodness. They are rather signs of the goodness of the Creator, goodness under compulsion; they are not signs of the person's inner goodness. They are *imitations* of the spontaneous manifestations of life—mercy, love, and trust which empower us even without our decision. They are imitations, but when the original is lacking, the imitation is not to be despised.

Finally, inasmuch as they are imitations, they accuse the doer inwardly, toward the "heart." When God constrains, the accusation always lies hidden in the constraint. When the law provokes to deeds, its "first use," there is enclosed within it the law's "second use," its pointing out of the absence of spontaneity. If, without any conscious decision on our part, we treat our neighbor's sorrow as though it were our own, we will then be able to judge what is genuine. This ability to judge will also free us from the notion that we are good just because we come to the aid of someone in need. Indeed, the clearer the picture we have of our actual *spontaneous* life-expressions, the more we will be able to resist feeling self-righteous when we do something good. A conviction of our own ethical emptiness goes very well with practical action for the benefit of others.

God's Image

When we talk about a spontaneity that empowers a person, we are talking about creation rather than law. This is a creation that gradually unfolds as spontaneous life-expressions occur. Yet it is pure creation; the constraint is lacking. The person is wholeheartedly involved in the action; indeed, it is only after one has acted that one becomes aware of what it was that moved one to action.

If this is the original, uncoerced spontaneity of creation, then Christ is the definitive reappearance of that freedom. Jesus' life is a single, complete "spontaneous life-manifestation" without anything subtracted from it, or to use the language of Hebrews, "tempted as we are, yet without sinning" (Heb. 4:15). Before there was law there was pure creation; after the law there was once again pure creation. The law has intervened (cf. Rom. 5:20; Gal. 3:19).

About both the created person and Christ, the biblical texts use the term "God's image" in a surprising variety of forms (Gen. 1:26f.; Col. 1:15f.; 2 Cor. 3:18; also Phil. 3:21; Eph. 4:24; 2 Cor. 4:4; 1 John 3:2, and deepest of all, Rom. 6:3-11). If one understands Adam to be an individual in history in the same sense as Jesus, one tends to arrange creation, the law, and Jesus' life as three separate entities in a time sequence with years attached to them even if one does not know exactly what the years are. Some argue for this sort of historical sequence because they see a need to anchor Jesus in history, somewhere in the general area of Herod and Pilate, Caesar

Augustus, Nero, and others. But with this approach to the matter
it is almost certain that we will miss the main point of what the
biblical utterances intend to convey.

For the point is that *each* person, if that person is in Christ, goes
through this history. Years and dates can be found, but they are
different for each of us. Our birth is creation; our pain in holding
ourself upright is life under the law; our baptism is our entrance
into a process of dawning life although under a blanket of death;
the consummation of baptism is our bodily dying, which constitutes
the end of the reign of law. Therefore, it means life, freedom, and
praise.

The setting in which this human life-process takes place can be
observed by everyone. It is as public and observable as Israel's history, the life of Jesus, or the reign of a Roman emperor. When one
looks back across one's life span and sees all the moments of which
it is comprised—the few flashes of fresh spontaneity (which no one
can cause to return but which were once given), the demanding years
of hard work, and the impending death—one notices in the midst of
all this, the story about a life other than one's own, a "gospel." It is
only when the story of the life of Jesus is told over and over again,
in naive and anthropomorphic language, that the bond can be tied
between the gospel and the fate of the individual person.

In each individual's existence there is creation and law; they
belong to our existence, and they are the basis for our waiting for
"him who is to come." We who live surrounded by constraints and
facing death cannot help but think about the future in images from
the gospel's story of Jesus. The New Testament uses such images
or symbols in its description of "heaven"; it uses symbols that cor-
respond to Jesus' earthly activity—his fellowship at meals, his service toward those he meets: ". . . he will gird himself and have them
sit at table, and he will come and serve them" (Luke 12:37).[9]

Whatever this symbol may mean, one thing is sure: it does not
mean that eternal life is the ongoing dominion of God's law. Heaven,
according to Christian faith, will be characterized by freedom
and praise.

O God, you who are love, release me from the chill in my own heart. Days and weeks pass and I remain locked into my own self, and find no way out to others. Let the simple deeds I perform in my everyday work reach and support someone, even if it be only one person. You have woven us all together, and you see the threads that bind into an invisible fellowship the tired and the strong, the fair-hearted and the brave. I know that I am in your hand, and I know that I daily receive good gifts from many who find it harder to believe than I do. Take my ordinary, everyday actions, and send them where you will.

Lord teach me to become accustomed to the night. When my duties wear away at my strength, let me recognize in that weariness my coming death—and let me preserve faith's certainty that death is life for all who are in Jesus Christ. O God, I thank you that he has lived and been one of us. No darkness is without light when he is with me.

The Second Article
The Son

Christ

. . . as one from whom men hide their faces he was despised, and we esteemed him not.

(Isa. 53:3)

Although he was a Son, he learned obedience through what he suffered.

(Heb. 5:8)

III

Works

THE RESTORED CREATION

Jesus' life can be said to constitute the reconquest of the created order, the halting of destruction. This is true of both his birth and his public ministry.

Jesus' Birth

When one moves from our time back to the early church, to the church that produced both the Apostles' and the Nicene Creeds, one makes a surprising observation concerning the teaching about Jesus' birth. That he is born of a woman is the great marvel—as great a marvel as that he suffered on the cross. One would not expect either of these deviant and ungodlike happenings to intrude into the story of God's Son.

That the woman was a virgin does not diminish the miracle at all. This is interpreted in such a way that the virgin birth becomes another evidence of Jesus' likeness to Adam: both are "born of God" (compare the startling turn in the genealogy in Luke 3:38: "who was the son of Adam, who was the son of God"). The term "adam" thereby remains a designation for "humanity," precisely as in the Hebrew. The virgin birth like the crucifixion is interpreted as a manifestation of Jesus' "human nature."

The background is certainly Gnosticism which preserved a Greek concept of God. It was as inconceivable within that framework that God should enter the body of a woman as that he should weep and feel anguish in the garden of Gethsemane. The absence of the male

in conception did not improve the situation from the viewpoint of
the Gnostics. The birth remained as repugnant as before. Against
this fear of the human, the Creed makes its confession: ". . . born
of the virgin Mary, suffered under Pontius Pilate."

This is the reason that it was self-evident to the early church that
Jesus was born of a virgin. The doctrine was embraced after the
Gnostics had expelled the dissidents, even those who opposed the
teaching about Jesus' divinity (the Adoptionists, Arians, etc.). It
does not appear, therefore, that the doctrine of the virgin birth constituted any protection for the doctrine of Christ's divine nature.
In the third century, Paul of Samosata and his associates fought
against all talk of Jesus as the Son of God, but all believed in the
virgin birth and drew the inference from it that Jesus was *human*.[1]

These are the historical facts that contradict present talk about
the virgin birth being a guarantee of Christ's divinity. Such facts
are surprising enough but the early church provides other facts
that are equally surprising. In all accounts of the earliest Christian
proclamation, Jesus' death and resurrection are specifically named,
but no mention is made of his birth (1 Cor. 15:1-4; Acts 2:22-36;
3:12-26; 4:8-12; 5:29-32). The powerful impact of the resurrection
expresses itself in the fact that "the first day of the week"—a usual
Jewish workday corresponding to Monday in contemporary practice
—immediately became a day of worship. This was the case the very
first week after the resurrection, and it continued throughout the
New Testament period (John 20:26; Acts 20:7; 1 Cor. 16:2; Rev.
1:10). But nowhere are we told that Jesus' birthday was celebrated
by anyone.

This becomes even more apparent as the yearly holidays gradually
developed. Easter was celebrated very early, already in the second
century. But there was no Christmas celebration for three centuries.
No one knew when Jesus was born. When the celebration of Christmas began in the fourth century, it was with the aim of wiping out
the heathen sun-worship, which had its big festival at the end of
December. The celebration of the birth of Jesus was intended to
replace "the unconquered sun's day," December 25th.[2] The celebration of Jesus' birth would not have been shifted around like this if
it had been considered a part of the fundamental faith from the
very beginning. Easter and Sunday *were* celebrated from the beginning (each Sunday is an Easter, and Sundays were celebrated from
the beginning).

To this we must add the testimony of Paul, the author of the
earliest writings of the New Testament. He never mentions the
virgin birth, and his statement "born of woman, born under the

law" (Gal. 4:4) rather suggests an entirely normal birth. Over
against this evidence, we have the two birth accounts in Matthew
and Luke, both of them late texts and embellished with legendary
features, and we have the use of the word "virgin" in the second
article of both the Apostles' Creed and the Nicene Creed. This constitutes the support for the virgin birth. It is certain that there were
early Christian congregations that did not know of this teaching.

This is a case in which two different points of view must be characterized as *Christian*.[3] One can take the point of view that Jesus
was born as a result of an ordinary conception, and that the dramatic, unexplainable, creative act of God is to be found in the resurrection. It was this that the first disciples believed; that is why the
empty tomb was so unbelievable to them. On the other hand, one can
with support from later texts hold the thesis that Jesus was born
"without the cooperation of man." In that case, the essential miracle
is already present in the birth. The cross and the resurrection are
subordinated to the basic miracle of his birth, and this is reflected
also in liturgical ways. In churches with a highly developed incarnation theology of the type prevalent in the fourth century, one bows
one's head in reverence when in the worship service one comes to the
point where the Creed mentions the birth, while one listens with a
straight neck to words about the suffering on the cross.

But this puts the question in a new setting. Above, we were able
to accept two different points of view in this matter and characterize
both of them as Christian. We must now assert that there are good
grounds in our time for stating the case for the position that Jesus
was born exactly as we.

The reason for this is that—in distinction from the early church—
we cannot think of the virgin birth as a sign of *humanness*. For us
the virgin birth stands as a guarantee that Jesus is *God*, who has
broken out of ordinary human life which has been defaced by destroying powers. We find ourselves today in a cultural climate in
which Jesus' humanity and his divinity are set against one another.
If we had been given the assignment of choosing texts concerning a
divine Savior out of that rich collection of narrative material, we
would never have included that episode in Gethsemane where the
Savior weeps "with loud cries and tears," where "his sweat became
like great drops of blood falling down upon the ground" (Heb. 5:7;
Luke 22:44). Earliest Christianity could hold onto both divinity and
unrestricted humanity as one; for us this is a problem.

When such a problematic situation prevails, and two points of view
can both be said to be Christian, one ought to weigh carefully the
arguments, each against the other. Where do modern churches devi-

ate most noticeably from classical Christianity? The answer is given almost before the question is asked—in the interpretation of the cross and the resurrection. To actually win the *victory* on the cross is something that we cannot conceive of unless the struggle is genuine, that is, unless the outcome could have been other than it was, or unless Jesus could have given way under the attacks of the destroyer. Temptation is temptation only if the possibility of yielding to it is present. Otherwise the temptation is only an appearance.

Today we seem to regard Jesus' temptation as nothing more than mere appearance. This becomes apparent in many details of Christian worship, in songs and prayers. (It can be seen also in the development of an independent secular picture of Jesus in films, operas, and novels—a picture of Jesus with only a human nature. The churches are free to cultivate the divine nature.) The docetic features of the church's interpretation are most clearly evident in its representation of the passion history. Even the moments of anguish tend to become manifestations of Jesus' tranquility as the Messiah. He cries out: "My God, my God, why hast thou forsaken me?" (Mark 15:34) because it is proper that the Messiah should cite the messianic psalm (Ps. 22:1) before his death. We cannot combine this majestic citation with the *actual feeling of anguish* on Jesus' part, as earlier generations could.[4]

If we are to understand the cross and resurrection as the center of the gospel, we must now (in contrast to earlier times) take seriously the humanity of Jesus in the temptation experience. This means that the scales must be tilted toward "ordinary human birth" and not to the "virgin birth." But, as has already been said, both points of view are Christian. And it needs further to be said that no concession is being made to rationalism by the deletion of the virgin birth, for the resurrection is at least as offensive to reason as is the virgin birth. Above all, there is the fact that the oldest Christian tradition does not know about a virgin birth, while all Christian proclamation begins and is based upon the amazing message that "he is risen."

His Ministry

The earliest church fathers did not, as a rule, think that God "became man" through Jesus' birth in Bethlehem. To be sure, the incarnation began there. But it continued as long as Jesus ministered to human need. Jesus had to pass through all the situations of human life in order to be completely human. To these situations belong temptation and death. Therefore it is sometimes said that only on the cross did Jesus "complete the incarnation," that is, enter into all that belongs to the flesh or the human.

Granted, this is a later interpretation, coming from about the end of the second century. But there is an aspect of the original New Testament which fits well into this interpretation. We refer to the placing of the temptation account immediately after the baptism in the Jordan (Mark 1:12f.; Matt. 4:1f.; Luke 4:1f.). The three synoptics report how Jesus immediately after the baptism is driven out into the wilderness, and they agree that it was the *Spirit* who drove him out. His life work cannot begin at any other place than in the wilderness, and alone.

What this means is that Jesus' baptism in the Jordan is understood as an initiation into the sacrificial death on the cross. His temptation in the wilderness is the temptation to exercise power for personal gain. When Jesus resists the temptation and overcomes it, he does this as an obedient human being. All the Old Testament texts he cites are words which refer to a human being in simple and helpless obedience. A divine being could hardly utter them. In the answer Jesus gives to the three successive temptations, God is standing *above* Jesus. All three times Jesus talks about God as one who stands over him and demands obedience of his child. "Man shall not live by bread alone, but by every word that proceeds from the mouth of God" (Matt. 4:4); "You shall not tempt the Lord your God" (Matt. 4:7); and finally, "You shall worship the Lord your God and him only shall you serve" (Matt. 4:10). These are the same accents one hears in Gethsemane.

For what then shall messianic power be used, if not for one's own gain? The answer is given in those oft-repeated words about the servant being the greatest. This pattern is expressly set against the usual pattern according to which the powerful use the weak (Mark 10:41-45, and parallels). The whole of Jesus' ministry can be subsumed under the word *servant*—the healing of the sick, the proclamation about the coming kingdom of heaven for the poor and the hungry, the granting of forgiveness. Jesus' ministry is one whole and undivided deed—from birth, baptism in the Jordan, temptation in the wilderness, all the way to his death on the cross.

But this whole and undivided deed can be seen from different points of view: it restores the created order, it points forward toward a coming future, and it consists of simple services with short-range benefits extended to individuals (giving bread, etc.). It is not, however, that some parts of his ministry restore (and hence point back), while other parts give hope (and thus point forward), while still others constitute short-range services (and hence focus on the present). *All these three are one.* When a man who has lost the capacity to move takes up his bed and walks, he wins back a lost capacity for movement, and then the present is filled with unexpected joy. Then, too, the man has been given a future toward which he may move—a future of recovered health. A rich present, an open future—all these are held together at once.

Our contemporary culture has no difficulty retaining this simple and unified conception. On the contrary, the attempts to split these three aspects of Jesus' ministry and make different, incompatible entities out of them is felt to be unnatural and contrived.

DEEDS ARE SIGNS POINTING TO THE FUTURE

Jesus' role as a public figure is summarized by Matthew in two activities: he preached the gospel, and he healed the sick (Matt. 4:23). The kingdom comes through both of them.

Healing and Proclaiming

The proclamation of the gospel is directly described as a communication concerning the coming of the kingdom (Mark 1:15). This message is combined with a call to repentance. Consequently, in the proclamation of the gospel something is coming to us from without, something which we could not ourselves bring forth if it were not given. On the other hand, something is happening within us: we believe, we turn around (for repentance means a reversal of the direction in which we are moving). In precisely the same way, healing implies that something comes to us from outside, at the same time that a change is taking place in our personal well-being. "If it is by the finger of God that I cast out demons, then the kingdom of God has come upon you" (Luke 11:20). As individuals we become healthy, and at the same time the environment in which we exist is changed through the coming of a new "kingdom."

"Kingdom" means having dominion over something. To rule is to act against an enemy (see 1 Cor. 15:24-26). Therefore the coming of a kingdom points forward toward the future, precisely as does the preaching of the gospel. Healing and proclaiming have, therefore, the same character: both give something now, and, as a result of what they give now, both contain promises for the future. There was for quite a long time a discussion within biblical theology about the present and the future—that is, about the kingdom of heaven which is both present and being awaited. At times this discussion centered on grammatical terms: the tension between the indicative (something is) and the imperative (something ought to be in the future). But Paul uses both terms when he says that evil has died (Rom. 6:2) and also that evil ought to die (Rom. 6:12).

These grammatical terms can be applied to the spoken word, but they may be less useful in describing actions. Even though it might be difficult to think of an action of Jesus as being both indicative and imperative—at once present and future, yet his words and deeds do in fact have this character. They enter wholly into the present moment to heal an individual's present and specific need. Messianic acts so intentionally insignificant as those Jesus performed, do not fit what Judaism expected of a genuine Messiah. To devote hours to a single individual, to stop before a single sick person, is scandalous behavior on the part of one who presumes to bring about a new world order. But that is the way this Messiah acts—and precisely on that account he points forward to something which is entirely new.

Had Jesus undertaken to purge society through some grandiose action, he would have been following the usual pattern of society. What makes Jesus' action different is the element of Golgotha, the character of condescension, which is present even in Jesus' activity as healer in Galilee; it is present in the insignificance, in the focus on one person at a time.

This has implications also for our concept of the church. If one views the church in terms of Jesus' own deeds, then the church is seen to be most vulgar and shabby when it has "a strong position," which means that it is honored together with other organizations in society. The church's influence is most pure and genuine when it moves in where individuals are threatened, and where they do not get support from anyone else.

There is thus a relationship between words and deeds—both focus on the individual. Forgiveness, for example, is the spoken word focused on the individual. Healing and proclaiming are, according to the gospels, activities which function in the same way.[5] They seek out one who lacks something; they give and they raise up. This is connected with their being "sovereign life-expressions"; they break forth without any thought of organized activity. They are born entirely out of present human needs, and they approach us as though we alone were important. This is the only rank or status in the kingdom of heaven, as we catch glimpses of it in the parable about the final judgment, where the smallest and most easily forgotten actions are the greatest of all (Matt. 25:35-40).

These life-manifestations or expressions are sovereign also in the sense that they signify an actual *dominion*—the one who acts on them *rules*. For dominion triumphs over the destroying power, and

the root of destruction is desire on one's own behalf, "envy" as the
church fathers called it. The striking down of the evil dominion happens, therefore, only in those actions which are considered meaningless from the viewpoint of organized power; they are so small that
they are already considered to have achieved their purpose when a
lame girl walks, a deaf person hears, one guilt-ridden is made free,
etc. And once again, this happens on the cross. This is evident from
the words to the malefactor on the side-cross (Luke 23:34, 43). Consistent with the inverted rank, it is a king who dies on the cross.
Death itself is sovereign; there is not the least concession to the
desire for power.

We must keep all this in mind if we are to understand martyrdom
in the early church. The worldly power which moved against the
martyrs with violence was already the loser because of the nature
of its actions. That this power could cause outward harm was not
something that gave those who exercised it a share in the future.
The harm their power could inflict did not deprive the martyrs of
anything. Quite the contrary. The martyrs now had majesty be-
stowed upon them just as Jesus had earlier. This laid the founda-
tions for a future kingdom with an entirely new evaluation of "high"
and "low," a new kingdom which had the radical effect of making
this world all at once a thing of the past. Pilate was helpless when
Jesus died; Caesar in Rome was helpless when the martyrs died.

All of this is implicit in the deeds of Jesus. It lies imbedded in
the very character of forgiveness and healing for the individual.
(See Mark 2:2-11 concerning the combination of these two.) That is
why the deeds of Jesus are signs that point forward.[6]

Short-term Resurrection

Stories about how Jesus awakened the dead are few in number.
Whether we see behind them historical events or interpret them as
legendary embellishments of Jesus' work as a healer, the purpose of
the texts is clear. Those who were awakened through the power of
Jesus' word were raised up to a brief period of health and were not,
as in the case of Jesus on the third day, raised up to an eternal
dominion over the whole of humanity. Furthermore, the widow's son
in Nain, Lazarus, and the others do not forgive sins. They grow old
and die just as we do. Their short-term resurrections are, like the
rest of Jesus' deeds, signs that point forward.

There is a typology in these isolated awakenings from the dead.
A good deal of mischief has been done in modern theology with the
term "typology." It is sometimes said in the New Testament that an

Old Testament even is a type of that which is to come (about Adam and Christ in Rom. 5:14, cf. on Hagar and Sarah in Gal. 4:24). In our time such passages are often interpreted in such a way that the older event is completely emptied of its significance; the only meaning it seems to have lies in its reference to Christ. The picture we are given is of an aloof God whose only interest is in establishing a royal family. He wants to place a regent, Jesus, on the throne. Before the regent comes, God sets up signs whose function is to point forward—only forward. Such a Jesus also becomes heartless and aloof when he occupies the royal throne in the church.

The only typology that succeeds in pointing to Jesus as he actually *is* according to the gospels, the only event which is able to point forward, is the event which is complete in itself, and is meaningful in its simplicity. Other events can no doubt point forward to all sorts of possible rulers (who turn upside down God's priorities and who are destructive in their use of power). But only creation—meaningful in itself, meaningful by virtue of the simple fact that it is created—can point to Jesus.

That sublime list of believers in Hebrews 11 consists of people who have trusted in earthly things to the extent that earthly things are meaningful—boats which are able to carry one in the floods (11:7), countries to which one can migrate (11:8), overage women who give birth to children (11:11), and other such things recounted throughout the whole chapter (see especially 11:32-38). Inasmuch as they believed and persisted in these small matters, they could point forward to that which was even better (11:39f.).

The point in the evangelist's accounts of how the dead were awakened to life lies precisely here—like the Creator, Jesus does not feel that a fleeting gift is too small to give to a person. What happens to the woman of Nain is characteristic. Jesus' deed involved a short-term gift to a widow: "He gave him to his mother" (Luke 7:15). If one is a widow, to have a son is especially important.

We will soon say more about Jesus' deeds as *service*. But now our theme is Jesus' deeds as *signs pointing forward*. This theme is illustrated in those texts that deal with a short-term resurrection life.

A comparison is drawn in these accounts: when this happens, how much more then shall not. . . . This is the way Jesus talks about the lilies of the field in the Sermon on the Mount (Matt. 6:30). Just because the lilies, like the birds (Matt. 6:26), can instruct us about freedom from anxiety, this does not imply that the lilies and the birds are reduced to empty signs whose only meaning is that they point to something else. They are not like road signs; if the town the sign points to does not exist, the sign does not have any meaning.

But a lily is in itself meaningful, and a bird is in itself meaningful—
and for that reason they can demonstrate to us that we have value,
and therefore they can help us out of our anxiety.

Descriptions of creation in the book of Job (e.g. Job 39) have the
same clarity in tone as the Sermon on the Mount. All creatures in
nature are meaningful in themselves—the lion, the raven, the mountain goat, the wild ass, the horse, the falcon. It would be nonsense
to argue that these animals must "mean something spiritual"—and
if they do not, what business have they in the Bible? But something
of this has found its way into the talk about typology. The reason, as
usual, is that the first article has been ignored.

The only plausible position is embodied in the following two general theses:

1) Something given in creation can be a sign that points to Christ
because it is meaningful in our earthly existence (e.g. the grain of
wheat that dies and yields a harvest).

2) A miracle of healing, or an awakening from the dead carried
out by Jesus during his lifetime, can be a sign pointing forward,
having in view eternal life, because Jesus' concrete actions (such as
in Nain, Capernaum, or Bethany), fulfilled an ordinary everyday
function. It is the single act of service, unreservedly aimed at the
present—just as unreservedly as the grain of wheat gives itself at
the time of planting—which points beyond the present to the harvest,
to eternal life.

Hope

What has just been said has important consequences for the question of Christian hope. One cannot set the expectations we have when
faced by earthly and short-term difficulties over against our hope for
eternal life. Since Marxism works with political utopias as a necessary ingredient in human life, the question of hope has become a
meeting place for dialog between Marxists and Christians. It would
be absurd to allow Marxism to take over all earthly hope, as if Christianity were concerned only with the hope of eternal life. This would
be a misinterpretation of the biblical material.[7]

The decisive difference between Christianity and Marxism does
not lie in the fact that the former adds an eternal hope to the tem-
poral expectations for a better society which Marxism entertains.
The biblical material reviewed above shows that people can be encom-
passed by an eternal hope and at the same time hold earthly expectations. The decisive difference between the biblical and Marxist views

is to be found in their different understandings of the forces of destruction (a point to which we shall return later).

For Marxism the evil is a certain economic system. This is why the good is to be achieved by tearing down this system and bringing in a different order of society. To be sure, the cultivation of a new person is also needed in order to reach this goal. The Marxists charge that capitalism denigrates people so that they do not really know who they are. Capitalism does not allow the workers to retain the products of their own hands, but takes away that to which the workers have a right. It is this drawing off of profits by a few, at the expense of the many, which is destructive.[8]

Marxist hope, therefore, depends on a change in society—and also incites strenuous efforts to achieve this goal. The system of private capitalism which Marxism regards as wholly destructive, is at the same time viewed as good by other people. They perceive free competition to be a system which is good in itself. Neither in Marxism nor in the system built on private gain does one consider that destruction has affected the individual person. The debate between the two conflicting systems is limited to how the economy should be structured. In the one case, the hope is for a change in society so that the power of capital will be diminished; in the other case, the hope is for freedom in the economy so that one's own profits will be forthcoming in the future.

Where two such systems vie for the loyalty of people, and then absorb their hope, the people become burdened by many intense hopes and longings that remain unarticulated and unfulfilled. They have no public language with which to clothe these hopes. People continue to hope, they continue to look for a renewal which will re-create their lives. The only words that can give voice to this hope are personal, private words (poetry, conversation, etc.). In the public and political language the person is made a thing. He is "clientele," "work force," "purchasing power," "factor in production," or a similar mechanically-viewed concept.

What is unique about the gospel accounts of Jesus' deeds is the direct connection between his deeds and the hope (i.e., the prayer) which is to be found in existence itself—not in the needs of any certain group, but in every person's hope and prayer. The specifically Christian does not stand in opposition to the human, but rather answers the cry for help which comes from within the human heart (that is why the gospel is a story about how God lives in a human person). The church, which proclaims the gospel, misses the decisive point when it identifies its hope with the expectations from different social structures, which are served by the different "isms." When the church makes this mistake it does not become more human, which it sometimes seems to imply, but rather less human. The church then begins to think in terms of power, a concept foreign to the church and one which makes people into things.

This does not mean that the church stands outside of the opinion-forming process. Church members clearly stand within it, but they cannot make the choice between political or economic systems the ultimate choice. As Christians we take part in all of this, but at a distance. We do this, not because we have an extra hope about eternity in addition to all our other hopes, but because we see in society another and more devastating destruction than can result from a poor economic system. This deeper destruction is illustrated by Jesus' deeds, which are directed toward individuals.

DEEDS ARE ACTS OF SERVICE

Here we return to the connection between the apparently insignificant everyday deeds of Jesus on the one hand, and the cross on the other. There is the same sort of paradoxicality in both; meaning is to be found in the apparently meaningless.

To Heal and to Give

The spotlight has too long been focused on the difficulty of reconciling the healing miracles with natural laws. Because of this focus, our judgment about them has been off-center. To eat with publicans and sinners does not conflict with natural laws, but these meals also constituted deeds, and were just as shocking (and for the same reason) as was healing the lame. For the real shock when the lame man was healed did not consist of the fact that he walked, but in something else—the forgiveness of sins (Mark 2:7). At that time people accepted the fact that "wonders" could be performed by powerful people, either in the service of God or the devil (see Matt. 24:24). The remarkable thing does not lie in the miraculous itself, but in the *kind* of miraculous deed Jesus performed. To understand that specific kind of miraculous deed, one must study them all—the healings, the feedings, and the forgiveness of sins.

Let us summarize the features of Jesus' deeds, beginning with the negative. Not a single deed of Jesus was national; not a single one was intended to give support to Israel as a people. This is a remarkable difference between Jesus and the Old Testament. In the earlier time, the great wonders of grace had to do with the people—the deliverance out of Egypt, the crossing of the Red Sea, the return from Babylon. Jesus, on the contrary, expressed himself sarcastically about his own people, and quoted Old Testament passages that emphasized God's grace toward the *outsider*—Nineveh, the queen of Sheba (Matt. 12:41f.), the widow of Zarephath, Naaman the Syrian (Luke 4:25-27), not to mention the most derided of all, the Samaritans, to whom Jesus returned again and again, always with a positive evaluation.

Two aliens also had a share in Jesus' healing activity: the Roman officer (Luke 7:2), and the Greek woman, who was Syrophoenician by birth (Mark 7:26). In this way the narrator of the gospel notes that the diakonia activity of Christians after Jesus' death, among Greeks and Romans, had support from Jesus. He had himself acted thus, at least occasionally. There is agreement among historians and sociologists that such service toward the weak and the sick has been characteristic of Europe and constitutes a part of the general western culture in distinction from the cultures of Asia and Africa. In our time, this western trend is sometimes more strongly accented outside the church than within it.

The fact that none of Jesus' deeds was national in character has two implications for those who would be his followers 1) we are called to a service that crosses boundaries between people, and 2) we are called to take account of the needs of others. The real problems of the needy are not solved by laws; the forces of destruction lie so deep that no law can reach them.

A second feature of Jesus' deeds is that none of them was cultural in character. The art of writing was not utilized. Neither was there a well-equipped organization. Jesus dealt with individuals, and he spoke to them orally—that is all. If he had not become known in the literature of the world through the writings of others, he would have been forgotten by everyone after a few decades. That is clearly the way he wants others after him to live also. The deeds which are praised in the final judgment are without significance from the viewpoint of world history—to give food, to bring a cup of water, or to visit the sick.

These deeds affirm everyday life. There is not one ounce of that feeling of being elevated above the ordinary which characterizes Buddha. Jesus is just as solicitous about life as is a good midwife, elementary school teacher, or nurse, to name three callings which care for life but do not produce external, tangible products that remain after the work is done. Jesus' deeds are characterized by their focus on one person at a time, and at points at which that person is threatened with destruction. And he expends his life in such deeds, fully conscious of the cost and willing to pay it (Mark 10:45).[9]

At the present time, Jesus' priority of the individual person over against narrow national values is generally understood. But some would still be shocked if in a disastrous fire Jesus put the rescue of a child above the rescue of a Rembrandt painting. And those few who would not be shocked by such a setting of priorities would be disappointed to hear Jesus say that the rescue of a little child is more important than the successful implementation of a political program resulting in a higher standard of living for large groups of people. But these three priorities—the person over the nation, the person over the cultural products, and the person over economic programs—are all expressions for one and the same thing: the offensive determination to be as the grain of wheat, to fall into the ground and die for the individual well-being of many.

Therefore one can say in summary: The true fruit of the earthly deeds of Jesus are people who live as grains of wheat, and who consequently care for and support life by offering up their own. They do not give rise to great cultural products, but there will be a harvest—new grains of wheat, people willing to devote their lives to the care and support of those in need.

The Unity of Cross and Deeds

This giving up of one's life raises a problem for the church which is the custodian of Jesus' deed in the world. It is correct to say that the culmination of Jesus' life consists in his death on the cross. But his death on the cross actually began with the temptation in the wilderness where Jesus turned back the vision of a life devoted to his own gain and elected instead a life of service to others. The same death occurs, bit by bit, in all his works. If he continues to do the kind of things he had chosen to do, it is clear that the cross will be the end. Then he will die like the grain of wheat.

Such a life has its own inner need and its anxiety. Jesus experienced anxiety in a unique form in Gethsemane and at Golgotha. But all those who live as his followers taste doubt, though in lesser degree. The doubt we speak of is not about the validity of statements but about the meaning of our own existence. When the grain of wheat falls there is no harvest to be seen; nevertheless, we are to fall, to expend our life on little deeds. Many have lived thus without knowing that they lived "in Christ."

This is a problem for today's church. For in the church the interpretation of Jesus' death was formulated into statements. Sometimes one church had an interpretation which was contradicted by the interpretation in another church. Often the conflict between the interpretations was justified by the facts, because there were absurd and destructive interpretations to be found within the church which needed to be opposed. But what was especially disastrous about the emphasis on statements was the shift in the nature of doubt—doubt became intellectual distrust of theological statements. From the biblical point of view, this whole emphasis and concern about doctrinal statements is a false concern regardless of whether one answers yes or no to the statements. Jesus never summoned anyone to a struggle over theological statements.

At the same time that the doctrinal concerns of the churches have become distorted, the effect of Jesus' earthly deeds has penetrated further into actual human lives and has resulted in service to others. We speak of "the social Jesus," or as some say, "liberal theology." No doctrinal conflict arises on account of the use of such a cliché because those who have this label applied to them do not reply with any statements about their own purity of doctrine; on the contrary they are apt to say, "I am not a Christian but . . ."

Dietrich von Oppen has coined the harsh allegation that the world follows Christ, not the churches.[10] This is an exaggeration, but it points to a real task that now confronts the church. It is the task of recognizing the genuine connection between the death of Jesus on the cross and all activity in society which has the character of service. Such activity often involves people working with a Red Cross or with other groups that use biblical names for their work (e.g., "Samaritans" of various kinds). These aspects of our life together have their origin in the deeds of Jesus. But the deeds and the cross are a unity.

Those who pattern their own actions after the deeds of Jesus will be identified with more than his deeds. In the pattern of action that follows Jesus' deeds there is always the example of the grain of wheat in which the doubt about the meaning of existence gradually gives way to the faith that spends itself in service to others.

*O God, you are the God of all people. You consider all
oppression to be evil, without regard to which people
may be the oppressors and which people may be the
victims. We belong to that humanity which you have
created, and we know that you want to use us to heal
all the wounds inflicted by the enemy. Give us endurance.
Keep us from being worn down by all the evil we witness.*

*It strengthens our hearts to know that Jesus endured.
We thank you that the image of him has been burned
into our consciences, so that we can never find peace
when we try to forget. We have no explanation for the
mystery there was in his life, or for his unaccountable
presence everywhere. We are captive to his example,
and we cannot be true persons if we cease to follow him.*

*God, your humanity awaits our deeds. Give us that
faithfulness which endures when no one sees any
meaning. Help us in the darkness to hear the footfalls
of him who has gone on ahead.*

IV

The Cross

Very early in the history of dogma, Jesus' nature came to be understood as twofold—divine and human. These concepts were used as aids for understanding what happened in Jesus, but they are not found in the Bible. They took form later in a milieu that was stamped by Greek philosophy. They have had a fateful effect on the interpretation of the crucifixion.

These two interpretations—one "from above," and one "from below"—are very difficult to combine. According to the former, God in Christ is dealing with destruction and the victory belongs to God. All the emphasis falls on Jesus' *divine* nature. According to the other interpretation, God needs to receive something from below, from humanity, before he can be reconciled. Hence, terms like "sacrifice" and "satisfaction" play a large role. The chief emphasis then falls on the *human* nature of Jesus, and the crucified one is considered to represent humanity over against God. To be sure, one who is merely human could not measure up to the standards of the perfect sacrificial act, and therefore the divine nature must be present in a secondary way as the necessary condition for Jesus' obedience.[1]

It is our object in this chapter to avoid any talk about the two natures of Christ and also to break down the alternative "from above" versus "from below." Instead, we will be talking about Jesus' humiliation and his victory, and will defend the thesis that victory is won in the deepest humiliation.

98   THE SONTHE SON

THE HUMILIATION

The crucifixion of Jesus took place after judgment had been pronounced by a worldly court. His execution was carried out by soldiers from the local military force. Such a procedure is always painful, but it is not necessarily always humiliating. Some who have died in this manner have suffered only physically. In their consciences they were secure.

But for Jesus that could not be so. He wanted to renew God's own people. He lived on the basis of the holy writings of Israel, totally and without reservation. What his death on the cross implied was that he was both repudiated by God's chosen people and condemned by God's holy law. Both imply that he suffered in conscience and was unsure about his cause. Therein lay his humiliation.

Repudiated by God's People

A "chosen people of God," can mean two things. Israel with its twelve tribes had been chosen by God and rescued by him. As a representative of this Israel, Jesus had himself chosen twelve apostles. Jesus was repudiated by God's people in both meanings of the word. The torment he experienced because of this is clearly expressed in the New Testament. "Did I not choose you, the twelve, and one of you is a devil?" (John 6:70). The evangelist feels called upon in his commentary to repeat "the twelve." "He spoke of Judas the son of Simon Iscariot . . . one of the twelve" (John 6:71).

To be left alone does not always bring anguish. If the goal of my activity is to achieve material gain, I may be quite willing to see personal ties broken and feel no loss in my quest to be successful. But if the goal of my activities is to gather a fellowship, my very existence is shattered when I am forsaken; it is shattered long before my biological existence comes to an end. Jesus' existence was an existence for others, but when the end came, the others were nowhere to be found. Even Peter, the one who was chosen to be "the rock" in that new fellowship, had expressly explained three times, in the presence of the worldly powers, "I do not know the man" (Matt. 26:69-74).

It must be added that those who forsook him and fled had clear support for their actions in the scriptures. Those places in the Old Testament that speak of a suffering Messiah must be hunted for with light and lantern. It is not even likely that those passages (e.g. Isa. 53:3-12) originally had reference to a coming Messiah, or that they were interpreted as messianic even by the groups that gathered around Jesus until *after* his death. When his death was still in the future, those who fled had "God's Word" on their side, while the one who was left alone to be executed, had many holy words of God directed against him. The number of passages that talk about a victorious Messiah is overwhelming. There is a great deal of biblical material on the side of Peter's denial, the treachery of Judas, and the image of the victorious Messiah that was in the minds of those who waited to be the instruments of Jesus' execution.

The situation is this: He is rejected by all who belong to God's people, and the clearest words in the Holy Scriptures are against him. Later efforts to place the disciples at the cross of Jesus (clearest in John 19:26) bear the marks of having been constructed after the fact and cannot be reconciled with the short and all-inclusive statement of Mark "They all forsook him and fled" (14:50). He was all alone on the path which he had travelled for the specific purpose of building a fellowship. The choosing of the twelve, the table fellowship, the miracles of healing, all had the aim of gathering people together. Now, instead, there is complete dispersion of those he had gathered; there is fulfillment of a word out of Zechariah "Strike the shepherd, that the sheep may be scattered" (13:7), a word which surely did not have in mind an individual future Messiah but which Jesus interpreted as a word about the totally new kingdom.[2]

When it comes to interpreting what happened at the crucifixion, the difficulty is that all systematic concepts tend to go awry—the doctrine of the two natures is no exception. The distinction between humiliation and victory also becomes blurred if one means by humiliation a descent from one level to a deeper one until the direction is reversed and an ascent begins that soon leads to victory. On the contrary, the humiliation goes on without ceasing, but victory is found in the humiliation! As the victorious one, Jesus continues to gather in the same people as before—those that have been left out. We do not know who the witness was at the scene when the soldiers threw dice for his clothing, or who the witnesses were to his conversation with the malefactors on the side-crosses. But we do know that when this was recounted it meant something important: it meant that Jesus was fulfilling his work of gathering people in.

There were no holy ones to gather in; there never were. Now that Jesus is at the depth of his humiliation, he sets about gathering in

"what is low and despised in the world, even things that are not."
This is Paul's interpretation of "the folly of the cross" (1 Cor.
1:23-28). One must go to the Pauline letters to get an interpretation of what happened in the Gospels. When Paul interprets what
happened he uses the verb "chose," the classical word for the gathering together of a holy band (the same Greek word is used for the
choosing of the twelve apostles in John 6:70 and the choice of "the
low and despised" in 1 Cor. 1:28).

The evangelists narrate the events at Golgotha in simple epic
form; they tell what happened after Jesus had been mocked and
abandoned. This simple epic without appended analysis is the only
adequate language to explain what happened. They tell about a culminating humiliation, an execution that increases the shame. In this
action on the cross Jesus carries his earthly work through to victory;
or, we might more appropriately say, here he *begins* his work. For
here the old covenant withers away, here begins "antiquity's slave-
rebellion," as Nietzsche labeled those whom Jesus gathered.

If this series of events is a fulfillment of the Old Testament, then
"fulfillment" must mean that through Christ's cross the God of
Israel changed! He became something different from what he had
been before. This is what some older doctrines of the atonement
wanted to say and they tried to explain it with complicated juridical
concepts and with an emphasis on the two natures. But naive, anthropomorphic language is better suited to explain how God has
become different.

Condemned by God's Law

In one sense the Jewish critics of Jesus had the law on their side.
Jesus takes issue not only with misinterpretations of the law but
with the law itself. When Jesus tells people that their sins are forgiven, he is committing blasphemy against God, as the reaction to
the healing of the lame man clearly shows (Mark 2:7). Such reactions do not imply any misinterpretation of the law. No matter how
far one searches in the classical prophetic tradition in Israel, one
never comes upon a prophet who displays such flagrant independence over against what the law declares. No prophet dares to say,
"Your sins are forgiven."

It is entirely consistent with this sovereign freedom over against
the law, that Jesus deletes all expressions of vengeance when he
quotes from the Old Testament. This is true both in the sermon in
Nazareth on Isaiah 61:1-2 recorded in Luke 4, and in his reply to

the Baptist in Luke 7:20-23 (where the signs are that the blind see and the lame walk).

In the first instance (Luke 4:17-19), Jesus has a clear text on vengeance before him (61:2 "To proclaim the year of the Lord's favor, and the day of vengeance of our God"). He simply deletes the reference to vengeance. In the second instance, John the Baptist asked if one who heals, raises up, and forgives, but does not judge can be the one who is to come. Jesus answers with a free combination of three citations from Isaiah (35:4-6; 29:18-20; and again 61:1). At various points in these three citations Isaiah speaks about vengeance, wrath, or punishment, not only about healing and restored health. But Jesus omits the references to vengeance and punishment from the citations.[3] His work is healing and gospel. These deletions show that Jesus understood the gospel to be good news against vengeance, which means against the law (Luke 7:22f.).

Law is constraint and force. No state exists that does not contemplate the use of force, although the force may take a relatively mild form (such as the transportation of a person from one place to another, or temporary imprisonment). Israel's law included elements of force, which were regarded as expressions of God's wrath and punishment. But Jesus was convinced that the Father in heaven wanted something else—and that something else would come precisely through his *Son* (Matt. 11:25-30). This new activity which has been entrusted to Jesus, and which he carries out with one person at a time, is to heal and forgive even *against the law*.

Now it is time to tie together some threads from the presentation on creation, law, and the sovereign life-expressions. The law with its constraint and harshness is conditioned by the fact that people do not want to love their neighbors as they love themselves. It is God who is at work in the law, but he works covertly in a world which is characterized by destruction. God is the source of that coercion which those under the law feel when they resist the demand for service to others. But what the law inwardly aims at is *voluntary* service, *spontaneous* love without coercion, such as existed in the undamaged creation. In the presence of Christ, the law is struck dumb, because he freely gives himself in a life totally dedicated to serving others. This leads to the cross, but even there a new creation breaks forth. There on the cross the law yields the field and the new kingdom takes over. However, the completeness of the new cannot be realized before death, but will be known first in heaven.

Here on earth, where opposition to God prevails and where the coercion of law is in charge, the new is realized only bit by bit, in spontaneous acts which no one including Christians can accomplish on their own. But even when the new is not realized because of the lack of spontaneous acts of service, an imitation of the new is forced into existence by the law. Even in the imitation there is something original, something of "God's image." However, no one can penetrate the mystery of true goodness in one's judgment of others. The unveiling of that mystery lies beyond all human possibilities; it belongs to the "last day."

These are a few threads drawn from our earlier analysis of the law. To return now to Jesus' conflict with the law we must recognize that the law was in the right against him! Jesus did in fact violate the law, or, looked at from the other direction, he was found guilty by God's law. It is beside the point here to talk about the Jews or about a fired-up mob, etc., as if a humane and wise interpretation of the law would have been able to accept the work of Jesus. *Jesus is and he remains the one who breaks the law.* He cannot be accommodated into any society's legislation without friction. This applies to our contemporary society also. If someone maintains that the laws of a certain society express the will of Jesus, we can be sure that the Jesus that person is talking about is not the same as the Jesus of the New Testament.

If Jesus is against the law, then the law is right in condemning him.[4] This has to include even the violence of the crucifixion. To stand against violence and vengeance can only be done in one way—by standing in the way of violence and allowing oneself to be struck by it. Violence is built into the law. It cannot be abolished in this world. But Jesus who created the new, against the law, could allow his own body to take the blows. This is what happened on Golgotha.

To be justly condemned by God's law is humiliation, just as it is humiliation to be rejected by God's people. And yet that which was the aim of the law, the free giving, has never been so fulfilled as in the crucifixion. The line that goes downward into humiliation does not turn around and proceed upward into victory. It goes downward without interruption, but victory is found in the utmost depths. Rejected by God's people and condemned by God's law are two expressions for the same thing. He who gathers together a holy people of God at a place of execution and allows a malefactor to be the first in paradise (Luke 23:43), is in the depths as far as the law is concerned. But victory lies at the deepest point of humiliation! And there in the depths Jesus brings it about that God becomes different. This difference implies a new understanding of God and of what he requires of us.

THE VICTORY

We have already touched upon Jesus' victory in the crucifixion. It remains for us now to discuss this victory more extensively. We shall organize our discussion around four separate points. The first is that since the destruction of creation comes from seeking after gain, the absence of any personal gain at the cross is a victory. Second, this absence of personal gain means that free course is restored to the previously blocked flow of the bubbling spring of creation. The third aspect is the harvest, the sacrificed grain of wheat yields a new abundant crop. Finally, we will return to a point already touched upon earlier, namely that through the cross God becomes different; his relationship to us and our access to him has been changed because of the cross. It is our intention, in all of this, to avoid talking about the two natures and to avoid anticipating the resurrection.

No Personal Gain

It would be impossible for a person to use the maxim, "no personal gain," as a practical rule of action. To allow such a rule would be to go bankrupt. But the reason this is so is because we live in the age of destruction, the age after the fall. In its own mystical language Genesis says that in this age the struggle for one's own existence is a necessity. But Genesis does not consider this struggle for existence to be part of God's original creation. Only when corruption has come into the world do we hear that "In the sweat of your face you shall eat bread" (Gen. 3:19).

On the other hand, Jesus lived according to the maxim, "no personal gain." When he accepted the rule, he also accepted its consequences even if it meant "to give his life as a ransom for many" (Mark 10:45). Jesus thus leaves behind him an ethical rule which it is impossible to live by, an "impossible ethical ideal" as Reinhold Niebuhr often called it. For on the lips of Jesus the word about death is only the culmination of a great program of action consisting of service. That it has to do with an ethical ideal, intended to be realized among the disciples, is clear (Mark 10:42-45). In part, the ideal can be realized. The actions called for are described as small, and easy to accomplish—give food, give drink, visit the sick and those in prison (Matt. 25:34-40).

This is the reason that our presentation of the Creed has dealt with deeds or works in a separate chapter (Chapter 3 above). There is a type of quite ordinary activity that begins with the example of

Jesus and moves through the centuries from small Christian congregations out into the world at large. The cross and the resurrection have not accompanied this activity into the world. That part
of the Creed has become more and more isolated within the church
bodies. There is a certain justification for this, because the creeds,
both the Apostolic and the Nicene, make a remarkable leap from
Jesus' birth to his crucifixion. Jesus' actions in word and deed are
not mentioned. (The false teachings of the heretics which were
rejected through the creedal statements were specifically teachings
about the birth and the crucifixion.)

If one compares the gospel with various isms or views of life, the
gospel's combination of simple, life-affirming actions for others on
the one hand, and Jesus' death on the cross on the other, constitutes
an excellent point of comparison. There is no parallel either in
world religions or in modern views of life (humanism, Marxism,
existentialism) to the way Jesus functions in relation to the be-
liever. The other forms of faith operate with the assumption that
a certain truth has been discovered, or that a rule of action has been
given, but the object of faith (or of obedience) does not have the
many-sided role Jesus has in Christianity. The unique position
Jesus occupies compared to other messianic figures is based on two
features firmly anchored in the gospel tradition: first, the combination of everyday deeds and death on a cross, and second, Jesus'
two-fold attitude that combines ethical rigor with generosity and
unconditional forgiveness. Here the demand and the gift are one.

The example of Jesus, both in its ethical rigor and in its unconditional forgiveness, is the key ingredient in building a Christian
fellowship. Jesus is the pattern for everyday actions. No one needs
to go to school or be a deep thinker in order to follow his example.
The deed lies hidden and waiting in human existence, and it can be
carried out even by one who is illiterate. No one has yet followed
perfectly the example of the crucified one. His example is always an
impossible ideal. Yet the one who falls short still meets in Jesus the
model for action, the one who affirms and accepts the failing person
and offers unconditional forgiveness.

This availability of unconditional forgiveness remained as a fel-
lowship-creating factor after Jesus' death on the cross as well.
Moreover it was the key factor in the good news which spread to
the uttermost parts of the world. In this sense, the cross is victory.
Jesus embraces our everyday life and calls us to action; when misfortune comes he faces our predicament and heals it. In the social
arena, he impels us to action. In our relationships to other people, he
helps us live on the basis of the forgiveness of sins. He forms us

into groups that work together but do not pass judgment on one another. No one has realized this impossible ethical demand, no one, that is, except Jesus the crucified one, the one lifted up above all others, the one who, at this highest peak of humiliation, forgives those who crucify him, and welcomes a malefactor into paradise.

This combination of contradictory elements has no parallel in any of the other views of life.[5]

Creation's Spring

Here we shall introduce a metaphor, and talk about a spring. Two features of the metaphor are especially relevant—a spring has been in existence under the surface long before it gushes forth; a spring is a life-giving reality which one reaches by bending down. We speak symbolically and imprecisely in both respects, and therefore the reader must not take metaphorical language literally. But the symbol has value, nonetheless, because it enables us to understand how the early church delineated the connection between Jesus and Adam (where Adam means the whole of humanity).

This involves both the incarnation and the ascension. We say that Jesus "stepped down" and became man, and afterwards that he "arose" and received divine power. But the stepping down is not understood in a spatial sense, as though Jesus descended from a higher level to the manger where he was born. Rather one should use Adam as the original model. Jesus must go through everything that Adam endured—hunger, temptation, suffering and death—and he must do it all *without being disobedient*. By doing this Jesus turns the Adamic pattern around, away from destruction and upwards toward heaven. Consequently through the gospel, Jesus is present everywhere bringing salvation to all the suffering. From Adam came death, from Jesus comes life (Rom. 5:15-19). The point at which the turning about takes place is the death on the cross, and above all in the obedience (cf. Phil. 2:8; Heb. 5:8). In such a death, resurrection has already been won.

In mystical language it is said that Jesus has come down to the spring of creation, to that which existed before Adam's disobedience. Through Jesus' baptism, resurrection, ascension, and through the Lord's Supper, the original spring of creation again flows forth. As a result, those in Christ's congregation are cleansed of their inhumanity and become what they were created to be, "God's image" (this is the content of the word *recapitulatio*). Only by consistently going *downward* can Jesus come to the depth where creation's spring pours forth. Thus, he conquers at the point that is

106   THE SON

farthest down in the depths. And the fruit of the victory is a spring out of which humanity can drink forever (so the sacraments are understood in the church).[6]

In this line of thought from the ancient church it is not possible to separate a divine nature in Jesus from a human nature. In his humiliation he is totally and completely human. But at the very depth of his humiliation is a point where the Creator has free course in human fellowship, and where God himself removes the obstacles to such fellowship. Divine and human cannot here be separated.

Let us now leave the mythical language with its references to Adam as the forefather of all humanity. The Hebrew word "adam" is not a personal name but means, quite simply, "human" (every one of us). The life-expressions in all of us cannot be dated and assigned to some ancient period before the human race had spread across the globe. Neither can the fall into sin be dated at a certain point somewhat later than creation. Nevertheless, we are justified in using the prepositions "before" and "after" in describing the various life-manifestations. What makes such language adequate is not the chronology of the life-manifestations but their nature.

The church fathers chose a very appropriate word, *envy*, to characterize original sin. The best way to illustrate envy is to first describe a positive life-supporting event, and then show how envy is a negative reaction to that event. Envy is by its very nature something secondary. The same holds true all across the board—hate, jealousy, slander—they are always "after," and they do not set forth anything positive but prey upon something which already exists "before" they come to be.

This is true also in a phenomenological sense. If we observe human fellowship today we can see life expressions such as love, mercy, and trust, that nourish and sustain life in the face of peril. And we can also see how these life expressions are tested in everyday living as distrust, envy, and slander begin their destructive work. It is then that "the others" play a key role.

It is possible for me to interpret both envy and hatred as life-affirming if by life-affirming I mean the affirming of my own lifestyle, good or bad. But the problem here is that if my own family, group, or race lives at the expense of others, then even my so-called love is nothing but planned egotism, the will to power. When negative qualities such as envy are called life affirming, the kind of life that is affirmed is selfish and closed off to others. Only if the others whose lives I affirm are *not* arbitrarily chosen by me, only if my affirmation of life applies to *all* those who happen to be here, then and only then do my life-manifestations become free and sovereign.

If we have ever hesitated between the sovereign, free manifestations of life, and the selfish, locked-in impulses, we know which of
these is healthy and which is sick. We want to do what is healthy
but we cannot; we simply are not able. This is the reason that people
in wholly different cultures recognize Jesus in the crucifixion as a
sovereign, a king as the biblical language has it. He does not choose
who is to be around him, he allows "the others" to come into his
presence regardless of who those others might be. Everyone has
needs, and Jesus answers those needs.

Again we have reason to underscore how inadequate are the terms
divine nature and human nature. One gets nowhere with them.[7]
The sovereign life-manifestations are human actions that also imply
the on-going activity of God. If these actions are quenched, humanity is damaged, and opposition arises against God. If these actions
spring forth anew, a fresh and natural humanity is again realized.
This is a humanity that became possible only because God conquered
envy in the humiliation of Golgotha. This enemy, envy, has no vio-
lent, outwardly diabolical features. On the contrary, envy appears
undemonic and trivial. Anyone can meet this enemy any day.

When God and the devil are thought of in this way, they are to
some extent demythologized. Nevertheless, we have reason to talk
about creation as something "before" all else and about destruction
as coming "after" creation. There is also reason for talking about
Jesus' crucifixion as a "descent into hell" and a battle to the finish
which resulted in victory over God's enemy. All of these terms
belong to a naive and anthropomorphic language, which for our
purpose is the only adequate language.

The Harvest

Harvest is life coming to fruition, but it is life that is contingent
on something having died, the seed. If the seed that has been sown
here were to be rescued from death and preserved, the harvest would
not occur. This symbol has been widely used in the New Testament,
both in the gospels and in the letters. The account of the temptation of Jesus compares a life that is forfeited or lost with a rescued
life that bears no fruit. The trial on the cross seems to be a repetition and culmination of the introductory trial in the wilderness
(cf. Matt. 4:2-4 with Matt. 27:33-34; further 4:8-10 with 27:35-37;
finally 4:5-7 with 27:38-50).[8]

In the relation between seed and harvest there is both continuity
and discontinuity. In other views of life the individual receives at
the beginning a pattern one can develop and obey. Life is to be

lived in unswerving progress toward that goal which is visible from the beginning. One can observe one's own progress in advancing closer and closer to the goal. In the Christian faith there is a break in one's progress toward the goal, a break which means that the individual cannot see the goal and is therefore thrown back on faith. The seed actually goes into the ground, and not all seeds yield a harvest. When the deposited seed seems to have been wasted, and the individual has been deprived of any result from the sowing, one has no other resource by which to live than faith.

There is a parallel to this in Marxism where exhaustion must precede revolution. From the Marxist point of view it is a good sign when capitalist society gets worse and worse; this means the fruit is ripening. It is possible that the Marxist pattern is actually borrowed from biblical teaching about the birth pangs of the last days (Matt. 24:3-36). But the political pattern talks only about classes and says nothing about the individual's personal difficulties. This is one of the reasons that Marxism in modern times has begun to be combined with other views of life which "fill out its anthropological vacuum" (the existentialism of Sartre has been a chief partner in this alliance).

In Christianity, on the contrary, the individual is taken seriously from beginning to end. The individual person is at the center of the tension between the seed and the harvest. There is one person who dies alone at Golgotha, and no matter where he looks from the cross there is not the least sign of any result. It was into such a death that Jesus entered, as a grain of wheat falls without receiving anything immediate in return. The harvest Jesus wins is not a group of people who can enjoy more "favorable" forms of loss and death, but people who share a universal human condition—a condition that affirms life even though it at times seems meaningless. Christianity does not claim to have a monopoly on such people; they can be found in the most surprising surroundings, without apparent "religion" and without ideology. No one can explain why.

But it is clear that the "harvest" of the cross in similar meaningless circumstances is more than mere endurance. But such meaningless circumstances have inspired the most emphatic songs of praise in the history of the church. Almost all political utopians talk about "the final strife," a time of struggle which is temporary and which results in gain. It is in anticipation of the nearness of the goal that one sings. But in the early church it was nearly the opposite. Suffering was not understood to be a passageway into something else, it was understood to be a *presence,* the presence of a *sovereign.*

When the martyrs stood in the presence of worldly power they stood in the place where Jesus had stood at Golgotha; they stood at the point we have called "creation's spring." This identification is apparent at the stoning of Stephen, and it can also be observed in the accounts of the martyrs in the first centuries (see Acts 7:55-60). In later years, however, this interpretation of suffering took a different tack; people began to seek out suffering egocentrically instead of having it laid upon them, as was the case in the beginning. The Reformers are unbelievably sarcastic about "self-chosen crosses," but the original view of the suffering laid upon one from without as constituting the presence of Christ breaks through at many points, not least in Luther's critique of the egotistic dream of the satisfactions of heaven. His famous words about heaven and hell apply here: "If I have to choose between heaven, when Christ is absent from it, and hell when Christ is there, I will choose to be in hell—with *him*."

These are very telling words inasmuch as they focus on the cross of Christ, not on his resurrection. The same is true of the words of the martyrs in the early church—they are utterances which bind together the individual's suffering with praise, and with Christ's sovereign death at Golgotha. When one reads such words as these one should remember that eternal life is thought to consist of praise. The view of the present as empty in itself (but rich inasmuch as it is a passageway to something greater) which is characteristic of the pilgrim-myth,[9] is turned around full circle. *Now* we have arrived, in the midst of our tribulation; *now* we are at creation's spring, we drink at Golgotha's well; *now* all of our dead partake in our worship, our songs of praise encompass heaven and earth.

This is a total view, which holds "Christ's body" together. When individuals seek to escape from this earth one by one, and one by one cross the boundary of life in order that they may see their dear ones, they are not thinking about the "body of Christ" but only about the self and its wishes. A summary of what the "harvest" from Christ's cross ought to mean can be formulated thus: *The harvest is the song of praise in the body of Christ.* In such a formulation two things join together, that which lies within our earthly existence and that which lies beyond death. The date of death is only a part of the great process of death which confronts everyone. But in the body of Christ the whole of death is swallowed up in victory.

God Becomes Different

Through the use of legal concepts, the old atonement doctrines intended to assert that through the work of Jesus God had become different. God was appeased and ceased being angry. The innermost being of God was revealed in the death of Jesus. According to these atonement theories, it was God himself who had arranged Jesus' reconciling death.

The historians of religion say much the same thing in different language. Original Christianity did not recognize any other God than the Old Testament Yahweh. Everything that happens through the death and resurrection of Jesus and the world mission which follows from it, is interpreted as the fulfillment of the Old Testament. But at the same time something entirely new is coming into being, another "religion" is being born. If it is the same God, he must have changed, he must have become different in some ways.

Neither of these two ways of looking at the matter has been used in our presentation of the death on the cross.[10] Nevertheless, we have used the phrase, "God has become different." Our discussion has always begun with human existence understood as life with others— *either* a life of free, spontaneous, sovereign activity, which we cannot generate by ourselves but which in fact empowers us, *or* a life of coercion under a law which demands service toward the needy. Whether in freedom or under coercion, we always live in mutual dependence on one another.

Jesus of Nazareth is a person like us. His existence is existence for others. When those forces which normally quench the spontaneous life expressions attack him, they do not accomplish their usual effect. The cross is the definitive demonstration that his giving of himself to others cannot be suppressed. Inasmuch as the stifling of spontaneous love and mercy is the form which our surrender to destruction takes, and inasmuch as this surrender does not happen in Jesus' case, the cross is victory. The law (that is, God's law in the biblical writings and at the same time God's law in the legislation of the community) does not stand over him as a definitive compulsion. The law is silenced when the imitation of love which the law can produce no longer fills any function in relation to love itself. Where the original is, the imitation is meaningless. The law is not eternal.

The term "original" here means creation without destruction. Where human life is unspoiled, God is at work without hindrance. What happens in the law is the action of the Creator, but it is his action in the world of destruction, with hindrances to his action still strong. If that which hinders were to disappear, God would be near us with his new creation in a manner unique in human history. But the hindrance is a hindrance in the *human*. It is in people like us that the life-giving streams are constantly being polluted, and it is in us that walls are built up against others through our concentration on ourselves.

Because such walls are not built by Jesus, not even when he is forsaken by God's people and condemned by God's law, creation's flow is no longer restrained by anything. On the cross the victory is as yet only an inner victory. The outward course of events looks like a defeat for life—a death has taken place and, moreover, a death in shame. But the powers which triumph in external matters are the destroying powers. There is only one point where they cannot reach —the dying one's inner self, Jesus' "heart" is undamaged.

The victory occurs in a person, but it does not happen in action "from below"; the victory is not something that rises up and influences a remote God who has been passive and uninvolved up to this point. On the contrary, it is the Creator who is the active one. It is the Creator, working through a pure and healthy person, who makes new. But this does not mean that the victory comes "from above"; the victory occurs within a human community. One who is being executed is confronted by his executioners, by onlookers, and even by others who are also being executed.

What the evangelists relate are concrete happenings that are typical of the destructive forces in human life. There are basically only two ways of destroying our sense of community with other people: there is the aggressive way, and the way of withdrawal, the way of revenge or the way of neglect, hatred toward those who injure us or forgetting about the suffering of others. Our fellowship with others is polluted by these two poisons, both of which surge up like a floodtide against the cross. But they do not have their usual effect; they cannot pollute or destroy the victory of the cross. The prayer for the soldier and the promise to the malefactor on the side-cross are audible expressions of a deeper victory which cannot be heard and is not seen—the victory over destruction in its entirety.

With this, the new creation is active again. The hindrance is removed by a person who simply was "obedient," the New Testament way of describing an ethical victory (Phil. 2:8; Heb. 5:8).[11] When that which blocks the flow is removed through the obedience on the cross, the result has to be that a fountain springs up in the world, life flows from the crucified victor out to others in an ever-widening circle. This is what the resurrection means.

*O God, you hold the whole world in your hand. For you
a thousand years are as a day. Our brother, Jesus Christ,
who struggled here on earth, is not generations removed
from us. He is as close as our own life. Our fields are
still warm from his body. We thank and praise you
that you allowed him to be a man among us, that his
tears have fallen on our earth, and that he has awaited a
new day from the same sun which now shines upon us.
Nothing that has happened on this earth is greater than
that which happened in him.*

*But most of all we thank you for his victory. No evil
thrusting itself up against his cross could take him in
its power. Our valleys and mountains, our cities and our
homes are still illumined by his purity, the purity of
the unconquered one.*

*And greatest of all, that which he won he gave away,
and he gave it not to those without fault but to those
who were, like us, prisoners under the power of evil.
Golgotha's well never dries up. Its water flows for each
and every one who is thirsty. The song of praise rises
in eternity, O God, from the earth where the cross
was raised.*

V

The Resurrection

That an ethical victory should result in a physical event does not seem likely. Further on in this chapter we will have occasion to deal more extensively with the relation between the ethical and the physical. But before we do that we must attempt to indicate what it is that is new about the resurrection. At that point the *future* plays a decisive role.

HE WHO COMES FROM THE FUTURE

As a European one easily falls in with the idea that Jesus has been a causal force in our history. If one believes in the miracle of the resurrection, it is easy to include the resurrection also into this sort of reflection. The resurrection is seen as pouring forth new powers into the human arena, powers principally channeled through the church which subsequently spread farther and farther into the world. With this perspective one loses an important biblical aspect of the resurrection. As risen, Christ dwells in the future; it is from the future, not from the past, that he comes to meet us when we live with our faces toward the future.

The Unbiblical Injection Idea

Within Anglican and Roman theology it is customary to call the church "an extension of the incarnation." Often this thought about an extension is combined with the idea of a succession in office such that the deposit which was left with the apostles is passed on from

one generation to another. In this way the church becomes a channel
through which something which was injected by Jesus moves forward. Power comes from the past into the present where we live.

It is self-evident that such an office ideology has the effect of chok-
ing off all expectations of Christs's "coming." Such expectations are
turned in quite another direction. They presuppose that some form
of Christ's presence is lacking now, and that what is lacking now will
be given only in the future. The great churches in Europe have lived
with the concept of grace as something deposited in the church and
passed on by the church from the past to the future. The simpler
sects have been left to cultivate the opposite perspective, that of
waiting for a Christ who moves from the future toward the present
where we live.

The idea of the church as a channel is entirely foreign to the New
Testament. When this idea of the channel is combined with the idea
that the validity of the means of grace depends on the laying on of
hands, then that which happened in Christ comes to be viewed as an
injection of grace which is passed on from one generation to another
through external contact. What cannot be expressed in such a framework is something which was very clear to the early church, namely,
that Jesus when he "comes" stands over against even the church; he
examines, he probes, he judges (clearest in 1 Peter 4:17, but also in
Rom. 2:6 and 2 Cor. 5:10; Col. 3:24f.) [1] The letters to the seven
churches in the book of Revelation make this church-critical function
of Christ their chief subject (Rev. 2-3). Those who are most carefully
examined and judged are the officeholders in the church.

When a very inclusive group of biblical expositors (in this case,
representing the large confessional churches, crossing all national
boundaries) displays such a solid one-sidedness in their understanding of the church, this has unfortunate consequences for those who
disagree, such as the apocalyptic sects. But these sects also have an
inadequate understanding of the church because of their overempha-
sis on Christ's second coming. This emphasis is applied in the name
of faithfulness to the Bible, but it lacks adequate support in the New
Testament. The point in the original Christian writings is not that
Christ has come once in the past, and that he will come once again
in the future. The point is that in relation to the church, he is "the
one who is coming." His very presence is a "coming" or "revelation"
(cf. John 21:1, 14). Christ does not come from within the soul;
rather, the individual is *confronted* by him.

If we are going to talk about Jesus' second coming, as the apocalyptic sects do, it will be necessary for us to call the meeting between
Peter and Jesus at the Sea of Tiberias a second coming just for

Peter, a second coming which meant restoration and forgiveness and the renewal of his shepherd role. This observation is more basic and more important in terms of principle than we may suspect at first glance. Peter is also in this respect the representative of the whole church; that which happens to him, happens to everyone. Also what Paul describes when he talks about his "weakness" (2 Cor. 12:9) is also a coming, a "power" of Christ which descends upon the one who is weak (cf. Phil. 3:10-21).

The element of judgment and discipline regularly enters into New Testament references to confrontations with the coming Christ. One does not join Christ in the fellowship of the resurrected life in any other way than through some form of death (this is the heart of the long section in Rom. 6-8). Only if we hold fast to this perspective can we understand the unique certainty that everything is moving forward which was the mark of the early church as it faced martyrdom. This certainly would have been impossible had the injection idea been the guiding star.

If one holds this unbiblical idea about an injection given in the past, one is likely to share the feeling which is characteristic of the European churches today: Christ's contribution is deposited with us; when there are reverses for us, statistically and in the opinion of the masses, there are reverses for Christ here on earth. There is not one single place in the whole New Testament where this mentality is reflected. On the contrary, when Christ won his dominion he went through much greater reverses statistically and in the opinion of the masses than we experience now. The thought that *he* could lose the future through our suffering is utterly excluded; the question is only whether *we* shall endure suffering in such a way that we will be his when he comes. His future is assured, our future is to be tested by him.

When we take as our starting point the fact that Jesus won his dominion at the very depth of his apparent defeat, everything is changed by what happened on the third day. Now we get a different understanding of life than Israel and Judaism had (and a different understanding than the churches have now, because they have come to resemble Judaism). For Judaism, the outward reverses experienced by the chosen people was a problem, even a problem of conscience. God could not be identified with those who suffered reverses, especially not if the reverses appeared to be permanent. But in the case of Jesus, it was on account of the reverses which Jesus himself experienced that the congregations that follow him become able to interpret death, suffering, and disgrace.

Christ Is Ahead of Us

If one is to understand this specifically Christian feeling about life, however, one must cease thinking about death as being tied to a date. This should not be difficult in the light of modern scientific knowledge. On the day we refer to as the day of death there is cessation of breathing and of the heart's activity (for that matter we debate whether in certain cases an entirely different day, the day when the brain dies, should not be called the day of death). We know that some life-functions weaken and even cease much sooner than the day of death. Death is in fact a drawn-out process that is combined with the processes of life. Paul talks about everyone's life when he says, "I die every day" (1 Cor. 15:31). To say that Christ is ahead of us does not mean that he is confined to a time after the date of my death. Ahead is really *here*, as I make my way through this day's difficulties (that is, this day's quota of death).

The feeling about life which is created by the resurrection is characterized by the realization that the difficulties and the resistance *taste* differently than before; they taste of life, victory, gain, in spite of the fact that nothing that one can point to is victory or gain. The difficulties encountered are life-giving in that they break down, especially when the difficulties come as a part of the individual's service to the neighbor. It is doubtful whether there is any parallel to this Christian view of life. The closest parallel is Marxism where it is the class that occupies the center. But personal and unpolitical difficulties cannot be directly interpreted by the individual. For the Christian faith, on the other hand, there is no kind of death which is left uninterpreted or unconstrued.

A multitude of different elements in the Creed here come together into a unity. First, there is faith in Christ, the crucified one. We taste the fellowship with him in the personal experience of meeting death daily, an experience which means equally germinating life (that is, movement forward toward resurrection). There is further our faith about creation, which presupposes that new life is possible, in a world in which destruction rules, only on the same condition as that by which the grain of wheat lives ("Whoever loses his life for my sake will find it"—Matt. 16:25). There is, moreover, the fundamental Christian conviction that evil is found not only in the economic system but also in the heart of each individual, therefore also in me. I encounter the demand for sacrifice and in faith I am driven to interpret the difficulties of this day as my own real life under the mantle of death.

Other elements can be added: a) the consciousness that all humanity constitutes "one body" and that mutual service is the way of life for the future for this body; b) the realization that baptism constitutes a dedication to dying and rising with Christ (Rom. 6:1-14); and c) the Lord's Supper, which is a constant return to "the night in which he was betrayed" but which anticipates a future mealtime in heaven.

There is no significant strand in the Christian faith that lies outside of this feeling about life which functions in the everyday world. Everything is integrated in the most trivial everyday action, such as an encounter with ailments, with slander, with inflated prices— whatever else.[2] In the remote distance one catches glimpses of the day of death, which in principle is no different from these "everyday deaths." Even one's own grave is integrated into this focus on the future, sunlit as on the third day, "very early . . . when the sun had risen" (Mark 16:2).

"Judge" and "Author of Life"

An outstanding example of how this basic pattern breaks through can be seen in Peter's sermon in Caesarea as recorded in Acts 10:34-43. There we are told not only about Jesus' death and resurrection but also about his activities in Galilee and "in the country of the Jews." Nevertheless, the "forgiveness of sins through his name" is not something which comes to us from the resurrection of Jesus as an event in the distant past. Instead the sequence of thought is quite different: forgiveness does not come from one who speaks to us out of the past, but on the contrary, from one who stands in the future and speaks to us here in the present.

Jesus of Nazareth has been designated by God to be the judge of the living and the dead. This Lord of the future communicates even now through the gospel that "every one who believes in him receives forgiveness of sins" (Acts 10:43). What is given in the forgiveness of sins is a word of judgment from a future judge. Christ is up ahead, not in the past; he comes to meet us as the years go by. The statement which was subsequently incorporated into the words of the second article, "whence he shall come to judge the living and the dead," is the bridge to what the third article has to say about the forgiveness of sins, that unique gift which the church exists in order to give (cf. Acts 17:31). At this important point, both the Apostles' and the Nicene Creeds are constructed in the same way.[3]

Christ comes from the future with power, and he uses his power in the same way that he did during his life on earth. Then it was the power to forgive sins illustrated in the healing of the lame man.

Jesus heals bodies in order to demonstrate visibly that forgiveness from his lips is the same as God's own forgiveness (Mark 2:9-11). Therefore Jesus' position as "the Author of Life" (Acts 3:15), and therefore the renewer of life, even the life of the body, is closely tied to his position as the one who is able to forgive. He is the judge and the Author of life who comes from the future into the present, and who uses his power in activities that are restoring in their effect.

But at this point difficulties arise for us who live in an age of technological advances in the natural sciences. The book of Acts tells about apostles who perform two closely-linked kinds of activities, both or them in the name of Jesus: they heal the sick and they forgive sins. Contemporary proclaimers proceed directly to the latter because they have with few exceptions ceased doing the first. Where this easy, problem-free forgiveness stands by itself, almost as a sort of churchly friendliness expressed in words, one wonders if the radicality of forgiveness remains. One wonders whether it is really the Lord of the *future* who is forgiving, that is, the one who removes the consequences of one's evil for all eternity. Because, when it is so understood, forgiveness has implications that are both bodily and physical: it may do away with social ostracism, and also bring about a new integration of the person's soul and instincts.

Forgiveness is restored health. The ethical and the physical join together and become one. This sort of unity is conceivable only where that faith concerning creation confessed in the first article actually functions. It was quickly lost in European culture after the Enlightenment, and has remained absent not only in the theology of liberalism but also in Bultmann's demythologizing. Bultmann says that the story of the empty grave and the reports of events on the third day in general are much too corporeal. According to Bultmann, Christ's resurrection is the kerygma, the preaching *about* Christ. We can never get behind the kerygma—and the kerygma makes its basic appeal to us with a message about our own new existence in faith.

For Bultmann, the essence of Christ's resurrection is the resurrection of the person who listens to the kerygma, and *that* resurrection can never be a "fact." The new self lives only in and with faith. Outside of faith, new life cannot be found. To ask that Christ's resurrection be presented as a fact in the gospel, means that one wishes to be relieved of the necessity of living with decision. But this would mean that we would also be relieved of the need to live by the gospel. Yet we desire certainty, and this includes words from the Bible; we want everything to be as sure as money in the bank.

There are good theological grounds for the charges the demythologizing prophets present against the fundamentalists' demand for a

secure faith (which, deep down is a claim of ownership). But these
critical objections can never rightly be directed against the bodily
or the physical in and of itself. Our physical health is as brief and
fragile as is our faith or our psychological equilibrium. The transitoriness and the fragility of the physical good which Jesus gives in
the gospels is entirely clear. It is never a question about his giving
health which someone can keep forever; it is not a question of "certainty." The criticism directed against the physical which has characterized European theology since the Enlightenment is a general
phenomenon. It runs through liberal theology to Bultmann and his
disciples, and it is tied in with a general antithesis between body
and spirit, which is in principle an "idealism" of the Greek-philo-
sophic type.[4]

This body-spirit antithesis has also had its effect on the historical
judgments concerning the source materials dealing with the resurrection on the third day. What is historically uncontested is that
Jesus and his disciples came from Galilee and only occasionally vis-
ited Jerusalem; it is further agreed that the crucifixion and the
burial took place in Jerusalem which was relatively unfamiliar to
Jesus and the disciples; and finally, that the preaching about the
resurrected Christ began in that same unfamiliar city soon after
Jesus' death and burial (in a very short time this proclamation had
already spread out into the country, to Antioch and Damascus).

Imagine a group of people from Värmland whose leader had been
executed and buried in Stockholm, but who soon after reappeared
preaching in Stockholm. Would it be reasonable to think that they
could believe such a miracle solely through some visionary experiences they might have had back in Värmland? Do not the Stockholm-
ers have the resources for putting an end to any such miraculous
claims? After all, his grave is located within their own boundaries.

Given such source material, how could we account for someone
affirming the visions in the home province while rejecting the empty
grave in the capital city? Such an interpreter would have to approach
the material with two presuppositions: 1) the desire to relieve the
proclamation of the painful rationale about the empty tomb with its
mistakes and inconsistencies, and 2) the acceptance of the antithesis
between body and spirit. The visions can be allowed to stand, but
nothing more.

What we have been discussing is the most offensive point in the
entire Creed, and moreover, it lies at the very center of the Creed.
We do not know any early Christian kerygma which includes the
virgin birth, and we do not know of any in which the resurrection
is lacking. Indeed, it would not have occurred to anyone to have gath-

ered together the little stories about the historical Jesus which we now have in the four gospels, if there had not been *first* the certainty that he was risen.

ETHICAL AND PHYSICAL

The Visions and the Empty Grave

All through the Bible nature is involved in both the ruination and the rescue of humanity. The belief that God creates life through the sexual act in both humans and animals is, when one thinks about how this act is performed, offensively naturalistic. One can easily understand the view of the Gnostics, who found this belief repulsive. Luke describes a scene in a mountain village where Mary and Elizabeth, both pregnant, meet each other and the child jumps for joy in the body of the one at the greeting of the other (Luke 1:39-45). As a description of God's salvation history, this scene is fantastic in its physicality. It is no less fantastic when one recalls that the two baby boys after their birth journeyed toward execution, through beheading and crucifixion respectively. And it was through their executions that they went toward victory.

Our whole created world sighs and groans because people have been gripped by madness. Surely no one can doubt this who has seen the birds of the sea fight for their lives after an insane dumping of oil by the crown of creation, man. But it is not so clear that salvation in a religious sense should include release from this sort of misery; this is regarded as being incompatible with the idealistic antithesis between flesh and spirit. It is, however, biblical through and through, and is in complete agreement with Genesis, Job, the Psalms, and Isaiah (cf. Rom. 8:18-23).

When one stands before the early Christian kerygma about Jesus, one must distinguish between two kinds of offenses to reason occasioned by the kerygma. The first and most serious offense is the idea that the rescue of all people could come about through what happens in *a single one*—one individual out of all the multitudes that have ever lived. As long as Christ is preached this offense remains. We do not reduce the offense in even the smallest degree by limiting the resurrection to inner, psychic phenomena, that is, to the visions of the disciples.

The other offense to reason is relatively bearable. It consists of the claim that this particular individual has been able to function on the human, physical level differently than we are otherwise accustomed to (that he functions in a unique way with regard to our inner persons we have already affirmed). When we find the physical side of the event unbearable it is because we are conditioned by a general discomfort with the thought that God gets mixed up with bodies at all. It is typical that those theologians who set themselves most frenetically against the need even to touch upon the problem of the empty grave are also theologians without a doctrine of creation (liberals, existentialists).

The empty grave does not mean anything else than continuity with creation. In early Christianity there is no evidence of any belief that the risen Jesus exists with flesh and blood. He is transformed; about that there is no doubt. The visions also bear witness to this. But there is the same continuity between the crucified one and the risen one that there is between the seed and the harvest (1 Cor. 15:33-49). Here, once again, we catch a glimpse of the grain of wheat, this time in Paul (1 Cor. 15:37); the Greek word here is the same as that in John 12:24. This Jesus who was sowed as a seed, who anguished in Gethsemane and who cried out on the cross, lives now among those who believe in him—it is not just the memory of him that lives. The outward sign of that continuity is the empty grave.

The empty grave is nothing more than that. It does not awaken faith and it does not constitute proof, any more than the grain of wheat that is planted, covered up, and decayed, can in itself awaken faith or constitute proof of the harvest. That which is planted and dead is regarded as nothing unless it can be seen together with the harvest. In the case of Jesus, his death must be seen together with the life-giving powers which were set in motion after his total sacrifice. This means that we are concerned with the life which comes out of baptism and the Lord's Supper, including the visions (they belong there) and fellowship with others, all in the certainty that in Christ even death is life, and moreover, it is an enhancement of the life which has hitherto existed in the world. But if we combine the picture of the insignificant grain of wheat which is planted and dies, with the picture of a glorious harvest, we will understand that nothing, no matter how ordinary it may be, can now be lacking in hope.

The cross on Golgotha plus the empty tomb gives rise to a confident migration toward the future and a sovereignty over against outward dangers, which the experiences of visions alone could never give. The key to the young church's unbelievable history is to be found in this combination of Golgotha and Easter. The material and physical aspects are related to the emphasis on the future which we spoke about earlier in this chapter. Christ is ahead of us; whatever the congregation may experience or encounter, he is always ahead, in the light, by the gate into which the tunnel of suffering opens. It is not meaningless to be hanged on a cross, or to be thrown to the wild animals in the arena (1 Cor. 15:32), or buried in an anonymous grave somewhere in the empire. Everything that can happen to us is victory (Rom. 8:37).

That is the way the original Christian faith was construed. The axis around which everything turns is death and resurrection. The ascension is sometimes mentioned as a separate event (Mark 16:19f.; Luke 24:50f.; Acts 1:9), but it is not a necessary ingredient (neither Matthew nor John report it). The resurrection is originally conceived in such a way that the assumption of having gone to heaven is included in it. He who is the Lord of the future, installed as judge with the right to forgive, is in heaven and has God's power of being everywhere throughout all the coming days (Mark 16:20; Matt. 28:18-20).

This is the way the original situation appears when one looks at it historically. Christianity entered the territory around the Mediterranean with a certain set of ideas, in which the crucifixion and the resurrection, both physical events, were at the center.[5] If you eliminate the physical, these events become incomprehensible.

Our situation today, on the other hand, is quite different. We live in a culture in which one goes to the hospital for everything physical; then alongside of this one may accept a "purely religious" belief in God. However, if we wish to have a proper understanding of what should be called Christian, we should begin with that which is central in the New Testament: *everything* which is told about Jesus was *gospel*, that is, something which made life easier to live. Nothing was added on as a requirement for faith. When the physical aspect of the resurrection becomes a burden for our intellectual conscience, then the word no longer liberates, even if through some mental gymnastics we are able to affirm the biblical record. Where this is the situation, it is useless to foist the old and original belief in the resurrection on people today. But where such a belief is held without intellectual maneuvers that coerce the soul, we would have to say that a relatively original form of Christian faith exists.

More than that one cannot say. One does more damage by trying to force the Christian faith into existence than by accepting honest doubt. For doubt is at home in the church. That is the way it was from the beginning, even in the earliest Christian period. Among the eleven, who according to Matthew 28:17 were sent out into the world there were some who doubted. This group of eleven men, among whom there was doubt, consisted without exception of apostles.

Resurrection and Forgiveness

The difficulty the modern westerner has with the physical aspects of the resurrection is only partly of an intellectual nature. In addition, there is the emotional opposition to combining God and bodily functions. This feeling does not come from our encounter with contemporary science but from our ancient platonic heritage. When Jesus heals a man who was born blind by spitting on the ground and making a paste of the spittle (John 9:6), our intellect may object to the miracle but our emotional reaction toward such unusual behavior is stronger than any doubt about the miracle itself. God, saliva, and earth cannot be mixed; it goes against etiquette, it is not good form.

Christianity is, however, a global reality. Africans, who do not have Greek philosophy as a part of their cultural heritage, readily accept emotionally those aspects of Christianity that seem very strange in Europe. The African has a greater possibility than we have of achieving that combination of the ethical and the physical which is characteristic of the Creed: the belief in creation, the view of the incarnation, the belief in the resurrection, as well as the outflow of this in a sacramental, corporeal, worship service. In the ecumenical and international era in which we live it is well to remember how incidental European culture is from the viewpoint of the gospel; it is but one of many cultures in which Christianity lives and grows, and from present appearances it is by no means certain that it is a particularly important one.

But if we are to attempt to fit the belief in the resurrection into the general framework we have given above which presupposes the cultural climate of Europe since the Enlightenment, with all the difficulties that are inherent in that climate (for instance, if we are to attempt to make belief in creation and the notion of a divine activity in and through universal law intelligible), the following six points are of special weight. All six of these points have been touched upon previously in separate connections.

1. The cross on Golgotha means that a person has lived in this world in which destruction prevails, without his human life having been broken down. The whole of Christ's human existence is a triumphant manifestation of life, and therefore it sets free the life that creates. In Christ the original becomes visible—that original which is only imitated in the actions which have to be forced, actions done "in obedience to the law."

2. Christ's resurrection means that the victory won on the cross now expresses itself in the whole of humanity, as health flowing from

the victor to all the ailing imitators. Therefore, the resurrection, and the ascension which is included in it, is directly associated with the sending out of the gospel to all people. There is no message about Christ's victory which is not also a message about the sending out of the gospel. Any thought of health and ethical purity which flows from the resurrection being hoarded rather than shared would be incongruous with the New Testament. If the purity is "retained," it becomes impure since destruction consists precisely in such private gaining and retaining.

3. Non-human nature—trees, flowers, and animals—are the victims of human wrongheadedness. They groan continuously under the dominion of destruction. Therefore, the resurrection, like the crucifixion, also has a relation to the non-human. The song of praise which begins to be sung in the Christian congregation means that people now join in the song that "the heavens and the earth" are already singing. The end of it all is the eschatological song of praise that wells forth from all creation. The life of the congregation is a future-oriented expectation of the final subjection of the destroying power.

4. This time of waiting is a time in which the law still rules, a time in which imitations of genuine love must be coerced into existence. On this point there is no difference between Israel's law, which is written in the biblical books, and those laws that govern our various communities, which are enacted by human jurisdictions. All human life, even where no religious faith is present, is in this sense expectation and waiting. Each person waits for the simple spontaneous manifestations of life—such as to love and to be loved, to trust in someone and to encounter confidence toward oneself—which sometimes break through the imitation. We all hope for the healing of those injuries that we have caused others when we fail to meet their expectations.

5. The gospel speaks directly to our human situation. This is the decisive point. Our betrayal of the expectations of others (that is, ethical negation) destroys spontaneity, both on our part and on the part of our neighbor, and it implies ultimately the destruction of life (that is, physical negation). The ethical and the physical are not two widely separated entities. On the contrary, they are intimately connected. This is the case in each individual's self-appraisal regardless of whether or not one has religious faith. The gospel paints a picture in our day of a person who in the crucifixion stood the test; he did not withhold but gave forth, and this says to the listener also today that the crucified one lives. In his resurrection lies forgive-

ness; to say that he is raised is identical with saying that he restores those whom he meets in the kerygma. The ethical and the physical thus come together in the offer which the gospel makes. *The resurrection and the justification of the hearer are one.*[6]

6. The one who accepts the restoration of his own life is drawn into that journey toward the future which is the heart of the new life that the gospel offers. The resurrection life, even though it is lived under the conditions of destruction here on earth and under the reign of law, means fellowship with Christ in his suffering, that is eventual death for the old world. And it means, above all, that we willingly and gladly live so that we interpret the difficulties we meet not as loss, but as signs of life and of approaching morning. The loss lay instead with the old deceit, which has now been erased by forgiveness.

Nowhere in the New Testament is this unity between resurrection, forgiveness, and entrance into a life that faces forward so clear as in the story about Peter. In this respect, Peter is exemplary since it is on him that the whole church is built.

Peter

Most illuminating from this point of view is the addition to John's gospel, John 21:14-19.[7] Whether or not this addition to the fourth gospel presents historical events is not important. What is historically certain is that Peter denied Jesus before the execution, and that this same Peter (or Cephas) played a central role in the early church throughout the empire.

It is important to keep together the following four elements in the story:

1. Christ meets the man whom he himself has chosen to be the church's rock, and he meets him as judge and as the renewer of life. The church is likewise confronted by Christ; the church is not his "extended arm."

2. Judgment and restoration are one—these two must be held together. In the threefold question to Peter (John 21:15-17) there is a reminder of the threefold denial, and hence an element of judgment. But the threefold question is built into a renewed commission to "Feed my sheep," that is, to live for *other* people. Faithfulness to Christ expresses itself in being turned toward these others.

3. The one who is Lord of the church and who "comes" to the church in the eucharistic meal (for it is a meal that is taking place

on the shore, John 21:5-13) holds the future in his hand. In the text this sovereignty over the future expresses itself in a number of sayings about the future (John 21:18-23) all of which include Jesus' knowledge of and lordship over the coming life and death of the disciples. When they move toward the future, everything that happens to them is a part of their fellowship with Christ. This point leads directly to the final one: the positive role of suffering.

4. For the fact that Peter is restored does not imply that he will be free from pain and trouble in the future. If that were the case Peter would not be in fellowship with the one who was crucified. In this fourth point we can see most clearly the distance between original and modern Christianity, a distance which presumably rests on the fact that the "myth" (that is, the physical nature of the event) has been lost. The least resistance becomes a problem for a modern Christian. "Why should this happen to me?" In the text about Peter, on the other hand, it is the *undesired* event—"and carry you where you do not wish to go" (John 21:18)—which is interpreted as *victory* ("glorify God" John 21:19).

If one is to find a contemporary ideology which has preserved its myth, one will probably have to examine Marxism. Its confessors can spend decades in prison without losing their conviction.

When in the current church-centered theological atmosphere, one describes Christ's presence as an uninterrupted *coming*, one always gets the response that this concept dissolves every form of real presence. What is left, it is said, is just something intermittent.

Well, how is the sunshine present in the world? One cannot store it up and then channel it forward in time through some sort of succession. It comes from without and continues always to be something that one must wait for. Still its presence is not intermittent.

This symbol is not modern but very ancient. It is found applied to Jesus already in the prologue to John's gospel. Moreover, it is in the text of the Creed itself: "Light of Light" (Nicene, second article).[8]

*O God, my life is a little ripple on a sea of centuries.
After a few years no one will recognize my name. And
yet you surrounded me on all sides. Wherever I turn
I meet your solicitude, as though I were your only child.
Jesus revealed the thought of your heart when he let
the very least be as precious as the whole world.*

*Give me that confidence in you which enables me to
find meaning in the transient and the humble. Each
week is a week with you, with workdays that become a
part of your work of creation. Each Sunday is a
resurrection and a promise which you give me. My
whole existence consists of moving forward toward the
eternal future. All my days are open toward the song
of praise in your kingdom.*

*This hope is given to me because the cross was raised
here on this earth, on one long and triumphant Friday.
O God, when the final evening comes, let me gladly go to
rest after the week of work is over. Teach me not to
fear the grave but instead go to sleep, quietly as a child
awaiting the festival of Sunday.*

VI

The Gospel

The four gospels cover the same series of events as recounted in the second article. Even in the New Testament epistles and in the Acts of the Apostles the words "gospel" and "kerygma" designate a series of events, not a list of doctrinal statements. Christ's death and resurrection are always in the center of this series of events. Therefore our discussion of the second article must include an analysis of the gospel. The gospel is also sent forth and results in churches being built throughout the world. We are then standing on the threshold of the third article. It is convenient for our purpose to begin with the sending forth of the messengers.

THE SENDING FORTH

Each of the four gospels closes with the sending out of the messengers. In two cases the sending out of the messengers is tied to an account of the ascension. The same connection is repeated in the introductory chapter of the Acts of the Apostles.

The Ascent into Heaven

It is only Mark and Luke who talk about the ascension, and in Mark the account is not a part of the original text. Mark 16:9-20 is placed in brackets in a number of modern translations and there are good reasons for this arrangement. The only evangelist who places any weight on the ascension as a separate event is Luke. He reports

128

on it twice, first in the last chapter of his gospel (Luke 24:44-51)
and then in the first chapter of Acts (1:6-11).

Matthew is most interesting with respect to this matter. At the
place where the others report the ascension, Matthew quotes Jesus
as saying, "All authority in heaven and on earth has been given to
me" (Matt. 28:18). This is also the heart of the appended conclusion to Mark, as well as the two texts in Luke, although in these
cases the point is made in the form of *movement through space*. For
the people of that time who sometimes used God and "heaven" inter-
changeably (cf. Luke 15:18) and for whom it was self-evident that
God as the creator of everything was everywhere, such a movement
through space did not necessarily imply putting distance between
himself and the surface of the earth. In one sense, it could be said
that the movement upwards meant a closer and more sovereign
presence everywhere. Just as God in heaven is everywhere and no
one can escape from him no matter where one may go (Ps. 139:7-12),
so now Christ, through his resurrection, is near to all his own
throughout the whole world, "wherever two or three are gathered
together."

To be sure, there is a movement through space that all these
texts have in common, but it is an entirely different kind of movement. It is not a movement from below upwards but from one
place on the face of the earth to all other places on earth. This is
the case with all the texts. In all three reports of the ascension it
is this outward movement that is at the center. The exhortation
given in Mark is, "Go into all the world and preach the gospel to
the whole creation" (Mark 16:15) and the final verse in Mark
shows that this missionary command is being obeyed (Mark 16:20).
In the last chapter of Luke we encounter the same reality in the
form of a simple declaration: "Repentance and forgiveness of sins
should be preached in his name to all the nations, beginning from
Jerusalem" (Luke 24:27). The same evangelist repeats his statement in Acts 1:8, after which the ascension follows in Acts 1:9.

The entire book of Acts is a detailed confirmation of the fact that
the command of Jesus was obeyed; we have accounts of continuous
journeys by the apostles culminating in Paul's arrival at Rome
(Acts 28:14-31). Without mentioning the ascension at all, Matthew
looks ahead to just such travels when, from the circumstance that
Jesus has "all authority in heaven and on earth," he draws the conclusion that the apostles are to move out among "all nations," with
the specific purpose that people everywhere should become disciples
(Matt. 28:19).

It may be easiest for us to understand that the ascension is tied directly to the sending out of the messengers in all three of the texts in which it is mentioned, if we focus on the text that talks about the sending out *without* saying anything at all about the ascension, namely Matthew 28:18-20. There the sending forth of the apostles is clearly anchored in that reality which is at the heart of all three of the texts dealing with the ascension—Jesus' power over heaven and earth.

As usual, the Gospel of John is the most radical. The final chapter—which is Chapter 20, not the added Chapter 21—speaks of the sending forth of the apostles, but it also has a pentecost story. We are told, "he breathed on them and said to them, 'Receive the Holy Spirit' " (John 20:22). The sending likewise occurs in the simplest possible form: "As the Father has sent me, even so I send you" (20:21). But there is also added to this the account of doubting Thomas, which contains the kernel in the whole incident: "Blessed are those who have not seen and yet believe" (20:29). This means that up until now people have been enslaved by the need to see. Now the time of "the blessed" begins when one does not need to see; now we can believe on the basis of what one hears proclaimed by those who have been sent out. The age of world missions during which Christ will draw all people to himself (12:32) has come. Both ascension and pentecost have already happened.[1]

Then the gospel moves as a spoken word from city to city around the Mediterranean. It would gradually be heard farther away and would spread across the known world. Christ is that word which, with the aid of human tongues and human lips, moves out over land and sea. The concept of the word as a word sent forth is common in the Bible. It is originally rooted in everyday life in the Semitic world (for example Gen. 44:10 and Judg. 11:12, where it is clear that the one who sends speaks through the mouth of the emissary). Something similar continues to be the case, for that matter, in our own culture, in the way we think of an ambassador in a foreign land. Jesus' presence everywhere hangs together with the sending out of his word "to the end of the earth" (Acts 1:8).

The Spoken Word

We are now at a central point in our discussion of the gospel—its oral character, and related to that, its constant reiteration. It has never been thought adequate to present the gospel message only once to each individual. From earliest times there have been regular worship services, with sermons retelling the biblical story.

The oral character of early Christianity ought to astonish us. Jesus and his disciples lived in a culture that was characterized by writings; it was filled with written scrolls. Yet there are no references in the Bible to Jesus writing anything, except for one significant moment when he "bent down and wrote with his finger on the ground"—significant because nothing is said about what he wrote (John 8:6). We are not justified in seeing any disparagement of the written word in this bookless development of early Christianity. It is not a sign of any tendency toward mysticism. Blocks of material were transmitted which contained the gospel in concentrated form (1 Cor. 15:1-5), but that transmission was oral. The four gospels all conclude with a section about the sending forth of persons by Jesus into the world with *words,* but these words are to be *spoken.*

These early accounts present the story of the risen Christ. We could take a critical position about the historical value of these accounts and assert that there are no factual events in these sections, that they were written many years after the fact, and that their purpose is not to write history or biography but to meet the needs of the church. Then the oral character of the message becomes even more astonishing. We know that the church as early as A.D. 70 had begun to prepare writings; reports and records came to be written down and not just spoken. If the church in retrospect could construct the events which are recorded at the end of the four gospels about Jesus' ascension and his sending forth the apostles, could not the church just as well have constructed a command from Jesus to write: "Write it down! Subscribe to this!" Such commands are found in the book of Revelation (1:11 et al.).

But that did not happen. No one put the word "Write!" into the mouth of Jesus as a commission to his followers. What we find is that the spoken word dominates completely. To this we must add that the Acts of the Apostles tells only about apostles who traveled and spoke. Add also that Christianity is already to be found in Damascus, a foreign area, when Paul as a fanatical anti-Christian is on his way there for the purpose of rooting out Christianity, even though there were no New Testament writings as a basis for that faith (Acts 9:2). Add also the fact that before Paul travels to Rome there is already a Christian congregation there for him to visit, even though there has been no New Testament writing available to them. Paul's letters are the oldest known Christian writings. His letter to Rome was written before his departure to Rome.

The oral character of primitive Christianity is a historical miracle. This miracle should be the basis for a closer look at the gospel. It is appropriate to express the relationship between the spoken word and the gospel in this pointed thesis: the gospel in its original purity is an oral report; it is *not* something written.

But this oral aspect of the gospel is not the most surprising sign of Christianity's dependence on the spoken word. Even in such carefully-written documents as the Lutheran Confessions, we cannot but be struck by the fact that the point of departure even here is the radically oral character of the gospel. According to Luther himself the real intention of the written words was to give birth to the spoken word. "It is not in accord with the New Testament to write books," he said. "There ought to be preachers without books in every locality." "That it became necessary to write books was itself a big interruption in the work of the Spirit and a diminuation of his presence." So says Luther about the production of the four gospels. Such a statement is highly offensive to a confessional Lutheran. But as usual, Luther is precisely on the mark as far as the historical situation is concerned at the beginning of the Christian movement.[2]

The need for repetition hangs together with the spoken character of the word. If an external event has taken place—and it is about external events that the gospels give us an account—then one would think that it would be preferable to present information about the events in written form, but orally if necessary. In this way the proper people would be informed about what happened. But this is not the way the gospel was communicated. It was repeated, and its retelling took a variety of forms. The word of the gospel is more than a word that communicates something. The situation into which the words are spoken is this everyday world in which destruction prevails; it is a world in which forces are at work to obliterate what is given in the gospel. Therefore, the words in the ear of the listener may be compared to food for the hungry. To stay with this physical terminology, we can say that everyone who accepts the word, who eats the word to satisfy a hunger, knows that they will need to eat again. The gospel is something that *happens* in the listener, and that which happens needs to happen again and again.

Now the parallel between the gospel, on the one hand, and baptism and the Lord's Supper on the other, should become clear. All of these constitute events that happen and that represent something; all of them allow that which is represented to happen over again—in the hearer, in the baptized one, in the communicant. However, they represent events in different ways, and this difference will occupy us later when we deal with the church. Here we must analyze in more detail the connection between the gospel and the sermon.

THE IMAGE

To Preach Is to Tell

For a long time the old gospel pericopes were the only texts assigned to be preached on in the worship service. The same text was
thus expounded before the congregation year after year. Behind
this arrangement lies the thought that we are really narrating the
year itself (or that the year itself is a "church year" as we now
call it). As soon as we have Christmas, Easter, and Pentecost, we
have the building blocks for the story of the year.

Since this is the case, it is clear that the day's chief text has to
be a text that is a story, not an analysis of doctrine. Consequently,
we can see that the system which places the gospel narratives in the
center of the Sunday worship constitutes an annual retelling of the
same events. Furthermore, this narrative is strengthened by the
permanent epic of baptism and the Lord's Supper, with the stepping
down into the water, the rising up, the breaking of the bread, etc.

Later, paintings on the walls of churches added a new dimension
to this retelling and repetition. These usually presented a series of
significant events drawn from the gospels. The picture of Jesus, the
only true person, the one who never aged, the one who was always
young, was the center of attention. No one has ever so renewed
European art, so inspired new impulses, with anywhere near the
power which Jesus has done despite his short life. And still it is not
his influence on art that has been most dramatic; it is his total in-
filtration of time which is the most remarkable. Entire cultures tell
the story of Jesus' life as they record events throughout the year[3]
—"It was just before Easter. . . . It was at Christmas that year. . . ."
That is the way people speak when they try to remember something.
And they speak the same gospel-telling language when they look
ahead and plan for the future. In each case what they are talking
about are the events in Jesus' life inserted into their own cultural
calendar.

The gospel texts for ordinary Sundays are similar to those for
the special festivals. Between Jesus' birth (Christmas) and his cross
and resurrection (Easter), the gospel texts relate either an activity
of Jesus or an event in which he was the center. The Sundays between Pentecost and Christmas continue with excerpts from the
gospel narrative and with other actions of Jesus. These texts are as
special in nature and as free of doctrinal teaching as are the texts
for the great festival days. Preaching throughout history has been
built on these epic texts. The oral nature of the written texts that
we now read in the service, implies that they should give birth to

oral speech and be heard by the people assembled at the worship
service.

To appreciate fully what this would have meant in times past one
would need to be illiterate. It is certainly true that most of those
who have told stories or listened to them during the history of the
world have been illiterate. Their capacity for narration or for listening was not lessened because of their shortcomings in the matter
of reading and writing. On the contrary, they were without doubt
more accomplished than we are both in the art of narrating and in
the art of listening. Communications of this sort among people in
times past may very well have been at a deeper level and have had
a more enduring effect than is the case with communication today
which often stops at the surface. The three following points are
especially important:

1) The text (and the sermon) paints a picture of a man on his
way from birth to death. The texts tell about Jesus and they fasten
his image on the consciousness of the listener. The listener is also
traveling the same road, between birth and death. There is immediately awakened in the listener an inclination to imitate the picture, to give oneself in "discipleship" to the one the gospel depicts.
This elemental summons to fall into step with the image is rooted in
the texts themselves and does not imply any moralistic misunderstanding of the gospel.

2) The text (and the sermon) colors in a large group of figures
around Jesus. There are the blind, the lame, the publicans, the adul-
terers. For all practical purposes, the chief figure is never alone.
This is the reason that the gospel can become gospel. If what we had
before us were teaching documents, it would be very proper to have
the teacher alone in the picture, or even better, alongside the picture. But now the text is a story about someone who does something; therefore he is surrounded by hundreds of others, all of whom
represent those with whom he accomplishes something. They all
represent "Adam," that is, humanity. What is remarkable is that
each of these exemplars are lacking something. Even the twelve
apostles as depicted in the gospels reflect misunderstanding; they
have not yet arrived at the goal, they are on the way, they are followers of the image. The illiterate listener in every age is entirely
capable of identifying with all of these.

3) The fellowship between the chief figure in these stories and
the other figures is never broken. This is what makes the gospel
"good news," this is the *ev* in the Greek *evangelion*. What gives rise

to the prefix *ev* in the message these texts contain, is that the listener is privileged to take the position of the addressee of the gospel. The listener is permitted to identify with those with whom the chief figure accomplishes something and who consequently are the recipients of the chief figure's restoring deeds (healing, forgiving, etc.). Thus the listener becomes a recipient. This is the aim of preaching, to transfer the chief figure's activity to new recipients, over and over again. The text assures these recipients that they do not need to be hindered from accepting what the good news offers because of their faults, mistakes, or weaknesses. Even a criminal about to be executed can be assured of receiving the whole kingdom of heaven. In that case, the criminal becomes the malefactor on the side-cross at Golgotha.

A text of epic character is much more effective than an abstract statement of doctrine. To say that "God justifies us without any merit of our own" is the same as telling the story of the prodigal son or the thief on the cross. In a theological dispute, the abstract statement of doctrine is the most effective. But to the one who listens to a sermon, an abstract statement of doctrine calls to mind no human image. When the church composed the narrative year which was to take into account the needs of all, it avoided placing abstract statements of doctrine in the center of the worship service. "The gospel for the day" became instead a story, in all the texts for all the services throughout the year. It is a great mistake to believe that such an arrangement is appropriate only for the illiterate. Even a modern, sophisticated, intellectual person may discover a new understanding of the gospel through encountering it, for instance, in a drama. There one meets the gospel in its original form. Suddenly the story-character is recovered and the *human picture* functions afresh.

The pattern of worship in many churches has long obscured this story-character of the texts. They have done this partly by preaching purely doctrinal and abstract sermons, and partly by attempting to be modern and current and hence giving up the text altogether, or at least giving up the epic element in the text. The renaissance of the image of Jesus in secular literature is, in this respect, a benefit to the churches.

"God's Fingers"

Irenaeus of Lyon speaks about both "God's hands" and about "God's fingers." He uses this anthropomorphic language for the pur-

pose of clarifying the relation between creation and salvation.[4] The
dogmas concerning the Trinity and Christ's action in the sacraments,
which often seem to us to be dry and irrelevant doctrines, were held
together with the help of this picture language of hands and fingers.
We shall approach this symbolic language in two stages: first to describe what Irenaeus meant, and then to understand its significance
today.

God is portrayed as a worker with two hands. The hands are the
Son and the Spirit. Thus we have the Trinity, for a person is a
unity with two hands. The Son and the Spirit are not something
other than God the Father, for a person's hands are of course part
of the person himself. But hands are designed for work. The material which God has shaped and touched with his hands and fingers
includes the created world, the experiences of Jesus and even our
worship services. We see the hands and fingers of God in the life,
ministry, and death of Jesus and because of what he has done there
has been a Christian congregation in the world.

Irenaeus also wants to explain with his picture language the
pluralistic element in the creation story: God said, "Let *us* make
man . . . " (Gen. 1:26). To whom was he speaking? Are there several gods? No, God is like an individual faced with a big work assignment. He looks at his own hands and says, "Now *we* are going
to get under way." And so he begins, with his two hands, to form
Adam.[5] But it is a long task, and the work is disturbed by the
destructive action of the enemy. The hands work on despite opposition: Jesus was born, was crucified, went to his grave, was raised
and now speaks through the gospel to the end of the earth, always
against opposition.

What is amazing about old, unromantic Irenaeus is that he draws
into this picture language some subtle insights about how we can
preserve our humanity and grow in faith, gratitude, and patience.
Reminding ourselves that we are the work of God's fingers is the
way to preserve "a meek and responsive heart," he says. Ungrateful
and bitter people lose themselves, forfeit their humanity and fall
out of the hands of the Creator, they lose "the print-marks of his
fingers." Even the soul comes into existence in a psychic event that
is part of the process of becoming a human fetus, and is the direct
consequence of physical intercourse. Each birth is a moment in the
original act of creation.

It is not difficult to translate this ancient way of speaking into
modern speech, even into technical psychiatric language of a rather
advanced kind. Of the range of possibilities which are open to a
child at birth, some are destroyed through the trauma of puberty

and through the attempts to live in community with others. A therapeutic program must always include some form of diagnosis of the
damage that has been done, as well as a model for leading the individual into one's own free development toward the possibilities
which are potentially present but which were choked out by previous destructive experiences. Thus far Irenaeus is fully in accord
with contemporary therapy. "Salvation" does not mean anything
else to him than this elementary objective of "becoming a human."

There are two problems. One is that the old church fathers believed that the picture of Jesus presented in the gospels illustrated
in the two-fold movement in baptism—down into the water (death)
and up out of the water (resurrection)—had a positive function in
the human healing process. The other problem is that they believed
that the goal of our becoming human lay on the other side of bodily death. This means that even when a person is on the way toward
death, even when one is dying, one awaits a sequence of events
through which one can always *become* something. The dying is incorporated into the continuing development in which the human
can continually achieve new form. One can become "the image of
the true person" even under the conditions brought about by destruction. To leave dying unexplained and uninterpreted while the
anaesthetized body sleeps away, takes away something from being
human.

Through both of these problems the old church fathers may
have a valuable word for us today. First, the positive role of the
image of Jesus in the healing process can be a point of departure
for a critique of modern denominations which often function as
purveyors of moralistic norms, and as critics rather than as support-
ers and sustainers of those who provide the services society needs.
Second, the positive role death plays in our becoming human can be
the point of departure for a critique of contemporary care of the
sick, which often stands completely perplexed before people who are
dying and which has patterns for dealing with people only when
physical health is in prospect.

"EV" MEANS REJOICING

The word "gospel" *(evangelion* in Greek) means "good news."
The prefix *ev* (which means "good," "joyful," "beautiful") cannot
be attached to any message whatever. Those toward whom the message is directed, must be relieved of something they have feared or
gain something for which they have hoped as a result of the message. When that happens, the listeners have heard an *ev*angel. The

information that God is Lord of all humanity is "good news" because it means God's victory over the enemy of all humanity.

The Will to Live

The term "will to live" is vague, and therefore it is a good word
in this connection. The reality designated by this term is variable
and shifts from time to time during a person's lifetime. What holds
together all these changing forms of the will to live is simply that
they make it possible for the individual to go unfrightened into
the new day which lies ahead. For the child the basis for this courage may be the confidence given by parents. In the course of time,
new factors such as companions, work, or one's own family may
replace parents. It is significant that when the synoptics (and even
the gospel of John) describe Jesus' activities, they relate the whole
of his impact to similar factors. After an encounter with him, people clearly have a new will to live, a new courage for life. This new
courage for life also includes the courage to die.[6]

Healing and forgiving are uppermost among those activities of
Jesus that strengthen people's will to live. Therefore it is important to emphasize that these two activities are an essential part of
the mission on which the disciples are sent forth (Luke 9:2; 10:9;
Mark 16:15-18). The Acts of the Apostles and other documents
from the earliest church, delineate a picture of a Christian congregation which functioned primarily with such activities at its
center.

These activities which gave support to people threatened by sickness or hunger were gradually shifted from the church to the community (the provincial assembly, the state). Let us imagine the
situation of a man living in past centuries who was not a partici-
pant in the worship of the church but who lived so close to the
congregation that he was able to see the effects of the congregation's
ministry in his everyday life. But a very significant change takes
place with the passing of time.

At the beginning, the secular society had few activities in which
the individual was *given* something necessary to maintain life and
health (it was up to the family to provide such). But the Christian
congregation in its formative years *was* engaged in giving something which strengthened the will to live. Afterwards, as the civil
organizations came to be governed by laws which were aimed at
securing the welfare of the individual, the state became more and
more like the church (and the local community became more and
more like the congregation). This meant that the church was emp-

tied of concern for "the body," and became increasingly engaged in expressing opinions, often opinions that differed from those of other people. The person who now lives near the church but does not actively participate in the worship begins to perceive a change in the church from a serving congregation to a pressure group. What issues from the church are primarily demands, rather than health and healing programs.

The church in the twentieth century is on its way out as a part of the total community apparatus, although it has not yet reached the status of being a minority. Therefore the twentieth century poses a particular challenge to the church if the church intends to keep the good news, the gospel at its center. The Christian congregation must continue to speak to the moral issues affecting people, without necessarily taking back from the state responsibility for the health care of people. What is said in the proclamation of "Christian norms" concerning sexuality, abortion, divorce, etc., has the purpose of supporting life and rescuing the weak, but it comes to the public as an addition to other forms of support and protection, also as an addition to the worship service. The information about what the church says concerning the norms is communicated beyond the congregation by the daily press and mass media and often appears to many people as a threat or constraint, without strengthening "the will to live."

In this modern period it is also clear that the will to live is deteriorating from other causes in the secular community. Novels, poetry, and the youth revolt all witness to this. Many factors contribute: technology, the fast working pace, and the dissolution of the small social units. In this situation, the Christian congregation cannot follow completely the original commission given to the disciples unless a complete and radical change occurs with respect to the view of the church and the world.

If it should occur to the church that the world is characterized by the absence of norms while the church has norms, the church should know that this thought is self-destructive. It is church-destroying even if it is true. There are many statements that are true but are nonetheless devastating. What the congregation has which it can spread abroad in the world must be determined on the basis of the sending out of the apostles to "all people" as it is reported in the New Testament. It is crystal clear that the commission to those who were sent out did not include the spreading of norms among the normless. The thought which must be placed in the center of the Christian congregation if it is to regain contact with its commission, is quite different.

In a world in which the will to live often gives way under severe pressure, the task of the church is to give people courage for life. Everything is included in that task, from young people's parks in Sweden to water wells in India to Holy Communion for the individual on the deathbed to confession and absolution, even norms and guidelines. Everything is included, but always within the framework of courage for life. To be sure, the norm can become a judgment even when it is embedded in something which is not a judgment, but the norm cannot in this framework become a form of moralistic pressure. Furthermore, there comes to be an element which is church-renewing in its effect when the courage for life, rather than the norms, is placed in the center. There is a positive point to the critical self-examination which is directed inward toward the worshiping congregation. There is no doubt that the congregation does have norms to hand out, but it is pertinent to ask whether it has courage for life.

The Eucharist

In both Baptism and the Lord's Supper there is an element of judgment, although the judgment is embedded in restoration.[7] Baptism is death for all that is old and at the same time it is resurrection and the beginning of a journey "in newness of life" (Rom. 6:4). The Lord's Supper contains the same two elements, both confession with absolution, and thanksgiving (eucharist). These two elements are not in conflict with one another, nor do they produce emotional feelings that nullify one another. To be sure, the matter is often interpreted this way, especially in discussions of the significance of the Lord's Supper, where the gloomy confessional element is said to contradict the eucharistic element, the song of praise.

But where this is the case, the confessional element has come to be dominated by the recounting of dark memories drawn from the individual's own history. The center of the confession is *not* the recounting of sins; it is *not* a scrupulous prying into the personal self. The center is the absolution, that which was earlier identified as "the power of the keys" and which is identified with the preaching of the gospel. This announcement of the forgiveness of sins means that the old is dead. The death moment is implicit in the forgiveness, and death brings joy; it is an enhancement of the will to live. It means that we are finally free from the bonds of the old; we are now free to move forward. Here lies the unity of the confession and the eucharist in the Holy Communion.

In spite of the fact that the eucharist has always been a mealtime for those that were baptized, and in this sense a worship service that was turned inward, the right to observe it without partaking in it has been acknowledged since ancient times. The observer can see and hear how others in an act of praise go forward and receive bread and wine; one witnesses how the bread is broken and distributed, and one sees how the cup is lifted and passed from hand to hand. To observe this is to receive the gospel in the form of a *picture*. That act has in itself a very strong missionary impact, in spite of the fact that the Lord's Supper was not included in the missionary command (as the spoken word and baptism were).[8]

The powerful impact of this picture of the gospel which the Lord's Supper presents is conditioned by the epic character of its institution on "the night in which he was betrayed." If one brings together the content of the gospel into a doctrinal and abstract form, one can say with Paul and the Reformers, that God "justifies the sinner without works" (or "without merit"). This abstract formulation, which almost cries out for some sort of illustration, is never so effectively portrayed as in the repeated act of Holy Communion.

It is the last night and *all* the guests at the Supper will abandon him in the presence of Golgotha. But in spite of this, Jesus does not, after his victory, build up his church from a new selection of better or more promising people. He takes the same apostles, forgives them, and sends them out into the world as his instruments. At every repetition of the Lord's Supper, there is portrayed a church which lives on the principle of "justification by faith without works."

*O God, you who have given us life and who would form
and fashion us. I know that all that happens to me is
filled with your presence. But I am as a dried out tree;
no life flows through me. I am a stranger to what
happens around me; it does not reach into my inward self.*

*Give me back, O God, the freedom that belongs to a
child. Give me the freedom to leave behind and to forget,
to choose anew, and to go farther. Through Jesus you
have told us that we must become like little children in
order to enter your kingdom. For the child every morning
is filled with newness. Give me a responsive heart, so
that the events of each day become great.*

*All this freedom lies within reach in the forgiveness
of sins. If I believed, I would be freed from all that is past
and open to all that is coming. Send your Spirit into my
heart, so that in the depths of my soul I may claim the
freedom which belongs to me. Make me soft and pliable in
your hand and create something whole out of me
before death comes.*

The Third Article
The Spirit

The Congregation and the Promise

When thou sendest forth thy Spirit, they are created; and thou renewest the face of the ground. (Ps. 104:30)

If the Spirit of him who raised Jesus from the dead dwells in you he who raised Christ Jesus from the dead will give life to your mortal bodies also through his Spirit which dwells in you (Rom. 8:11).

VII

The Congregation
in the World

As we begin the third article, about the Spirit, we must join together the contemporary congregation and eternal life in the future: "the forgiveness of sins, the resurrection of the body, and the life everlasting." The church (or the congregation) begins on the very first Pentecost to move out across the face of the earth. It is continuously and without exception directed toward the whole of humanity, and is therefore directed toward the eternal future. This movement of the congregation to the farthest corners of the world begins with the outpouring of the Spirit (Acts 1:8).

In the four sections of this chapter we will deal with the congregation in the world. Each section has as its rubric a New Testament citation in which the form "Spirit" occurs. The first section sets the congregation in relation to the world and to society; the second takes up the inner fellowship within the congregation (the body and its members); the third deals with the relation between the church and the world (in which the dissimilarities among the various confessions are pointed out); the fourth devotes particular attention to how the Spirit uses certain external physical means, as in the sacraments.

Within each division we will make brief comparisons with some other view of life: Marxism, humanism, existentialism, and mysticism (the relation to naturalism can be deferred to the next chapter in which we will deal with eternal life and discuss the attitude of the Christian in the presence of death).

144

"I WILL POUR OUT MY SPIRIT ON ALL FLESH"

In the time of the Old Testament prophets, Israel did not doubt that God was at work in the nation's history. From the same period there are a number of sayings which testify to the fact that the Spirit was believed to work in the present, as a contemporary reality (Isa. 48:16; Mic. 3:8; et al.). Later on, and especially in late Judaism, this certainty about God's presence in history weakened, and at the same time the Spirit tended to be pushed into the future. God will act eventually; the time will come when the Spirit will be poured out. For Joel that statement "I will pour out my spirit on all flesh" (2:28) was a strictly futuristic statement dealing with the last times. But in Acts 2:16-21, Peter argues that what had been promised for the future has now come to pass. At the same time, the preaching of the gospel to all people in the world begins. The coordination of a) external events which are a part of world history and b) the Spirit, remains as it was in the Old Testament.

The Church and the World

The history of the Christian church begins in this movement out to all nations. The birth of the church is tied in with two phenomena in Greek philosophy which were thought to contradict each other: partly a new, fresh association with the *world* and its many people; partly the pouring out of the *Spirit*. As soon as the Spirit is poured out, the bond with the world is in place.[1]

The Spirit's orientation toward the world is not as strange as may at first appear. It is Semitic thought that lies behind this imagery, and for the Semites both "Spirit" and "word" were thought to be tools of the Creator in the work of creation. Spirit proceeds from his mouth when he speaks. "By the word of the Lord the heavens were made, and all their host by the breath of his mouth" (Ps. 33:6) sounds to us like two quite separate statements, but in Old Testament times the second half provided a festive repetition of the first half.

God creates through the Spirit. "When thou sendest forth thy Spirit, they are created," is said about God's feeding of the animals in Psalm 104:30. The words which follow that statement are just as typical: "thou renewest the face of the ground" (concerning the combination of word and Spirit compare also the amazing statement about the animals in Isa. 34:15-16). In all these places the Spirit is spoken of as active in creation. It is not enough that God creates in the world through the Spirit; what he creates is corporeal. It consists of creatures and things.

In an earlier chapter we encountered the anthropomorphic and naive language about the Creator's hands and fingers. These were thought of as being occupied with the forming and shaping of the person all the way from the mother's womb through everything that happens after the child is born—including its dying. These fingers of the Creator show up again in the New Testament in connection with the Spirit. When there is strife about Jesus driving out the demons, Jesus replies, according to Matthew, "If it is by the Spirit of God that I cast out demons, then the kingdom of God has come upon you" (12:28). This is a situation with which we have become very familiar in this presentation: God gives health even where the forces of destruction are at work. In Luke the same passage reads thus: ". . . if it is by the finger of God that I cast out demons . . ." (11:20). So there is no real difference between "spirit" and "finger." Both designate something that God uses when he heals and creates.

Since the Spirit functions in this way, events which are different in our thinking—such as healing the sick, sanctification, the resurrection of the dead—can be held together in a single unified series. All are the work of the Spirit. Even Jesus' awakening from the grave is the Spirit's work; and this passes over directly into the awakening of a new person who as sanctified *acts* differently than the old destructive person acted. This new and different person will, like Jesus, rise up and live. His expressions of life can no more be quenched. Paul holds together these two apparently different happenings with extraordinary clarity when, for example, in the letter to the Romans (8:1-17), he sets forth what the new way of life consists of. If the Spirit dwells in the heart, he says, then there is that power within which called forth Jesus from death, and that power will make the person of faith alive eternally (Rom. 8:11).

This seems to be a mythology that will not endure. Here the ethical and the physical are mixed; moral action is associated with the healing of the sick. It is clear that some of this cannot be carried over into the present. But one thing that can and must be carried into the present if Christianity is to retain any continuity with its origin is the relationship between the Spirit and the world. To concentrate on the Spirit *against* interest in social activities in this world, implies a denial of the biblical teachings about the Spirit. That church which is born through the Spirit, is *by virtue of its spirituality*, a church for the world and in the world according to the New Testament.

Salt and Light

This position is underscored also by other New Testament citations concerning the function of the disciples. In the Sermon on the Mount are references to salt and light. Both expressions assign a task to the disciples, but it is a task which does not relate to their inner life in separation from the world. On the contrary, salt does not exist for the sake of salt but for the sake of food threatened by putrefaction. "The earth" is identified as the proper location where this function is to be performed, "You are the salt of the earth" (Matt. 5:13). This becomes apparent also in the parallel statement about light. There the location which is otherwise often appraised negatively, "the world," is the proper location for the functioning of the disciples: "You are the light of the world" (Matt. 5:14).[2] The earth and the world are thus the two fields in which the Spirit works. It is in these arenas that the congregation functions—when it functions! The salt can, of course, lose its saltness.

Behind this language lies the thought of creation. The first article is joined to the third article by a bridge called Christ. That food ought not be allowed to spoil is not written in the Sermon on the Mount. That the darkness ought not to be allowed to conquer is not directly stated in the Sermon either. In a peculiar way one of these two self-evident things (for everything that belongs to creation is self-evident) is intimated in a cryptic way in the creation account. There God gives names to both light and darkness ("day" and "night") but only light is said to be *good*. Darkness is from the beginning understood as something destructive, like putrefaction. Both threaten life. Existence needs salt and light to keep from going under.

All of these components—creation, destruction, healing of the threatened—are by now very familiar to us. We touched on them when we were describing the spontaneous expressions of life under the rubrics of the first article; we came upon them again in the analysis of the deeds of Jesus, his death and resurrection. What is new and specific in the third article is this: The focus is no longer on Jesus as a historical person with death still ahead of him, but instead the focus is on a group of people who worship in his name (his congregation). The destructive forces remain and continue their devastations, even though Jesus as Savior has fulfilled his work.

This is the situation in which *the congregation in the world* finds itself. The teaching about the Spirit deals with this congregation and with its holding fast to the promise (i.e., to eternal life). The problems implicit in the teaching about the Spirit derive from the situation of the congregation. The place where the congregation is to function is this world, this earth, and the boundary for its activity is the death of its members. The time in which the congregation is to function is the time after Jesus. An important point in teaching about the Spirit is the question of the means which proceed from Jesus and in which faith sees the presence of Jesus himself. Such "means" are baptism, the spoken word, and the eucharistic meal. In all of these there is a promise, an element which points forward to a time that includes the death of the one who receives it, and which assures us that death is life "in Christ."

Destruction, in the sense of death as something that threatens us, is thus drawn into the congregation's service of worship; it is explained and interpreted in the means of grace. The congregation acts in the world not in the service of destruction but in the service of life, in the service of "the will to live." It encounters suffering but it does not seek revenge. It is thus that the church is salt and light, but that is a role from which it is easy to fall.

Comparison with Marxism

One can undertake a comparison between Christianity and Marxism at several points. However, the difference between them comes out most clearly in the view of what constitutes destruction or evil. We have earlier dealt with the same point in connection with the analysis of Jesus' miracles of healing and of hope.

If we begin with the Christian idea of creation, we find that only God can be the subject of the verb "create." That is why the spontaneous expressions of life are something which only *enable* us to act in a certain way. We cannot just decide to trust someone, or to love someone, or to make ourselves glad. We can do it only if we are *enabled,* only if we are given the gift to do it. We can hope for it, even if we do not yet have the gift. The destruction of trust and love and the will to live, are things that we can accomplish. It is the nature of destruction (i.e., evil) that it corrodes what is good in itself, what is good only if it is being continuously created anew.

In Marxism, the person has taken the place of God. In the Marxist view of work it is clearly the person who creates. Destruction consists in the unnatural distribution of work and in private capitalism, which is connected with that maldistribution. The trouble is that the worker is not allowed to retain the product of his work (it is taken by the capitalist owner), and as a result one becomes a stranger to one's own existence (one becomes alienated).[3] In this view, destruction (in the form of private capitalism) also wears away at something good which is being constantly created, but those who are doing the creating are the working masses, those whose existence is being "siphoned off."

If we were to define salvation as bringing an end to the forces of destruction, we should realize that Marxism defines the decisive act in salvation as the breaking to pieces of a certain economic system. When private capitalism is crushed, creative powers are released which have always existed in the person and which have remained intact all the while. However, unnatural habits of thought ingrained in the person over a long period of time by the business community may make a period of "nurture" necessary after the revolution. But basically, there is nothing in the human being as such which hinders the development of the new socialist person.

In its view of what it means to be human, Marx is not as original as many seem to think. He is unique in his understanding of what sort of power it is that enslaves the human, and it is here that the dynamic of Marxism is to be found. Rudolf Bultmann has studied the Greek texts outside of the New Testament to see how they understood the terms "freedom" *(eleutheria)* and "free" *(eleutheros)*. He has concluded that whenever one encounters ideas outside the New Testament which are similar to Christian ideas, they differ in that they understand the enslavement of the person as coming from some irrational force that attacks the person from *without* (e.g., stoicism). According to the Greeks there is no destruction to be found *within* one's own inner being. This highly unGreek thesis in the New Testament can be found only in Paul and other primitive Christian authors.[4] All other Greek-speaking people considered the enslaving power to come from a false system outside of the individual.

The same situation exists in relation to Judaism. According to the Jewish view, if one has the law which explains what is good, one can then accomplish that good. Christianity has a contrary point of view; that is why when the gospel speaks of the truly human it describes someone other than myself. That is also why when all human resources have been exhausted, the gospel continues to be tenable. It can speak to us individually and give us something when by ourselves we can do nothing. However, the gospel has shown relatively little ability to change society where the majority prefer to maintain the status quo, even though adequate resources were available for changing society. The reason for this apparent passivity is sometimes considered to lie in the preoccupation of Christians with purely inward, individual concerns. In this way, say the Marxists, the church functions as opium, and is manipulated by capital.

If one looks at the history of the church, there is a good deal of evidence that supports the Marxist charge. The question is to what extent the history of the church actually reflects the message of the Bible. Where in the history of the church, for instance, does one find the biblical concept of the Spirit? The Bible presents the Spirit as creative, as active in external, worldly happenings such as the healing of the sick, the feeding of the hungry, even the awakening of the dead. This brings us back to the figures of salt and light again. Both of these figures receive their meaning from a relationship; they are not to be thought of as existing for themselves but in relation to the decay and darkness in the world. *"Spirit" has hardly ever been understood in this way in the entire history of the church.* Normally, when one says "spirit," one is thinking of an inner sphere, separated from the "body." When one says "purely spiritual," one thinks of a flight from social phenomena, a retreat into a private, inward "holiness."

This way of thinking implies that Greek philosophy has triumphed over the gospel. The Spirit is no longer regarded as implicit in our birth; rather, it is acquired through some form of experience generally tied to Jesus. After that experience the Spirit becomes encapsulated in the religious person. Some people, therefore, say they "have" the Spirit, in about the same way that one "has" intelligence. In this unbiblical Greek cleavage between body and spirit there is a devaluation of the body which expresses itself in many ways not only in ancient cultures, but in contemporary Indian culture as well. When Marxism criticizes Christianity it offers a broadside against all religion and not specifically the gospel. In fact, passivity with regard to the body and aversion toward outward change is much more characteristic of the religions that surrounded primitive Christianity than it is of biblical faith (which might more properly be regarded as a critique of traditional religion).

An unbiased historical view of Christianity and Marxism would yield two interesting results. Both have to do with total victory and with one hundred percent majorities.

Christianity operated somewhat in accord with its original nature while it was still on its way to acceptance in the Roman Empire. Then it lived in relation to something that was outside of itself. That is the way salt functions, and that is the way the Spirit functioned at Pentecost. But to remain salt when one is expected to be identified with "all flesh" is extraordinarily difficult, just as it is very difficult to preserve the Pentecost view of the Spirit when the church lives as a majority. One has to include the whole empire; all are inside the congregation. *This is the problem faced by the fourth century.* We have taken too little notice, up to this point, of the circumstance that it was in the fourth century that Christianity became a state religion, and it was in the fourth century that the monastic movement broke through in a big way. In the life of the cloister there was cultivated a view of spirit, as contrasted to body, which came from Greek philosophy and which was foreign to the primitive gospel. Spirit was now cultivated *in isolation.*

Marxism has characteristically had its strength in revolution itself, when a capitalist society is being overturned and when a revolution is under way. It has always had its weakness in the attempt to build a new and enduring system after the revolution. One can believe that this is because of Marxism's understanding of the nature of the destructive forces. If there is anything destructive to be found in the person, then Marxism is a romantic ideology, having the same difficulties to master as all other forms of romanticism. If one has in principle conceived of destruction as consisting of an improper external management of work, production, and capital, one can describe evil without ever talking about the individual human being. Then after the revolution, evil will be incomprehensible—this "counterrevolutionary force" will no longer keep cropping up. Marxists have no conceptual apparatus, and no terminology suited to the problems that exist after a revolution. In this lack of an ideological arsenal, and in the impotence that follows from it, Marxism resembles Christianity after its victory in the fourth century.

"BY ONE SPIRIT WE WERE ALL BAPTIZED INTO ONE BODY"

The New Testament very often joins together baptism and the Spirit.[5] When this is done, baptism is understood as death for the destructive forces and victory for the created life. Since what is to die is one's own private inclination to possess, and since it is service to others which is to live, we might expect that we would be required to give up our individual originality through baptism and to substitute for it a kind of conformism where all would be alike. The opposite is, however, the case. In that body which constitutes the congregation the individuals are to be *unlike* one another. Only in that way can they help each other.

The explanation of this lies in the fact that what is individual is not our own private possession. It is on the contrary something which we have been *given* for the purpose of functioning as a part of a body. The eye functions through seeing, the ear through hearing, etc. That which is specifically individual is something that is *created* and is not to be put to death. What is purely one's own private possession, and therefore destructive, is the selfish use of all that is created with the intention of receiving gain without service. Consequently, the congregation's life will reflect the flowering of the individual originality of its members because what is one's own and private is being subdued and put to death.

This is developed especially in the two great Pauline chapters about the congregation as a "body," Romans 12, and 1 Corinthians 12. It is from the latter chapter that the rubric for this section is taken: "by one Spirit we were all baptized into one body" (1 Cor. 12:13). The accent is on *one*, thus: "in one Spirit . . . into one body." After this double emphasis on unity, the argument for multiplicity and for individualized functions within the whole seems all the more noteworthy.

The Dissimilarity among Individuals

The eye and the ear in the human body are used by Paul to illustrate how the person functions in the congregation. "If the whole body were an eye, where would be the hearing?" A whole series of bodily organs are listed in the context for the purpose of making clear that a body can function as *one* body only on the presupposition that its different parts function *differently*—eye, ear, hand, foot, etc. The one who has created the body to be one with many parts is God (1 Cor. 12:12-26, esp. vv. 18, 24).

Consequently, the ordinary human body is not just used as a symbol. Among New Testament exegetes the inference is often made that Paul is only talking here about what God, through Christ or the Spirit, is doing in the congregation; as a pedagogical aid, it is thought, he uses a nonspiritual relationship, namely an ordinary human body (where it is presupposed that God is not at work). This is to do away with the entire meaning of the text. Paul says expressly that *God* has "arranged" the members in the body, and "adjusted" its parts (1 Cor. 12:18, 24). These are expressions which apply to any body whatever, and not specifically to the congregation. What is called a metaphor or a symbol is thus much more than just an illustration; it is *itself* a miracle of divine creation.

The same is true of the ordinary grain of wheat, with the sun and the rain. They are not only symbols. God himself acts in nature, and in addition he acts in the congregation, and he acts in a similar fashion. The words of the Sermon on the Mount about the lilies of the field and the birds of the air (Matt. 6:26-34) lose all meaning if what Jesus intended to say was that God concerns himself only about the disciples, and if the birds and the lilies were just an illustration. The whole point lies in the fact that God does actively care for the birds and the lilies—therefore, how much more will he care for the disciples of Jesus. It is here a question of accurate speech, and not only a question of metaphors. The same is true with those texts that talk about what God does with sun, rain, and grains of wheat (e.g., Matt. 5:45; 1 Cor. 15:36-38). *The Old Testament idea of creation in its entirety is carried over into the New Testament.*

This has significance for understanding the gifts of grace in the congregation. It is a mistake to think of these as being given only in specifically religious experiences in which the members of the congregation have participated subsequent to their entrance into the congregation (or in connection with their entrance). To have the ability to speak, to be physically strong, or to be able to handle strain, are not specifically religious gifts; they are common human qualities which in the church, understood as a body, can be used to help the whole. If they are used in service to others, these gifts given in creation also enable the congregation to fulfill its proper role. Then also the individuals who have been given the gifts bloom, even though at the same time what is one's own in a private sense dies, and thus the death of the old possessive self which is the goal toward which baptism points, is fulfilled.

"By one Spirit we were all baptized into one body"; in service we now become what in our innermost being we already are. Apart from the body our gifts would lie unused and would have no meaning. A foot that is cut off may be as whole as it ever was, and an eye that is torn out may still have its membranes and lens in perfect condition, but unless they are a part of a *body* the foot and the eye are nothing. The primitive Christian way of looking upon individual differences as an *enhancement* of the oneness instead of a diminution of it, involves an interpretation of originality and individuality, and gives an importance to divergences which has hardly ever been realized in the Christian church to this day. As the body is understood in the primitive church no one can be an observer, or belong to an awed audience observing a few who "have gotten the Spirit." All possess the Spirit, even the weakest, whose contribution to the whole is hidden from our view just as it may be in the human body (1 Cor. 12:22-26).[6]

This last fact is the most remarkable of all. One can present the theme of pneumatology in the following formula: It is the Spirit through whom Christ continues to work on earth. What was unique about Christ's victory was that it was won down in the depths, in the midst of deprivation. It may be said that the Spirit works

most effectively in the Christian congregation through those who
have no visible gifts—those who are the farthest down (as Christ
was), and who in the midst of their deprivation work against division and against envy (inasmuch as they do not possess anything
which can drive someone into competition and the search for pres-
tige). It is the poor and the despised who keep up the church; they
carry it on their shoulders.

But it is also a part of the teaching concerning the Spirit that no
one can say who these are, these "last who will be first" (Luke
13:30). To point them out would be in conflict with the eschatology
of the grain of wheat. To point out and to separate, this is an activity which does not belong to the congregation in this world. Its
function is to plant the seed—or expressed even more pointedly—
to fall into the earth and die.

Comparison with Humanism

When one sets out to compare Christianity with other views of
life, or "isms", attention is often concentrated improperly on those
isms that form groups, that are collective in nature. Among those
is of course, Marxism, but the same is also true of existentialism,
which at times in the period after World War II was identified
with certain kinds of dress and its own distinctive jargon. Among
the strengths of N. H. Søe's *Christian Ethic* is that it consciously
departs from such deference to the collective. He insistently sets
forth "idealism" or "human ethic" as the main alternatives to
Christianity, and he affirms just as insistently that Plato and his
dialogues continue to form the life-views of Europeans.[7]

Søe is surely right about this. But those whose views are shaped
by Plato (and other Greeks) have hardly ever read Plato. They are
shaped by his ideas nonetheless, through the prevailing culture
which influences them with its poetry, novels, and plays. In Sweden,
it was for a long time the cultural heritage of Victor Rydberg
which was the bearer of the Platonic thread. At a later period it
was Hans Larsson, author of a book with the revealing title, *Plato
and Our Times*. Few teachers at Lund University have exercised
such a strong influence as Larsson (professor in theoretical philosophy 1901-1927). But if one tries to give a name to the members
of the "group" which was influenced by him one often finds that
they had nothing to do with one another, sometimes did not even
know one another personally. This is typical of that ism which is
called "humanism."

Individuals detached from one another, without any confidence in unusual "experiences" but convinced that everyone through their own reason can participate in truth, and that all thinkers converge and mean basically the same thing—this is *humanism*. Hardly anything is so foreign to humanism as the New Testament idea of the body and its members. The differentiation in human tasks, and the idea that dissimilarity can be a plus and can enhance the unity that exists among people, from the viewpoint of humanism seems to imply a disdain for the human. It is assumed that the human expresses itself in an elite, and that this elite has a perfect right to keep others away. Such an elitist idea will also express itself in the concept of the body. That is the fate of every kind of corporatism unless we allow the revolutionary idea that the "last will be first" to permeate our view of the whole. In other words, we must maintain a strictly *Christocentric* interpretation of the fellowship within the body.

Every fellowship that is organically mature runs the risk of becoming a tyranny, and this is true to a higher degree in the family than in other kinds of associations. A family offers greater possibility of individual flowering, and greater opportunity for individual contributions by those of different ages, than does any comparable group. There also, as in the body of Christ, the weakest—a new-born child—can count for more than all the rest and hold the others together, so that "there may be no discord in the body" (1 Cor. 12:25). But if the strongest in the family oppress the other members, no human association, not even a political dictatorship can be as devilish as such a family. But humanism does not operate with the organically mature as its ideal. Humanism looks at the individual as free-standing, intact, and alone. As a corrective for the church, which keeps it from becoming derailed, humanism is a wholesome neighbor.

In the form of Neoplatonism, humanism is the oldest neighbor of the Christian congregation. In the early church, relations between Christianity and humanism were marked by two characteristic features. The first is that the early church asserted that the Greek philosophers had "borrowed from Moses," by which they meant that their idealism was equivalent to the law. The law was, of course, God's own law (even according to Paul, the works were "written on their [the Gentile's] hearts" Rom. 2:15). The same can be said about many isms also in the twentieth century. One cannot talk exclusively about the contrasts between the isms and Christianity, because to a certain degree they exist *within* the activity of God through his universal law. This is true even of Marxism and existentialism. The other characteristic of humanism in its

Neoplatonic form in the early church was that it was an *aristocratic* phenomenon. The simple folks remained on the outside.

So it remains today, even after the contributions made by Victor Rydberg and Hans Larsson. The reason for the inability of humanism to reach down to the masses is because it has no fellowship; it assumes that in a group each individual seeks out and arrives at the truth independently.[8] Among the nineteenth century philosophers only Marx was able to influence people from various levels of society, and this was the case because he thought in terms of social classes, not in terms of dissociated individuals. Humanism, on the other hand, has preserved the same view of "spirit" as it had in the fourth century when, during the powerful upswing of Neoplatonism it was able to create the cloisters. In spite of the fact that the cloister became the organ for folk-culture, and for other activities which promoted enlightenment even in practical affairs (horticulture, care of the sick, etc.), the inhabitants did all of this in separation from ordinary physical life. The Old Testament view of Spirit (the Hebrew *ruach*) was foreign to their central premise.

There is probably no area of Christian doctrine where ways of thinking foreign to the Bible have held such uncontested sway as in the doctrine of the Spirit. That God creates the whole world is an unacceptable thought for Greek philosophy; that the Son suffers death and is despised on earth is equally unacceptable to the Greek way of thinking. The first and the second articles have brought confrontations between Christianity and other views of life from the very beginning. But "spirit" is a term which opens doors and allows the substance to be reshaped and reinterpreted. Even today, "spiritual life" and "spiritual awakening" are understood in terms of the separation of the individual from everyday physical life; they suggest some sort of sublimation or flight. The potential to be found in the significant words of the gospel about the Spirit—"poured out over all flesh," "baptized into one body"—was squandered just when it was most needed.

A proper understanding of the biblical view of the Spirit was needed when factory workers had become the bottom layer of society, even though they were not only a part of the same body as others, they were the most necessary part (1 Cor. 12:22). They produced what the body lived by, but were also the "less honorable" part inasmuch as they were dirty and poor (12:23). The Spirit in the primitive Christian understanding would have said that these parts of the community in God's eyes were worthy of "greater honor" than all the others (12:24). But the Spirit in the nineteenth century could not say that. For more than a thousand years the Spirit had nothing to do with the body.

"THE SPIRIT SAYS TO THE CHURCHES"

The book of Revelation presents the Spirit in a manner which is unusual in the New Testament. Each of the seven churches seems to be regarded as having its own Spirit who speaks to it (Rev. 1:4; 3:1; 4:5; cf. also the phrase "the Spirit says to the churches" Rev. 2:7; 3:6, 22). The background for their being seven is to be found in a famous and influential Old Testament passage about the seven-fold Spirit to which the author of the Revelation is clearly alluding (cf. Rev. 5:5 with Isa. 11:2). It is clear that when the Spirit speaks to the congregation Christ is exercising his domination over the congregation.[9]

The Word and the Church

The Greek word *ekklesia* can be used both as the designation of a local congregation as is the case in Revelation, and as the designation of the whole church, as in the title we have given the third article of the Creed, "The Congregation and the Promise." In Swedish and in other languages as well, the word "school" functions in this same way. If one is debating the working conditions in "the school" one is thinking about all the schools in the country; at the same time, the "school" is a small local unit, perhaps with as few as a dozen pupils.

No one will deny that the congregation in both senses, universal as well as local, is tied to the sacred word. All churches, without regard to confessional branch, are constituted by the fact that they expound the biblical word, and that the word is for them the norm. They may describe their relationship to the norm in different ways, and they may add something to the word, but none of them fails to put the word first among all that they consider normative. Just as all confessions are constituted by the fact that a sacred word existed before they existed, so they all leave with the one who attends their worship service a word which has been given to the listener. As a rule, this word consists of the sermon, but it also includes the liturgy, hymns, and instructional programs. The Eastern Orthodox churches, which do the least talking, can sing the long portions of the Mass for hours. This is filled with biblical material; it is a presentation of the gospel in the form of action. That is how their liturgy is generally constructed.

Our problem is this: the Spirit in the Nicene Creed is called "the Lord and Giver of Life," and in Revelation and in other early Christian texts it confronts the congregation and *addresses the church*. In later church history, however, the Spirit often comes to be presented as a power that lives within the church and which expresses itself in the authority with which the congregation *addresses the people*. The word is then viewed as the word of the church, filled with the Spirit. But the church does not become filled with this power because of what the Spirit says to the church (as is the case in Revelation) but it becomes filled with power (i.e. with Spirit) because of something else, such as the rite of ordination, the succession of bishops, some form of primacy, etc. Something of what was originally Christian has been lost here. On the other hand, the Spirit can no longer talk to the church in the same way that it talks to the world. Some sort of dormant and permanent form of Spirit must be found in the church, something which the world does not have.

This is the problem, and it has been solved in different ways. Different churches distinguish themselves from one another in the way they resolve these problems. Some think of the Christian as being personally equipped with gifts of the Spirit given at the time of conversion (identified with new birth, or faith, or spiritual baptism). Others emphasize ordination, and above all the ordination of the bishop. This applies especially to those communions in which the word from the pulpit is not thought of as a means of grace, and where the Lord's Supper (especially the question of its validity) plays a large role. Again others—and Lutherans as a rule belong to this group—the word and the congregation are viewed as confronting one another in such a powerful fashion that the Spirit comes to be incorporated entirely into the word! The members of the church are considered just as empty of spirituality as is the world. When the word gets this exclusive role over against the congregation, it is customary for "the right proclamation of the word" to become much more strictly governed by the confessional writings. The confessions then become "possessed of the Spirit" in about the same way that the office of bishop or one's new birth is thought of by others as resulting in a sort of possession of or by the Spirit.

We will return shortly to the most important attempts by the church to solve this problem. Now, we want to say something that is very general in character. Peter is, as we have seen earlier, the paradigm for the whole congregation. What happens to him, the church's rock, happens to all. We do not often look closely at the uniqueness of the New Testament view of Peter. The texts which tell about his going to sleep in Gethsemane and about his denial the night before the execution, deprive Peter of that sort of spirituality which consists of possessing some deposit of the Spirit. In John's gospel we are told emphatically that the Spirit after Jesus' baptism in the Jordan, *remained* over Jesus (1:32-33). If one is to talk at all about the Spirit being associated with a human being, then one will have to restrict oneself to the assertion that the New Testament says this about Jesus (and about others only in a secondary sense, on the basis of their nearness to him).[10]

However, Peter is never severed from a relationship to this dormant and permanent Spirit. At the denial, the relationship may be said to be reflected only in his weeping, but in view of Paul's description of "the body" in 1 Corinthians 12 weeping is not something to be treated as a mere bagatelle. Do not the weakest and least honorable members of the body include such a one as Peter? And he surely did receive also "overflowing honor," more than the others in the body, which is to say more than others in the congregation or the whole church (1 Cor. 12:24). It is not without significance that the Spirit, according to Romans 8:15-27, expresses itself in our *sighing*, and what the Spirit cries out is the Aramaic word "Abba," the same word which Jesus cried out in Gethsemane (Mark 14:36). There is only one interpretation that can hold all of this together: The Spirit allows the congregation and each of its members *to die and rise again*. The needs of the dying, the sighing and the weeping, do not imply that the Spirit has departed. On the contrary, to pray and to cry out from the depths is a form which the presence of the Spirit takes.

This agrees very well with the contents of that *word* which the Spirit speaks. The word addressed to the congregation is throughout a word of judgment (i.e., death) and a word of restoration. It is consequently a life which, like that connected with Peter's restoration, is a life of forgiveness (i.e., resurrection). One may, perhaps, argue that this is not an abiding, permanent presence of the Spirit. But would one not acknowledge the permanent presence of oxygen in a person who is constantly breathing? The biblical word "spirit" (Hebrew, *ruach;* Greek, *pneuma)* designates air in movement—wind, breath. Wind and breath can be continuously present in spite of the constantly ongoing movement. The modern idea of the Spirit as quiescent and as something deposited in the church is one of the many indicators of how alien contemporary Christian thinking is from the viewpoint of the Bible.

If the word spoken to the congregation is judgment and restoration (death and resurrection), the word from the congregation to

the world will be of the same character. This is the consequence of
the word which the church receives and by which it lives. Death
and resurrection also constitute the process through which destruction in the human world is overcome and through which a healthy
humanity comes to be. But this transformation cannot take place in
the church unless the church turns to the world and invites those
living outside the congregation to participate in this goal—to be
free, to be human, to be a *whole* person. The congregation is the
beginning of a new humanity and it must remain open to the world;
for if it does not do this, the congregation does not resemble Christ.

One is entitled to ask what this idealized picture has to do with
the church that actually exists. The answer is that the Christian
church, built upon the tripartite Creed, actually saw its function in
the world to be "the new humanity" and to offer "salvation" which is
"whole and undamaged humanity," to all people. This claim did not
strike people as untrustworthy because the congregation did in fact
move out in service to the sick and the needy in the Roman empire.
According to this same Creed, the movement outward constituted
the church's life. If the congregation saw people weeping outside of
its borders, it was immediately on its way to them, and at the same
time on its way to that heaven where those who weep now shall
laugh (Luke 6:21). In its dream of heaven there was also the picture
of those who were to come from the east and from the west, those
who were now without but would soon be within.

The Views of Various Confessions

In the church of a later time, divided into various confessions,
there are to be found different interpretations of the Spirit. The three
most important confessional groups are presented here in outline
form: 1) the churches which give primary importance to the *office*
(Roman Catholic, Greek Orthodox, and Anglican); 2) the churches
which give primary importance to the *preaching of the biblical word*
(Lutheran, Reformed); 3) the churches which give primary importance to *the spiritual experiences of their members* (includes a number of churches which developed as free churches and were independent of any national church).

1) When the *office*, in one form or another, is considered to be the
Spirit's complete presence in the congregation, the role of the scriptural word comes to be dominated by certain instructions given by
Christ to the apostles. What proceeds from Christ is certainly gospel, and it falls to the ordained servants of the congregation to com-
municate this gospel to the world. But it is a mistake to think of

the gospel as any set of instructions which tells us how the official duties of the church should be organized. We have to seek in other New Testament writings than the gospels for such instructions. And since these instructional passages are so few, we must complement them through historical investigation about what took place during the first centuries (with regard to laying on of hands at the installation of the bishops, etc.).

Among the churches in this group, the Roman Catholic Church is the dominant one. The church of Rome points to a New Testament text in which Jesus apparently chooses Peter to be the first among the twelve, the rock on which "I will build my church" (Matt. 16:18). It can also cite early lists of the bishops of Rome which indicate that it was there that Peter became bishop. The Anglicans, who have no pope, must rest their case on early Christian texts which speak of the bishops as a collective unit. The same is true of the Eastern churches, which build their case, to a lesser degree than Rome and the Anglicans, on individual scriptural passages in the New Testament.

There is nothing to prevent the churches in this group from also accepting very subjective and observable evidence of the Spirit's presence in solitary individuals (for instance, in a saint), or in "awakening" phenomena of various kinds. They may even recognize the Spirit in expressions of love and goodness in secular, everyday life.[11] But these acknowledgements do not undo the basic doctrine about the congregation's need to have a certain office in order to receive the Spirit.

2) When the *preaching of the biblical word* is the guarantee of the full presence of the Spirit in the congregation, there always develop confessional writings which are to govern the correct exposition of the Scriptures. This is true of all the church bodies which grew out of the Reformation in the sixteenth century. The idea of offices, often strictly understood and firmly organized, is to be found also in these churches. But it is never ordination to the office which guarantees the purity of the proclamation (or, in other words, the presence of the Spirit). The authority of the office derives, on the contrary, from subordination to the message given in the Scriptures. Both the Lutherans and the Reformed, the two largest denominations in this group, came to be preoccupied during the seventeenth century with the content of the confessional writings, and at the same time with the doctrine of the verbal inspiration of the biblical word. Both of these seventeenth century phenomena are directly dependent on the view of the Spirit which was proclaimed by the Reformation.

These two denominations reveal interesting differences. Luther separated law and gospel and considered them to be two distinct activities on the part of God. The gospel and the Spirit are almost always joined together. The Spirit is given when the gospel word is received in faith. To be sure, Luther also connected the Spirit and law, especially in his exposition of the law's *accusing* function in conscience (the law's "spiritual use"). God's direction of the secular communities through the law is not, as a rule, regarded as a part of the Spirit's life-giving activity on earth (in spite of Ps. 104:30). As a result, the gospel has nothing directly to do with external progress in society or with the body in general. What the Spirit primarily accomplishes through the law and the gospel is that the individual is driven forward out of spiritual death and crucifixion toward spiritual resurrection.

Calvin, on the other hand, asserted that only one covenant is instituted by God with his people on earth. Old and New Testaments bear witness together to this single covenant. It is a covenant of grace even in its preaching of law. For Calvin, the highest and most important use of the law is "the third use," according to which the law guides the one who is born anew into new works. The prophetic proclamation in the Old Testament is an activity of the Spirit, even when it is talking about social injustices.[12]

The result of this doctrine in the Reformed churches has been a demanding moralism, by which these churches distinguish themselves from a sometimes more lax Lutheranism. Reformed piety is marked by an orientation toward the world which reminds one of the missionary character of the early church, but without possessing the same concentration on the gospel. Lutheranism concentrates on the gospel, but in the matter of social questions tends to allow the laws of the individual countries (rather than the Old Testament words of the prophets) to be the expression of what God wants in the present.

3) When *spiritual experiences of the individual* are viewed as the guarantee of the Spirit's full presence in the congregation, the power which expresses itself in the activities of the congregation depends on the presence among the members of persons through whom the Spirit can work (believing, true Christians, those born anew). Neither ordination, nor the presence of the biblical word in the congregation are enough.

Types of external order to be found in these churches vary greatly. Generally there is found among them a certain opposition to infant baptism as a way of entrance into the congregation. Their view of the Spirit is to a great degree conditioned by the fact that these churches have often been free churches among people who have had a national church. They have then taken a critical attitude toward the large, nationwide churches which were based on infant baptism and which did not require of their members any testimony concerning their own personal experiences. Therefore, the tendency among these opposition church bodies becomes strongly *subjective* in orientation; the Spirit is known through "experiences."

It is not possible to regard any one of these three confessional groups as the bearer of the entire early Christian message concerning the Spirit. They are all negatively conditioned by one another, and they have all emphasized certain points in the total view of the early church against each other; the office against the scriptural word, and the scriptural word against individual experiences. All of them are much more strongly focused on the problem of the church's external form than was the case in the early church. Even when the third group (the spiritualistic group) talks about individuals and their expressions of life, it is still talking about one kind of church organization set over against other types.

Comparison with Existentialism

The most important existential philosopher is Martin Heidegger. He has directly influenced such unlike authors as Rudolf Bultmann and Jean Paul Sartre, and by way of these two he has built bridges which have made it possible to interpret the gospel in existentialist categories and to interpret Marx in similar thought patterns. Heidegger is clearly dependent on Kierkegaard, whose conception of "human existence" he shares—minus, however, God, Christ, the incarnation, etc.

The threads of theology which are still to be found in Heidegger in spite of his more or less outspoken atheism, have led analytic philosophers to view the whole Heideggerian analysis of human existence as an unscientific conceptualization of faith. They charge that although the idea of God has been formally deleted it remains hidden in the peculiar terminology which Heidegger uses to describe what "human" is in distinction from everything else. We humans can live "authentically" or "inauthentically"; we can fall from our authentic existence and become lost in the universal "man"; we can also in the act of decision listen to our conscience (that is, our authentic self) and choose our true existence, thus wrenching ourselves loose from the universal "man" and becoming an individual. In almost every term we have now mentioned, Heidegger is a copy of Kierkegaard. All of the terms can, with minor alterations, be used by Bultmann for New Testament exegesis.[13]

The critical judgment concerning Heidegger offered by the analytic philosophers is of course correct; he *is* a philosopher without a concept of God, living in a cultural situation in which a concept of God is considered untenable. What the analytic philosophers as a rule overlook is that even in a post-Christian culture we must have some tools with which to distinguish between humans on the one side and animals and objects on the other (that is, unless we go along with the naturalists and assume that a human being is one of the animals and that the words humans leave behind are among the objects). Heidegger fills this need for an anthropology, and he is in fact one of the very few contemporary philosophers who do fill that need. That is what accounts for his exceptional influence in many different directions, not only in modern New Testament exegesis, and not only in advanced forms of Western Marxism. Psychiatry and drama are also influenced by existentialism, to cite only two additional cases. The flora is very rich.

In a comparison of Christianity as delineated in the tripartite Creed, with existentialism, the decisive question will be, "What judgment shall we make about Kierkegaard, not as a philosopher but as a theologian?" If it is reasonable to regard Kierkegaard as one who helps us understand the credo of Christianity, then existentialism must be regarded as an ism that stands close to Christianity. But now we must make a contrary judgment about Kierkegaard. Of all the authors who tried to interpret the content of Christianity during the nineteenth century, none hindered people from having access to the three articles of the Creed as much as Kierkegaard. It is not an overstatement to assert that Kierkegaard actually hated creation faith in the form found in the Old Testament and in Christianity and as developed in the Reformation.

The difficulties which European theology has had in comprehending the biblical understanding of creation come from one single person—Kierkegaard. It is not surprising, therefore, that Løgstrup in his attempt to make creation faith understandable, has found it necessary to devote an entire book to just this matter *(Opgør med Kierkegaard* [1968]). Christian action for Kierkegaard implies breaking out of the natural and basic conditions of human existence; therefore he consciously repudiated all spontaneous expressions of life. Such a negation in the area covered by the first article brings with it negative consequences for the entire Creed. This negation has propagated itself in Heidegger, and specifically in his view of "authentic" human existence as being identical with the breaking away of the individual from the universal "man." Spirit is cultivated through separation from the body, as in idealism.

Since the problem in the relation between Christianity and existentialism lies in the understanding of man, it is of little significance whether existentialism affirms God's existence or not. Several philosophers who have affirmed God's existence have only made it more difficult to understand the basic features of the Creed. It is typical that the book by John Macquarrie, *Existentialism,* includes various analyses of the thought of Kierkegaard and Heidegger, and views atheism as an important question for the theologian, but has not a word to say about Løgstrup.[14]

"ALL WERE MADE TO DRINK OF ONE SPIRIT"

It is not easy to understand and translate the last phrase in 1 Corinthians 12:13. The correct translation would appear to be: "We received a single Spirit to drink." The correct understanding of it would appear to be that the statement completes the first line in the same verse: "For by one Spirit we were all baptized into one body." Taken together both utterances emphasize that the human as a part of the congregation is surrounded by the Spirit and without interruption walks by the Spirit (Gal. 5:16).

Paul's language about a drinking of the Spirit has an interesting history. It is not likely that the word in 1 Corinthians 12:13 originally had reference to the Lord's Supper. The symbolic speech used in the earliest Christian period was so filled with physical imagery that one could very well have talked about eating and drinking (as for example in John 6:48-58) without specifically thinking about the event of the Lord's Supper. The external action which dominated the imagination of the primitive church was in the first instance baptism, not the Lord's Supper. Baptism was the act by which one was grafted into the body of Christ; most of the people one met during the week were unbaptized. Baptism was preceded by instruction, and when the person was ready, it was a great event symbolizing one's dying with Christ and being raised with him (through the stepping down into the water and rising up out of it). The original Christian ethic was built on baptism: lay aside the old, put on the new, put to death the members, rise to new life, etc.

Body and Mealtime

This original ethic quickly changed when everyone was baptized, generally as infants, and when church discipline associated with the Lord's Supper became the secular domain's form of folk nurture.

Now that the Lord's Supper moved to the center, people began to look for New Testament references to the Spirit coming to them in the Supper. In the early church, one cries out for the Spirit, one prays for the Spirit to come to the bread and wine and to draw near in worship, so that one's heart may be filled by the Spirit. One of the most important citations in this regard is 1 Corinthians 12:13 which concludes, "all were made to drink of one Spirit." [15]

How the importance of baptism overshadowed everything else in early Christianity can be noted also in the Creeds, where only baptism is mentioned and not the Lord's Supper (the third article of the Nicene Creed speaks of "one Baptism for the remission of sins"). In distinction from baptism which can only happen once, the Lord's Supper is a repeated act; it does not add anything to baptism but brings to fruition what baptism contains, namely, walking by the Spirit. Just as the congregation could admonish the baptized to "walk by the Spirit" (Gal. 5:16), so the congregation could pray for the Spirit, and thus behave as though they had not already received it, as though they were "spiritless." But it only seems to be so, because to pray is already evidence of the work of the Spirit (Rom. 8:26). But from another point of view it is not only an appearance, inasmuch as the congregation in its cry for the Spirit makes itself one with the spiritless world.

The congregation's worship and the Lord's Supper are activities which take place on behalf of all creation. The congregation is not separated from the rest of creation but is in fact "within" all the other created entities (Col. 1:16-20; Eph. 1:10-23) and represents all of them in its prayers. Therefore, it is no accident that in what is the central point in the worship service, the Lord's Supper, we find that which belongs to creation in general and which serves to nourish the bodies in daily life, bread and wine. These external things have the same goal as the grain of wheat: transformation, new creation, resurrection, harvest (see 1 Cor. 15:35-39). This connection between spiritual meaning and external nature played an extraordinary role in the early church. The vine and the grain of wheat are at once Christ; the congregation represents the promise of heaven.

The coming of the Spirit for which the congregation prays in the worship service is a reality to which the New Testament bears witness, although it is not so exclusively tied to the Lord's Supper as came to be the case later. The biblical foundation for the controversial word about the Spirit in the third article of the Nicene Creed, "who proceeds from the Father and the Son," is precarious and is capable of double interpretations. The chief text, John 15:26, says about the Spirit only that it "proceeds from the Father," and the

Eastern churches hold firmly to that single biblical statement. They will not consent to the addition, "and the Son," and they believe that the whole doctrine of the Trinity is jeopardized if those words are inserted here. For them the Father is the basis of everything; he is the Creator with two hands, the Son and the Spirit.

The Western churches have found additional support in other Johannine utterances: "he will take what is mine . . . All that the Father has is mine . . ." (John 16:14f.). An even stronger New Testament support for the Western position can be found in the teaching that the Spirit comes (Acts 1:8) when Christ's work is completed and that the Spirit is immediately called "the Spirit of Jesus Christ" (Phil. 1:19) and "the Spirit of his Son" (Gal. 4:4-6). There is, however, no way that the precariousness and the double interpretations of the New Testament at this point can be eliminated. Even such a citation as Galatians 4:4-6, which talks about "the Spirit of his Son" would seem to retain full parity between the sending of the Son (4:4) and the sending of the Spirit (4:6). Both proceed from God, hence from the Father, as the Eastern churches assert.[16]

This is one of many doctrinal points at which two positions must both be characterized as Christian. That different teachings are to be found in the church is in accord with both the New Testament and what we know about primitive Christianity. The strife about the little word *filioque* ("and of the Son") is one of the factors that has split the church into an eastern and a western bloc, although the differences between the two doctrinal points is less than the difference between Matthew and John. These differences in doctrine have been blown up to unreasonable proportions during the course of church history, while relatively little attention has been paid to the much greater difference that exists between *all* contemporary churches on the one side and the early church on the other. This difference consists in the absurd modern cleavage between baptism and the Lord's Supper in comparison with the original close connection between these two sacraments. Three important points need to be considered here:

1) In the primitive Christian period, baptism was the chief sacrament. It could happen to a person only once, whereas the Lord's Supper was repeated. Baptism meant being grafted into Christ's body, his death, and his resurrection. It embraced all of life, it embraced the death of the body, and it even included our participation in the life to come. The Lord's Supper gave the baptized ones nourishment for the journey toward this goal.

2) In modern times, the Lord's Supper is the chief sacrament.

Yet many denominations do not recognize each other's interpretation of the Lord's Supper. At the same time, most churches will accept baptisms performed by those "deviant" churches, as is evident by the fact that re-baptism is not required. Churches that make an issue out of the Lord's Supper but accept the baptism of churches they do not recognize, have degraded baptism and made it insignificant. The bizarre conclusion to which their practice leads is that a false church (which is not Christ's body), through its act of baptism grafts the person into the body of Christ! This devastating conclusion is inescapable.

3) The transformation which has taken place in comparison to the early church expresses itself also in liturgical conduct and in regulations regarding the office of the ministry. No one is going to understand the symbolism of stepping down into the kingdom of the dead and being raised up again when the pastor lightly dampens the child's head with a few drops of water. The Lord's Supper, by contrast, is surrounded by regulations that point out its Christocentricity and its dissimilarity from everything else. Often the rite of Communion is the only act that one must be ordained in order to perform; everything else a lay person can handle. There is no New Testament basis for this attitude toward the different elements of the worship service.

As we earlier affirmed that no contemporary confession could claim to represent the primitive Christian understanding of the Spirit and that all of them are in different ways deviations from the original, here we must now unequivocally assert that contemporary *universal* church practice is in fact a thoroughgoing departure from the primitive Christian pattern.

At the same time that we assert this to be true, we must also acknowledge that the gospel in its transforming power breaks through the absurd churchly patterns and works with its original power in the action of the Lord's Supper. While baptism is weak in its power to represent the gospel visually, the Lord's Supper has a strong spiritual effect especially on the "new" Christians who have come out of a secular environment without any knowledge of the Bible. The one who was betrayed, who broke bread on the last night, and who proclaimed the order of rank in the kingdom—"the servant of all shall be the greatest"—communicates in the Lord's Supper to many people now living *both* a mystic feeling that he lives and is present, *and* a shattering social judgment over those who take part. All of those socially and politically betrayed, who are "outside," ought of course to be inside the congregation. In fact, those who have been pushed out are basically the ones who are closest to Christ.

This means a number of things for a plausible comparison between Christian faith and mysticism.

Comparison with Mysticism

The term "mysticism" can refer to two different phenomena. On the one hand, it can mean the intense, deeply personal experiences of the presence of God or of Christ. But one can also define mysticism in such a way that what is Christian cannot be included in it. One can define it to mean that without the intervention of external words the individual experiences the inexpressible, a oneness with God (the whole), a sinking into total quiescence.[17] So understood, the mystical experience must be disturbed by the concreteness of the language of Christianity, for instance by its talk about a specific revealer (Jesus, or the word). The confrontation between Christianity and mysticism in this sense becomes meaningful.

Peculiarly enough, in today's debate it is the intensity of the experience which is the most common mark of mysticism. Individuals come to perceive the presence of Christ, they hear a word from Jesus with undeniable force and finally come to be "possessed by the word," they identify themselves with a biblical person and take over that person's role. If one calls this sort of experience "mysticism," in distinction from Christianity, it must be because one has experienced the church and Christianity as mechanical and conformist—one routinely goes to church, one regards the word as true without exception, or something else just as dead.

But ordinary Christianity has always involved the assuming of roles; it has always identified with the persons who surrounded Jesus. Christians therefore have felt possessed by the word (so that they physically hear the word within themselves), in intense experiences of the presence of Jesus. This is Christianity; it is ordinary, everyday Christianity, and it has always been Christianity.

The worship service exists so that this personal experience may continue. It is the place where that which has been given once is applied to new individuals and new situations, and therefore receives a new interpretation. It is only by such personally-conditioned changes that the continuing phenomenon of Christianity exists at all. In this sense, mysticism is a phenomenon within Christianity (as well as within Islam, etc.) and there is no reason to set Christianity and mysticism in opposition.

Of course one may define mysticism in such a way that nothing concrete enters into the experience, only the self and infinity. Then mysticism becomes a religion by itself, above Islam, above Christian-

ity, above any other religion; it becomes an experience of God independent of all concrete historical words. Christianity then, is viewed
as something circumscribed, something locked in to a limited revealer, Jesus, and to a restricted group, the church. It is true that
this sort of limitation exists. With that we have arrived at the problem of eternal life, which is the theme for the final chapter. The
limitation is to be found *in time*—but it is to be found there in order
that it may cease to exist.

> *O God, all the people on earth belong to you. You love
> them and you have given Jesus Christ for all of them.
> We do not know why we who now worship you have
> been chosen to bear witness concerning your name
> before the world. But you have told us that you want to
> use your congregation for the sake of others, as Jesus
> lived in order to serve the many.*
>
> *Give us pure hearts, so that we do not seek what is best
> for the church but what is best for humanity. We
> thank you for Christ's presence in our midst, and for his
> constant return to us in worship. Help us to look ahead
> toward your day, when many shall come from the east,
> west, north, and south to sit at table with you in your
> kingdom. Hold Christendom together throughout the
> world, and deliver us from division. Teach us to
> understand that we are members of a single body,
> and that we can be servants only if we are not alike.*
>
> *O God, I pray for myself. If someone must be the
> lowest in your congregation, let it be me.*

VIII

Eternal Life

This chapter, which concludes the presentation of the Creed, will attempt to make clear the relationship between what we have said up to this point and judgment on the one side, and eternal life on the other.

What is called eternal life in the New Testament is already a reality in the resurrection of Christ, and it is given through the congregation to its members. What is of great importance in this connection is baptism as understood in the oldest Christian writings. Baptism awaits a renaissance in our time, when so many people remain unbaptized. In this final chapter, a separate section will be devoted to the discussion of baptism which will give the key to understanding both judgment and praise.

ETERNAL LIFE

It is typical of Christianity that it does not think of eternal life in terms of the soul's liberation from the physical body within which it has been imprisoned (an understanding which was common in hellenistic surroundings). Eternal life consists of rescuing the life that has been lived by the person with a body (that is, "the resurrection of the body," as it is called in the Apostles' Creed).

The Spontaneous Expressions of Life

We have touched upon the spontaneous or sovereign expressions of life many times in this book. Now we will discuss this subject again from a particular point of view—the play of children.

Of the dogmatic studies published in Sweden during this century, none is as original as the one entitled *Evangelisk Fadervårsdyrkan* ("Evangelical Worship of Our Father") by Pehr Eklund (professor of dogmatics at Lund 1890-1911). These thin pamphlets or brochures published in 1904-05 were directly related to the Small Catechism, and set up in the form of tables using Eklund's own terminology. Some of it is very ingenious. When he comes to the third article and the question of how eternal life can be experienced in time, the principal answer is this: it is experienced in the joyful play of small children.[1]

Two things can be said about the play of children. The first is that from the point of view of productivity it serves no purpose, and consequently from this limited point of view it can be said to be meaningless. The second thing to be said is that the play of children immediately expresses joy: for them, it is fun to be alive. This very simple view of life is nearly forgotten in the western world but it is deeply biblical. The approach to nature which regards it as something beautiful but static, something that one can paint pictures of, is foreign to the Bible; in fact, the making of images is expressly forbidden. Instead, streams, trees, mountains, and sunrises are perceived to be engaged in a continuing song of praise to the Creator (Ps. 19:1-7; 89:6; Isa. 6:3; 42:10; Job 26:14). The whole world is full of the same sort of joy which expresses itself in the play of children.

To make gladness into an object is to destroy it. There is no representation of life as an object anywhere in the Old Testament; nor is any to be found in the teachings of Jesus. When the lame man "took up that on which he lay, and went home, glorifying God" (Luke 5:25) he behaved like a child at play. The healing miracles themselves announce that eternal life is coming near—it is, in fact, *here.* The crowds which surrounded the lame man and which also praised God for the miracle of life, would surely have considered it callous if someone had observed that the lame man had now received additional hours of productivity for the benefit of the community. While from our modern point of view such a reflection concerning the lame man's regained health may appear reasonable, from the biblical perspective it implies a very shabby view of the one who has been healed (he is reduced to a factor of production). The observation would also, if it were to be inserted into a biblical context, constitute blasphemy against God. Moreover, it turns an act by the Creator into a lifeless event that lies within the power of ordinary human beings. Thus, God is deprived of praise for the deed; the human makes a claim upon the health of the body and declares this health to be good *because* it achieves an improvement in production. This is what the denial of God implies; the creature allows its own creation (the productivity-apparatus) to take the place of praise to God.

If one has already denied God in one's attitude toward that which is human, it is not strange that one subsequently finds the grounds for affirming God to be very weak. Questions about God's existence are, as a rule, entirely meaningless. To put the whole matter as pointedly as possible: If one were to assert that "God is to be found" while retaining all the God-denying propositions concerning the *human*, that person would be farther from biblical faith in God than the atheist who never uses the word "God" but who places himself at the disposal of others, and who *is glad* (i.e., praises God) in both good and evil days. To praise God is to allow one's own personal existence to participate in the joy of existence which is to be found everywhere in creation. All the varied views of life (all "isms") can be included within faith in the sense here given.

A flower praises God by being a flower. A child praises God by being a child and by carrying out that activity which is "the office of the child," to use Luther's language—that is, to play. But everyone who says that sort of thing knows very well that the world is full of children who do not play. The many whose joy has been choked out are not themselves the cause of play dying. They are the victims of destroying forces over which no one person can be the master, and which cannot be subdued. There is a philosophy which suggests that when we are confronted with the sight of two children, one playing and the other inactive, we may value play as good and inactivity as bad, but we may also make a different evaluation in specific situations (for example: we may judge the former child to be unruly and the latter one to be quiet). When we look at this lofty elevation of theory over practice from the viewpoint of creation faith, we must regard it as a kind of nihilism.

We give positive value to the spontaneous expressions of life, and we sorrow over their absence. This does not apply only to such life expressions as the play of children and the joy expressed by a child; it applies also to our confidence and our will to live. When Jesus in the gospels is described as a support for these expressions of life, this colors the whole message about the resurrection: it means that he who raises us up is in our midst—he lives.

Christ's Resurrection

The accent on the nature miracles is foreign to the New Testament. There is not a single example of the apostles after Easter

being exhorted to go out among the people and proclaim that something has happened now which is contrary to the laws of nature.
All of the directives to the disciples had to do with preaching "the
forgiveness of sins" (that is, the gospel, healing the sick, etc.).
That is to say, the apostle who is sent out is commanded to carry
out the same kind of deeds of restoration that Jesus carried out
before Golgotha. The way Christ's resurrection expresses itself is
that such works of restoration continue to happen to people who
are in need.

Therefore the connection between the resurrection and the awakening of hope in us—a connection between an outer and an inner
event—is a *direct* connection: "we have been born anew to a living
hope through the resurrection of Jesus Christ from the dead" (1
Peter 1:3).[2] This direct connection becomes even more evident when
we observe that the Spirit is the subject throughout. The Spirit
awakens Jesus from the dead; the Spirit dwells in people now with
renewing power; and the Spirit will in the future make our bodies
alive. It is a series of spiritual deeds (Rom. 8:11). Eternal life is
here and now in view of the resurrection of Christ. The one who
hears the words of Jesus and believes has eternal life (John 5:24).
The Spirit, which is now the pledge and first installment of eternal
life, continues to have the destructive forces arrayed against it; they
are still to be subdued.

This yet-to-be-conquered destruction includes both ethically objectionable attitudes which remain with the believers and which
they are admonished to "put to death," and the biological fact that
life withers away. Such a combination seems strange to us. We do
not ordinarily link together ethical attitudes and biological health.
One of the few people in later European church life who retained
this combination was Grundtvig. He expressed it in practically
every hymn he wrote. For him, a person's joy, love, and fellowship
were threatened by the same enemy that threatend the health of
the body, the flowers and the birds, and indeed all of nature. As long
as death reigns "the last enemy" has not been conquered (cf. 1 Cor.
15:26). That is why eternal life at the present time must be hope.

Since this is the case, and in view of the fact that the family
plays such a central role in the biblical writings, it is surprising
that there is not a single place in the New Testament where hope
is family-centered. To the extent that hope in the face of death
functions in the contemporary world, the future eternal life is generally conceived to be an extension of the family's current life. This
is witnessed to by the poetic lines which often follow the death notices: father reaches out the hand and mother grasps it. Nothing

like that is to be found in the New Testament; on the contrary, it is negated by some very clear utterances. The wife with seven husbands is not bound to any of them in the resurrection of the dead, nor are they bound to her (Matt. 22:23-33).

What then is that "I" which now lives the life that is eternal and which also awaits that same life in overflowing measures in the future? If I peel away all the characteristics by which we are normally identified—being someone's child, someone's spouse, someone's parent—what sort of an "I" is there left which is to live eternal life? The play of the child, looked at as an overture to the song of praise which rises up in eternal life is the best illustration of the fellowship about which we are here speaking, a fellowship without any of the pressures of law. Such play is available to all who want to play, it transcends the boundaries of family and race—and it does this without thereby breaking up the family. It is only a wider, richer, and more elastic fellowship. This is indeed true of all spontaneous expressions of life: they are given in creation; they function in the twinkling of an eye; it is not possible to pressure them into existence by our own resolution. It is where all of this, which is given in creation, is *lacking* that we encounter laws, contracts, and fixed regulations. Marriage as an institution must be included among them.[3]

The fellowship we have been speaking about is physical without being bound by the civil laws of the community. This is implicit also in the character of baptism. Baptism is an act of birth; it gives an immediate and direct connection with Christ's resurrection, and it lays the foundation for a fellowship which is wider and more comprehensive than the fellowship into which we are placed by virtue of our physical birth. Also, baptism signifies the person's death and resurrection. It presupposes destruction and it opens up a futurist perspective of a situation which is on the other side of the destruction-conditioned boundaries which now prevail. It is only in such a life, on the other side of those boundaries, that we will be genuinely human, free, and able to sing our song of praise; we will be "recapitulated" forward into the undamaged creation[4].

BAPTISM

The act of baptism points back to a death which happened once for all, down in the depths of destruction; at the same time it points forward toward the baptized person's coming death, which is perceived in advance to be a misfortune, but which in reality cannot hurt that person. Both in pointing backward and in pointing forward baptism is speaking about the same reality—eternal life.

That Which Happened Once

The biblical content of the word "baptism" has been obscured by the external form of the baptismal rite in the churches. If one wishes to hear the original ring in the word one has to leave the churches and go into the world, to a secular use of the term. If someone is facing a particularly difficult test, it may be said, "This will be your baptism of fire." The implication is that if you make good in this test you will be able to handle that which is to follow.

That is how Jesus, according to Luke 12:49-53, understood his approaching death. He was going to go through "a baptism" and he anguished in advance over this baptism of fire. The Greek word for "baptism" used here with reference to the approaching death on the cross is the same word which is later used in connection with the baptism which the disciples go through, "baptized into his death" (Rom. 6:3). The same language meets us in the answer to the two sons of Zebedee, who ask for rank and are confronted with the question whether they can actually handle the same baptism as their Lord (Mark 10:38). In the context of both of these synoptic texts there is talk about a baptism which can separate one from the fellowship of one's family (Mark 10:28-45; Luke 12:49-53). That body into which the person is baptized is larger than all fellowships based on biology.

After the death of Jesus, people are "by one Spirit baptized into one body" which includes "Jews or Greeks, slaves or free" (1 Cor. 12:13). Then there is built up the new, worldwide and completely human fellowship on the foundation of *what happened once for all* —the great test at Golgotha, before which Jesus anguished but came through victoriously. One can say about Jesus' struggle at Golgotha what one usually says about those who have gone through a real baptism of fire and faced it successfully: they made good, they have cleared themselves, and thereby they are assured of the future. Such secular speech applied to Jesus is much closer to the biblical meaning than is the traditional churchly way of speaking about Jesus and baptism.

That which happened on Golgotha is the *real* baptism, or the "general baptism" as Cullmann calls it.[5] After he endured this baptism, Jesus pushed forward through humanity without being restrained in any way by the destruction that remains. The manner in which he moves forward is through new "baptisms," which means only through acts in which people allow themselves to die by passing through the same baptism as did Jesus, a baptism which he filled with life. In the early church people often postponed baptism and sometimes allowed it to be administered only on their deathbed (presumably out of fear that they would "sin after baptism," see Heb. 6:4-6, 10:26f.). Therefore, in the early church, it sometimes happened that someone would die a martyr's death without having been baptized. The martyr was then viewed as having been baptized with the specially powerful "blood baptism" (sometimes appealing to 1 John 5:6-8). The basic meaning of baptism is here very clear: death, life-giving death.

This death-element in baptism can still be heard in every contemporary baptism, in spite of the inroads which have been made on the baptismal ritual through the centuries, and it is reflected in the immersing of the one to be baptized. This element of death is determined by the fact that baptism is the renewal of life in *destruction's* domain. When the psychotherapist says that a person cannot regain health without pain, or a surgeon similarly tries to get a patient to understand the need for an operation, this is perceived as something realistic and believable, but a comparable rationale concerning baptism usually falls flat, or else is regarded as some sort of pastoral oppression. This is a clear indication of the lost sense of reality concerning churchly actions which has taken place through the years from primitive Christianity to the present.

Baptism should be viewed primarily as a completely secular event —an execution that takes place in full view of the public. Those people who accompany the executed one to baptism are also affected by this event in a way parallel to the surgeon's operation and the psychotherapeutic cures. The one baptized as well as the onlookers go through a "baptism of fire." The Reformation excels in seeing baptism realized everywhere, in all sorts of daily "crosses" and hardships. The language is taken directly out of the Small Catechism, which in turn borrows it from Romans 6, the foundation chapter for our understanding of baptism (see especially Rom. 6:6).

The watered-down churchly language concerning baptism cannot be brought into conformity with the classical sources, especially the synoptic gospels, until we are willing to call *that which happened once,* the event on Golgotha, baptism—not only *a* baptism, but baptism in its definitive form, *The Baptism.*

The Forward Movement

We have now come to the decisive point in our analysis. What is here called "the forward movement" receives its content from Christ's own power as the risen one, and it occurs as the work of the Spirit in people. By "forward" we mean three things, which may seem to have nothing to do with each other but which do in fact hang together, and at their base they are really one. We mean 1) geographically forward into new territories, 2) forward in history toward the future of the race, and 3) forward in the individual's life toward the final boundary which one approaches. That which happens in all three of these lines of movement is in the ancient church called *recapitulatio:* humanity is coming to be, inhumanity is being conquered. The presupposition for understanding this is a fact that is entirely commonplace: death is not something Christ or the Spirit invent and lay upon us. It is there already, it applies to everyone, it is inescapable.

That death is present in the situation is a part of what we have called "destruction." The forward movement along all three lines is liberation, the restoration of the inner freedom of the created. That is the way "the spread of Christianity" was conceived from the beginning, and that is the way it actually functions as long as the Christian congregation does not possess power, and as long as it is not tied in with the state. In the early church theologies developed in opposition to the Gnostics, there is an emphasis on the "freedom" of the human expressed in almost frenetic language. That freedom is understood to mean the unlimited possibility of saying either yes or no when the gospel is proclaimed. Up until the fourth century and the beginning of a state religion no one joined the church except by choice.

After Constantine the Great this gradually changed. The bearers of the gospel began to perceive a sort of "imperialism" in the forward movement of the church's world mission, a perception which still today marks the experience of large parts of the populations of Africa and Asia (missionary work was in fact often combined with some form of western colonialism). But it was not so from the beginning. Christianity moved forward through the oceans of people in the Roman empire because it was perceived to be a message of joy; *ev* was still retained in the *evangel.* Christ encountered people in the congregation (his "body"), in a way which restored them and which, more than any other force in the Roman kingdom represented the *humane.* This was especially true for the masses and for the poor.

So the movement forward among people, geographically, is a movement against destruction; inhumanity is being conquered. The same applies to the movement forward in the case of the individual. In each individual the Spirit is in conflict with something (Gal. 5:17), and what it is in conflict with is destructive at every point, not only for the individual but also for one's environment: "enmity, strife, jealousy, anger, selfishness, dissension, party spirit, envy" (Gal. 5:20f.). All of them destroy fellowship. To grow forward toward one's own individual death implies, providing the Spirit is guiding, a maturing of this destructive state and liberation out of it, so that the individual may be "formed by God's fingers" to be like the image, Christ. This is to become *human* according to the original decree of creation (Gen. 1:27).

But this movement forward of one insignificant human being becomes a part of humanity's great forward movement toward Christ's definitive revelation, when he will be visible to all (Rev. 1:7). According to the original Christian belief in the resurrection, Christ already dwells in the future. When people (that is, Adam) move forward through death, this implies that Christ, who is Judge and Author of Life is coming closer. He is approaching, and he approaches *everyone*. There are no destructive forces which will escape the encounter with him in judgment. But what is judged and rejected is only that which has oppressed and destroyed his people. Whatever has been of assistance to the least and the despised (food, drink, shelter, clothing, health care, visits to the imprisoned) lives eternally, and it lives as a song of praise (Matt. 25:31-46; Rev. 7:9-17). In the final judgment, there is no imperialism either.[6]

This has decisive importance for the interpretation of Jesus' words about rejection and judgment on the one hand, and his words about salvation and eternal life on the other, as these words meet us in the New Testament. All such words are spoken to us from the future, where he dwells as Judge and Author of Life; they are spoken to us in the present where we move forward toward the boundary which is the end of our individual existence. It is only within this eschatological framework that the interpretation of the words can be Christian. This is, in fact, our framework within which the words have been interpreted during those Christian centuries which retained a reasonably complete view of the biblical word (that is, a view oriented toward death and resurrection).

When the biblical word paints the final judgment as an epic scene before which the reader seems to be an observer, it is important to insist that the reader is not really an observer at all. If we believe that the scenes we read about are real, then the judgment happens. Then the Judge from the future *executes* the judgment over those who believe. That is the way the Hebrews understand "the word." In listening to the word, that about which the word speaks happens. An account about forgiveness is not merely an account which the listener (or the reader) is observing. Nor does "I believe" mean to hold a proposition to be true. Rather, it means to trust in the statement, to rely on it. If one relies on it, then that which the statement describes happens; then forgiveness is given to the one who trusts that such a thing can happen. It is the same with judgment. The parable about the unmerciful steward who is thrown into prison pronounces judgment upon each unmerciful person who hears it and is shaken by it.

The judgment occurs through the word about judgment. Forgiveness occurs through the word about forgiveness. Jesus, who by virtue of what once happened, has gone through his baptism of fire and become both the Judge "of the living and the dead" and Author of Life. This same Jesus speaks from the future to those who move forward toward him by way of death, and he judges them and makes them alive now through the words of life (see Acts 10:40-43 and 3:15; also 1 Cor. 4:15). The gospel of John, along with the Johannine letters, expresses these fundamental propositions concerning the presence here and now of both judgment and eternal life in a very forceful manner. This presence now is to be found in the words of Jesus:

"He who hears my word and believes him who sent me, has eternal life; he does not come into judgment, but has passed from death to life" (John 5:24).

"He who rejects me and does not receive my sayings has a judge; the word that I have spoken will be his judge on the last day" (John 12:48).

"As the Father has life in himself, so he has granted the Son also to have life in himself, and has given him authority to execute judgment, because he is the Son of man" (John 5:26f.).

"It is the Spirit that gives life, the flesh is of no avail; the words that I have spoken to you are spirit and life" (John 6:63, and several comparable places in the Johannine letters).[7]

These words of Jesus are present now; it is the function of the worship service and the task of the sermon to allow them to be constantly heard, expounded, and understood, anew. Both those now living and those who have gone before take part in the worship service. All of them are gathered around "the one who is coming"—and coming from the future, toward which all the participants in the worship service are being brought.

JUDGMENT

To accept one's own death willingly is to accept the judgment and to allow it to pass over oneself. Those who have crossed over the line of death have passed over the line of judgment; they have the baptism of fire behind them. No one can say to whom this has happened, not the congregation and not the one who expounds the word in all its truth. If we would be able to say that, we would ourselves have become judges. But now no one is judge; all people find themselves among those who are moving forward. Only one of all those who have ever lived has arrived at the future, and as a conqueror he inhabits the future. He alone is the Judge.

Death as Judgment

Death is, quite simply, a necessity—it is "appointed" that we should die. As a necessity it constitutes a judgment over the emptiness of human desires. To accept death without complaint is to bow oneself before God's judgment. There are not many modern theologians who accept and utilize the grim statements in Genesis on this point (Gen. 2:17 and 3:19). Simone Weil apparently more secure in her discernment than many professional theologians, draws from the New Testament, and specifically from what Jesus has to say about the grain of wheat, the possibility of interpreting death as appointed, necessary, and from the viewpoint of the individual, meaningless.[8]

In Jesus' word about the kernel's death (and subsequent life in other kernels) there is the same depth of self denial which one finds in the Pauline images of the different members of the body, where the point is never that the individual gains a private eternal life. On the contrary, the individual functions as one who gives life to others and thus lives as Christ and the grain of wheat live. When we as religious people elevate ourselves above the "one body" to which we belong, and demand eternal life of our own, we make the same demand on which Adam stumbled into death—the demand to be an owner (Gen. 3:4-6). Eschatological expectation as it is mirrored in prayers, hymns, and proclamation, throughout the history of the church, has always been marked by such an egotistic expectation. This is very much like the certainty of a privileged position before God which Jesus found in his Jewish contemporaries and against which he hurled his sarcastic comments.

When Jesus compares the despised Samaritans with the secure, peculiar people of God, this is a judgment against the chosen people. A purely historical exegesis misses the meaning of such expressions of judgment; they are therefore quite useless for proclamation in contemporary worship. If we are now to say anything about

the Samaritans in our worship service, we must first understand
that the regular people of God are today's church. And the Samaritans are then those atheists who, like the grain of wheat, offer
their days to the oppressed members of the community and who,
when death comes merely lie down and say, "Yes, now it is over.
The physician can do no more." That is the way to accept death as
appointed, necessary and, from the viewpoint of the individual,
without meaning.

What then becomes of Christian faith? Implicit in that question
is the idea which is very difficult to root out, that one can earn
blessedness through some deed. Pilgrimages and the mortification of
the flesh have now been eliminated from the catalog of works only
to be replaced by Christian statements of faith. One then thinks of
the last judgment as an examination in order to determine the final
end of the individual. One is thinking, "I gave personal expression
to my Christian faith before I died." The whole question about eternal life in that way becomes self-centered.

The final judgment is the definitive fulfillment of *recapitulatio;* it
is thus the healing of the human. Everything and everyone who have
helped heal "the human," sings praises and rejoices. Everything and
everyone who have harmed and despoiled have now been robbed of
their power (1 Cor. 15:24-26). The church, or the congregation,
does not exist in the world to offer a place to which individuals who
are in pursuit of their own spiritual gain can go for the purpose of
assuring themselves of eternal life after death. The church is the
mouth and body of Christ, and it exists in order to bear witness to
the *one* uncorrupted man in whom true human life—eternal life—
is given.

Nothing is more devastating for true human life once it has been
realized on earth, than the idea that the congregation, the human
"body" of this eternal life, should become a place where one seeks
personal gain. What should be the restoration of humanity becomes
distorted, and the real life of the grain of wheat (that is, the life
in Christ) may unexpectedly show up among the atheists instead of
in the church. This is the way it was with the Samaritan on the way
to Jericho, when the priest and the Levite had already gone by on
the other side.

The law is to be found already in the world; and judgment in the
form of death is also to be found already in the world. It is possible
to submit to the law and the judgment, to accept them "in obedience" as Simone Weil says, and thus fall into the earth as a grain
of wheat. No one knows in which of one's neighbors that happens.

To Assert and to Pray

In one of his earliest volumes on dogmatics, Karl Barth deals critically with the Calvinist doctrine concerning God's eternal decree, through which some are predestined to damnation and others to eternal blessedness. Barth asserts that there has been *one* person whom God rejected and sent to hell, Jesus Christ. In the same way, there has been *one* person to whom he has given eternal life, Jesus Christ.[9]

As always in Barth, an unacceptable framework surrounds these theological statements (a framework which we will not debate at this point). But his rationale leads us to a new and reasonable attitude toward the biblical sayings about rejection and salvation. That everyone should be saved is not an assertion of fact that has any biblical support. But it is something that one can certainly pray for. Everyone who talks about life and about judgment is included in the forward movement. No one has arrived. So, while we are in the process of moving toward the goal, we can pray what we cannot assert. For one thing, the New Testament clearly says that God wants everyone to be saved (1 Tim. 2:4). To pray for that which God wants is naturally appropriate to the movement forward.

We were earlier trying to look at the words of Jesus about judgment and eternal life as words spoken *now*, from the future, by the one who judges and makes alive. This means, we understand that Jesus' words already here and now carry out what they promise. We move forward toward the future while listening to the word about judgment and eternal life, and through our listening we allow judgment to happen and life to be born. The Christ who speaks in the word is the Christ who is drawing ever closer, the one who is coming.

Corresponding to these words of Jesus now spoken from the future, are our own words spoken in prayer as we move forward. The place and the time where the words of prayer are spoken are along the line of movement forward toward death. This is the end of all history for each individual. But our forward movement is part of that great movement toward the gathering of all "from east to west, and from north to south," as it is written in the primitive Christian symbolic language. "And behold, some are last who will be first" (Luke 13:29f.). By virtue of the fact that we believe in Christ and listen to him (that is, allow the judgment to occur and the new life to be born within us), we are praying members of the body, of his congregation in the world. Those from east, west,

north, and south are all who surround the congregations—all of
humanity on earth.

To pray in the congregation during the movement forward can
never mean that one prays with limited boundaries. The statement
that God wills the rescue of all includes everyone from east, west,
north and south. No one is outside of God's will and no one can be
left outside the prayer of the congregation as it moves forward
into the future. The boundaries between the congregation and the
general population will vanish in the life to come. Already in its
prayer and its worship, which are anticipations of eternal life, the
congregation reaches out across all visible boundaries. It can do no
other, since it knows that God desires that everyone be saved.[10]

This prayer does not ignore the fact that each second brings
individual and often lonely death to many people. Those who make
their way one by one across the chasm between life and death, join
the hosts from the east and the west, the north and the south. They
become part of that multitude about whom the congregation cannot
make any definite assertions, but for whom it can surely pray. In
view of the sharpness of Jesus' sarcasm toward God's own people,
the church can never assume the right to judge with respect to any
single death. Rather, the church must pray with uneasiness about
its own fate: "Make me, if possible, a Samaritan or a publican, an
outsider and lowly."

Comparison with Naturalism

When one takes note of the "isms" in the modern world which
may be regarded as constituting alternatives to the Christian faith,
one often works with intellectual elites. Existentialism and Marxism
attract the most attention. It is characteristic of Christianity that it
is spread quite evenly throughout the various levels of the population: the intellectuals do not constitute a majority in a congregation. This corresponds with what the New Testament has to say—
"not many of you were wise according to worldly standards . . ."
(1 Cor. 1:26). One can wander over many miles of Christian territory without bumping into a single existentialist. But on the other
hand, a fair number of Christians do live by the old humanistic
heritage, on the pale but tough remnants of the nineteenth-century
Swedish lyric: "The beautiful is eternal . . ." or "What you think
is right . . ."

The same is true of naturalism in its simplest form: the person
is an animal, somewhat more complicated than the other animals, but
in principle the same sort of animal as the rest. If one turns from

the literature and focuses on people, naturalism offers a much more intensive life principle than Marxism. One of the foremost marks of naturalism is that it explains everything causally. Therefore, it inserts the human into the natural process as the product of causes already at work.[11]

A comparison of Christianity and naturalism should begin with their internal similarity, which is to be found in their view of death. It is a likeness seldom noted, that naturalism develops the Old Testament thesis: "For the fate of the sons of men and the fate of beasts is the same; as one dies, so dies the other. They all have the same breath" (Eccles. 3:19). The presupposition of this citation is the classical statement in Genesis which has found its place in many Christian burial rites: "All are from the dust and all return to dust again" (Eccles. 3:20; cf. Gen. 3:19). It is very seldom that one finds such a clear inclusion of the human among the events of nature anywhere in the history of religion. This is also the reason that our comparison with naturalism takes place here in this section where we are dealing with death.

Naturalism teaches the human to accept death as appointed, and necessary, and from the viewpoint of the individual, meaningless. But it does this with a line of reason which is content with a causal explanation. The human should feel as little uneasiness in the presence of death as the animal, since the human is an animal. The Christian faith, on the contrary, accepts also the uneasiness in the presence of death and considers it to be something entirely human. Three points of view are important in this connection and they hang together with the three parts of the Creed: Father, Son, and Spirit.

First, Christianity affirms the sadness that humans feel at the transitoriness of the spontaneous expressions of life. One cannot see the play of children and perceive the joy it brings them, without wishing that those who play might forever be free from sorrow and tears. We often feel that it is unnatural that this carefree children's world should be replaced by bondage to work and by pain. Play and song seem to us to be the destiny for which we were created. To desire that such a life continue eternally and to complain when it breaks down is not irrationality and lack of insight into natural processes; it is rationality and also presentiment of eternal life.

The guilt we feel each time we corrupt another person's joy or restrain someone's play is for us a form of contact with the Creator of all life. For the Creator is at work in all that takes place in ordinary human life and in all that is perceived by each person. The Cre-

ator is also at work in the sadness, the complaint, and the consciousness of guilt.

The second observation is that Christianity does not say that as
human beings we have a number of characteristics that separate
us from the animals. We do have such characteristics, of course,
but the dog also has many characteristics which are lacking in the
tapeworm. At this level of argument, we can never separate ourselves from the animals. But what Christianity does say is that
there has lived *one* person in history who did not take away the
joy of others, but, on the contrary, directed his criticism against
those who laid on the burdens; it says there was one who was human
for all who are unfree, and who explained that the kingdom of heaven
belongs to *children*—to children at play.

The image of him already judges those who have spoiled the lives
of others. If we accept his judgment, the judgment has already taken
place, for all the future. Everyone who believes "has eternal life; he
does not come into judgment, but has passed from death into life"
(John 5:24). This judgment and forgiveness which is happening
now (and which is death and resurrection) is the work of the Son.

The third point to be made is that Christianity does not demand
of the human beings that we should be filled with spiritual life and
thereby separate ourselves from animals. Rather the Christian faith
interprets the human in such a way that the Spirit is already present when we pray—and we pray when we sigh without being able
to put into words what it is we are sighing for (Rom. 8:26). Confronted by the destruction which breaks creation down, and confronted by
our own guilty cooperation in that destruction, we pray when we
hope for an end to the evil that goes on. For hope is prayer, and it is
moreover a prayer in which the human is at one with nature (Rom.
8:20-23).

The eschatological promise—"Blessed are you that weep now, for
you shall laugh" (Luke 6:21)—is not a promise about a supernatural
addition to nature. What is promised is the conquest of destruction,
not anything else, and on the basis of the conquest we may join in
unceasing play in the presence of God. To be able to continue to hope
for this in the face of the death that is appointed and necessary
(yet from an individual point of view, meaningless), this is the Spirit's gift to mankind.

Christianity is distinguished from naturalism on all three of these
points. It is both differentiated and connected, for it interprets the
naturally-given expressions of life in man. The decisive point is that
what is now present can point *forward;* it need not be understood
exclusively in terms of what has happened before. To explain that

which is at hand causally, and to see it only as the product of something that existed earlier, is an arbitrary limitation of the possibilities of understanding. Every interpretation that points forward appeals to faith and hope. Evidence is not to be found.

THE SONG OF PRAISE

Eternal life is depicted in the New Testament as a song of praise. Even the primitive understanding that the ongoing worship service is a song of praise in which the departed ones also take part, implies a life after death that is independent of space. The term "heaven" in the primitive Christian period did not include the fantasy of being locked into a certain space; instead its reference seems to have been to freedom from boundaries; it implied the power to be everywhere. But it was possible for early Christianity, because of its image of the world, to think of many unfamiliar rooms. This is a possibility which we do not have. Therefore we seek to *demythologize* any specific fixed interpretation. Biblical statements that presuppose an older picture of the world become meaningful for us only when they are detached from that antiquated view of the world.[12]

After they have been detached, however, these biblical statements continue to appeal to faith and hope, yet still without proof. We will handle the song of praise here in two stages: first, the song of praise in the worship service during the movement forward to the future, and then the song of praise in the end when the goal has been achieved.

In the Present

In the liturgical tradition we find references to the sacramental and the sacrificial elements in the worship service. One could distinguish between these most easily by observing the movements of the officiating priest. When he turned his back to the congregation and his face to the altar, he was acting in behalf of the people in the presence of God, that is sacrificially. When he took the opposite position, he represented God to the people, hence this was a sacramental element. This use of language fits in well with the two natures of Christ, a divine and a human nature, and it fits well also with the two static realities "the heaven up there" and "the earth down here," and with the pair of concepts "transcendence" and "immanence." None of these terms has played any role whatever in the composition of this book, nor will they play any role now. We mention them here only so that the reader will know what language we are rejecting.

What is the worship service here and now, *in time?* It is something in which the whole of Christ's body—that human fellowship
which is guided by the Spirit—engages as it *moves forward.* The
Lord of the congregation, who is risen, "the first-born from the
dead" (Col. 1:18), dwells ahead in the future. He speaks into the
present to those who have not yet passed through the final gate.
Those who hear his words pray and celebrate in worship now, as
they move forward. Behind them is their baptism, their being grafted into death and resurrection, which is a life process that is repeated daily in their hardships and their joys. Tears and laughter
in the present are tears and laughter in Christ, and they point forward toward the final conquest of destruction, envy, and sorrow.

The God to whom we pray and whom we worship, the Creator, is
not overcome by death though we his creatures are. "Now he is not
the God of the dead, but of the living; *for all live to him*" (Luke
20:38). Those who now celebrate in worship remember their dead
as voices out of the past; they remember them only for a short time,
a generation or two perhaps. But with God they are not dead; if
they were, God would not be the Creator. For him all live, for him
all the voices are blended together when the worship is celebrated.
In worship the Swedish voices are blended with the Aramean and
with hundreds of other languages. This is what it means when in
the Lord's Supper we exult "with the faithful in all ages and with
all the heavenly hosts."

Other symbols are intertwined with the images of the choir and
of the many languages. We must of course refer again to the grain-
of-wheat eschatology in our imagery about eternal life. Otherwise
we would begin to chop up the whole into bits and pieces—one individual lived at such and such a time, then another began to live, etc.
These dead are grains of wheat and they *are still living.* They are
living in the harvest which grew up because the voices out of the
past were those of earthly people who went through that death
which is appointed, and necessary, and from an individual point of
view, meaningless. But what is meaningless when looked at from
an individual point of view is deeply meaningful when the individual
is seen as part of "the body," the congregation. And the body lives;
it is the congregation reaching out toward all people on earth.[13] So
the dead take part in the congregation's song of praise; there those
who "by one Spirit were all baptized into one body" (1 Cor. 12:13)
are alive.

It is significant that the existence of the dead according to the
classical Christian conviction, has been associated with the *worship
service,* rather than with individual experiences connected with

meditation, dreams, or the attempt to contact the departed. Such individual experiences are more or less self-centered. The worship service, on the other hand, is the gathering together of the worshiping community before the Father and Creator, and the offering of praise to him. Worship takes place while listening to words spoken by the Son, who has already arrived at the goal and who, from his place in the future, once spoke the same words to those who are now dead. That is the way members are joined into one body in the Spirit. This finally brings to an end the question about one's own private blessedness, which separates and destroys fellowship—as though there would be some value in being an ear apart from the body (1 Cor. 12:17).

Every person has a tone, or a voice, that belongs in a choir, and can thus be a part of a singing body. This is the profound implication in Pehr Eklund's thesis that if one wishes to see what eternal life is, one should observe children at play.

In Heaven

The various symbols of eternal life—the choir made up of many languages, the grain of wheat and its harvest, the body and its members—have one thing in common: they teach that life takes place in community, not in isolation. The meaningfulness in life comes from the wholeness and is related to the fact that the others in the fellowship are different and have roles which differ from mine.

Our imagery can conceive of the dead as taking part in the worship service here on earth which is arranged by those who have not yet died. It is, of course, not possible to see these dead ones in the room, but we can believe that they are joining in the song of praise. We can also visualize Christ as being present in the worship service in spite of the fact that he was once a specific, limited person, who spoke a specific language, and in spite of the fact that we cannot point out a certain place in the room where he now is. He is heard in his word. It is not difficult to understand that we can hear someone who has once lived; that is something we all have experienced when we read old letters or hear a radio program repeated.

But what can be the meaning of a song of praise that is sung when all have passed beyond death? Can we imagine that situation? The answer has to be No! When we talk about the heavenly song of praise we are talking about something we cannot imagine concretely.

If then we reject a future eternal life, we should be clear that our only alternative is what we have earlier called naturalism. We have to say that the human dies in the same way that everything else in nature dies. The Platonic idea of the immortality of the soul is not an alternative. We cannot conceive of a soul without some bodily foundation, that is, without some kind of localization in space. It is in fact much easier to imagine a song or a voice without having to locate it in space. A reverberating sound is everywhere and nowhere. The existentialist interpretation of eternal life as our own authentic existence, present to us as a possibility in a situation in which we choose, allows eternal life to be something thinkable in every situation except one—the situation of death. Existentialists can find hope everywhere, except at the nethermost point in our existence. Such an interpretation cannot be gospel, whatever else may be said about it.

We stand between two possibilities: naturalism or the hope of a heaven we cannot concretely imagine. It is only the latter which can be called "Christian." This hope has many genuinely Christian features in it, and we will return to it promptly. But before we summarize the specifically Christian elements in this grain-of-wheat eschatology, something negative needs to be said. A Christian cannot say more about the future eternal events than words of hope and prayer.

We cannot, in the first place, express judgments about other people. The New Testament reports of the final judgment are Jesus' own words, and they are spoken into our present from the future where he is. If we listen to these words of Jesus for any other purpose than to judge and cleanse our own hearts, we misuse them. We are then positioning ourselves as observers at the seat of judgment where others are being judged. This nullifies the intention of the New Testament witness.

In the second place, a Christian cannot talk about bodies, graves, clouds in the heavens, streets of gold, etc. Such language is to be found in the New Testament, to be sure. Often this was intended to be symbolic from the beginning, but sometimes it is intended to be taken literally. That people at that time thought thus is not any more strange than that they reclined at table, squirted oil and wine in sores, carried sandals and washed the feet of guests. But because of an unbiblical understanding of certain words, obsolete elements in the New Testament have become sacrosanct and unchangeable affirmations in the church.

It is as though a check for a fortune was made out to us but we were lamenting that the house number on the envelope was wrong. We could waste our time trying to prove that the faulty house number, looked at in a certain way, really was the right number. But it doesn't make any difference whether the house number is right or wrong. The gospel, the fortune, is obscured by all this meaningless discussion about the infallibility of the biblical text. If the end result is eternal life, this assures the victory of the gospel over everything that condemns. Nothing is lacking in eternal life.

But now to the five points that summarize the specifically Christian elements in eternal life viewed as a song of praise.[14] In all five points, the difference between the song of praise (which rests on the resurrection of the dead) and the immortality of the soul becomes apparent.

1) A song of praise is a bodily act. While it is not bound to a certain point in space but is, on the contrary, everywhere and nowhere, it is of necessity produced by a body (or more properly, by bodies). The body is entirely foreign to the idea of the immortality of the soul.

2) A song of praise, as it is described in the New Testament, is an act of fellowship. Many languages and many tongues go into it, but when each has contributed its voice and its tone, what is sung is a unified song (Rev. 7:9-17). Any kind of plurality is foreign to the immortality of the soul.

3) A song of praise is, by its very nature, directed toward someone other than those who sing. They are not only expressing their own satisfaction over their freedom from imprisonment in the body but they are praising one who has freed them. The one whom they praise is himself *human;* he himself bears the marks of earthly, human life. This focus is also foreign to the immortality of the soul. According to Platonism, that which is innermost in the person possesses the quality of immortality.

4) A song of praise such as that described in the New Testament springs forth from a completed act of creation. The decision to make human beings in God's image has been brought to fulfillment through this other one, who *is* God's image (Col. 1:15) and who creates a new people in union with himself (Eph. 2:15). This representation of a Creator who works without ceasing is foreign to the theory of an immortal soul which is presently locked into a material, unspiritual body.

5) A song of praise addressed to another following a liberation presupposes victory over destruction. The nature of destruction is enmity against God, but since God is creator, destruction also devastates the person God has created. To be saved is to become human; it is to be what one was created to be, to be made free. That is why the song of praise in heaven is a mass song, sung by many (destruction consisted of tearing apart, and in the lust after private possessions). That is also why the song of praise extols Christ (who

in his human existence refrained from being a private owner, and who broke down the walls that divide, cf. Phil 2:6-8 and Eph. 2:14-19). All of these features are foreign to the doctrine of the immortality of the soul.

The hope which expresses itself as a song of praise has all the features which are characteristic of the primitive Christian faith concerning the resurrection of the dead, as distinguished from the theory of the divine spark or the immortal soul. It is, however, necessary in our time to present this original Christian hope in its demythologized form if it is to be a *hope* for us at all. The demythologization has to do with the idea of the final judgment as well as with the eternal continuation of the cells in the body. At both of these points, what is at the heart of the New Testament is being obscured, especially in Sweden, through fundamentalistic tendencies, combined with the absence of any open discussion.

In the introduction to this book we set up the thesis that one cannot separate the content of the three articles of faith from one another. The whole Christian faith is creation faith, for the Creator acts in everything, from the beginning to the resurrection of the dead. In the same way, faith is altogether faith in the Son. What is human in a person and what constitutes the destruction of one's humanity can be identified only with the help of "God's image," the true man, who is Jesus of Nazareth. Finally, it can truly be said that all Christian faith is faith in the Spirit. We do not see God face to face and Jesus does not live as a historical person today. If we believe, it is because of the Spirit's invisible work in our heart.

The presentation which has now been concluded seems to have substantiated this thesis which was set forth at the beginning. But at the most controversial point—creation faith or the first article—one side of the matter bears repeating. There are in our time certain interpretations of faith which subsume everything under the viewpoint of Christology, the second article, and they do this with great success. We are beginning also to get comprehensive pneumatologies —interpretations of the faith which attempt to bring together everything under the viewpoint of the third article. But when someone tries to do the same thing with the first article, to bring everything together under the heading of creation faith, there is usually strong opposition.

It is said that creation theology is always reactionary theology. The two letters *re*, which imply *re*storation, *re*capitulation, are, it is said, expressions which refer to a dream about returning to a lost golden age, a dream that is reactionary in principle, seeking to hold fast to the status quo, without movement and without change. It is not often that, in dealing with something as complex as theology, one is able to express the exact opposite of the correct judgment, but the one who describes creation theology in this way has managed that dubious achievement.[15] *If it were possible for one to return to a previous situation, it would then be impossible to believe in a God who is Creator.*

To believe in the Creator is to believe in a God who cannot do other than constantly make new. Just as God, according to the Christian faith, cannot do other than love, so he cannot do other than create, which means *to make new*, against all that corrupts, against all death. The notion of a return to a condition that is gone is a notion that is godless and self-centered. The point in the Christian faith at which such thinking is especially out of place is the idea of creation.

If belief in the Creator has this implication, what do we then mean by the *re* in *re*storation, in *re*capitulation?

This question can be answered in many different ways. Today, when the work of Christ seems meaningful only in view of its focus on the future, and when the proclamation of the gospel strikes people as being uncontroversially Christian in its content while only creation faith is dubious, it is proper to answer the question with two statements.

The first is that if we include in Christ's work what he accomplished as the risen one we must also recognize the possibility that Christ could have chosen new instruments for his work in the world since the disciples at the crucifixion had betrayed him and fled. But the fact is that it is precisely these old, used-up disciples who are *again* installed to serve, they are *re*-instated. Peter, who had not only fled but had denied Jesus, is a paradigm of how God regularly acts. The gospel character of Christ's action in the world would have been weakened if new disciples had been allowed to take over. *It is the restoration which is the gospel.* In that very fact the Creator, who continually makes new in the face of destruction, steps forth and can be seen.

The second point is that this feature of restoration is also the heart of the proclaimed word; it is the gospel about "the forgiveness of sins." Youngsters demonstrating in the streets may effect some renewal, but the person who turns from a wasted life and prays for forgiveness is closer to the wellspring of the New Testament. Two gospel passages are decisive here. The one reads: "Those who are well have no need of a physician, but those who are sick." The other is found in the parable of the prodigal son: "your brother was dead and is alive; he was lost, and is found." It is the same point as in the story about Peter; it is the same point as in the first article of the Creed.

> *O God, every unselfish deed on earth comes from you.*
> *There is sorrow in heaven each time we harden*
> *ourselves against a suffering one. You alone know where*
> *love is real, and we tremble before the thought of*
> *your judgment upon us while the merciful Samaritans*
> *of the world stand before your throne praising you.*
> *Have mercy on us—your church, the people who claim*
> *to be your own.*
>
> *Even now heaven and earth are pouring forth their*
> *songs of praise to God for what Christ's sacrifice*
> *achieved. O God, we thank you that through our baptism*
> *we have been given a share in the eternal life he won.*
> *Let us, without complaint, accept death when it comes,*
> *and resign ourselves to the common fate of all people.*
> *You who have taught us to pray for all the world, hear*
> *now our prayer: let no single human be left outside, when*
> *you gather your own around you.*
>
> *Through Jesus you have promised that in heaven those*
> *who weep shall laugh, and that those who are hungry*
> *shall be satisfied. O God, give heed to the weeping and the*
> *hunger which fills the world, and which yearns for new*
> *heavens and a new earth.*

Notes

Foreword

1. "Creation faith" is used to translate *skapelsetron*. The Swedish original implies not only a belief in creation as event, or as a doctrine, but a view of creation as dynamic, ongoing, and pervasive. It shapes the meaning of "faith" as well as being something in which the Christian believes.
2. The Nicene Creed, in distinction from the Apostles' Creed has the expression "the resurrection of the dead" in the original text (. . . *et exspecto resurrectionem mortuorum*). Cf. Heinrich Vogel, *Das Nicaenische Glaubensbekenntnis* (Berlin: Lettner, 1963), pp. 196-209.

Introduction

1. Concerning the dogma of the incarnation, see Ragnar Bring, *Kristendomstolkningar i gammal och ny tid* (Lund, 1950), cf. pp. 127-132.
2. Wingren uses the noun with a definite article "the destruction" to describe not only a condition but that which causes the condition. It implies a dynamic evil and an active process of decay and deterioration which "the destruction" does not necessarily convey in English. We have sometimes used "forces of destruction" or "destroying powers" to translate what is quite uniformly conveyed in the original by "destructionen." Trans. note.
3. The temptation account is treated at length in Birger Gerhardsson's contribution, "Bibelns ethos" in the compilation *Etik och kristen tro* (Lund: Gleerup, 1971), pp. 42-44, 195.
4. No church father is as clear as Irenaeus on this point. Concerning envy, see my book *Man and the Incarnation: A Study in the Biblical Theology of Irenaeus*, trans. R. Mackenzie (Philadelphia: Muhlenberg, 1959), pp. 42-45, 195.
5. Wingren follows the Swedish version, "the resurrection of the dead."

6. Concerning the biblical stories of creation cf. Joh. Lindblom, *Israels religion i gammaltestamentlig tid*, 4th ed. 1967, pp. 142-144.
7. Løgstrup's presentation of the spontaneous and the locked-in expressions of life is scattered through a number of smaller writings. One can get an assembled picture of them from Lars-Olle Armgard's doctoral dissertation, *Anthropologi*, e.g. pp. 44-51, 170-173, 198, 204 and 214.
8. For a criticism of the modern concept of revelation, compare F. Gerald Downing, *Has Christianity a Revelation?* (London: SCM, 1964), pp. 278-282.
9. Gerhard Ebeling's essay appeared already in 1950, but it is still one of the most rewarding articles to be found on the subject. It is now included in his first large compilation of essays. "The Significance of the Critical Historical Method for Church and Theology in Protestantism" in *Word and Faith*, trans. James W. Leitch (Philadelphia: Fortress, 1963), pp. 17-61.

Chapter I: Creation

1. See here K. E. Løgstrup's pointed thesis in *The Ethical Demand*, trans. Theo S. Jensen (Philadelphia: Fortress, 1971), pp. 111-121.
2. This appears especially clearly in Jürgen Moltmann, for example in his *Umkehr zur Zukunft* (Munich: Siebenstern-Taschenbuck, 1970), pp. 113-132.
3. Concerning these two citations, see William Neil, *The Epistle of Paul to the Thessalonians* (New York: Harper, 1950), 2nd ed. 1965, p. 157 f. Further, in Bertil Gärtner, *Die rätselhaften Termini Nazoräer und Iskariot*, in Horae Soederblomianae 4, 1957, pp. 57-60.
4. See Oscar Cullmann, *Salvation in History*, trans. Sidney G. Somers et al (New York and Evanston: Harper and Row, 1967), pp. 143-150, 323f. Of great weight in this connection is Rom. 5:12-21.
5. Concerning Jesus in the destruction see K. E. Løgstrup, *Opgør med Kierkegaard* (Copenhagen: Gyldendal, 1968), pp. 22-25.
6. All deaths can be as shocking as the earthquake in Lisbon in 1755. Concerning the effect of this problem in more recent Swedish literature see Olov Hartman, *Jordbävningen i Lissabon*, 1968, pp. 68-127.
7. See, for example, Simone Weil, *Gravity and Grace*, trans. Emma Crawford (London: Routledge and Kegan Paul, 1952), pp. 28, 38-44, 157-160.
8. See here the classical presentation by A. M. Ramsey, *The Gospel and the Catholic Church*, 2nd ed., 1937 (London: Longmans, Green), pp. 21-24.
9. Cf. Gerhard von Rad, *Genesis: A Commentary*, trans. John H. Machi, G. E. Wright et al, The Old Testament Library (Philadelphia: Westminster, 1961), pp. 93-99.
10. See here the clarifying presentation in Per Erik Persson, *Att tolka Gud idag*, 1971, pp. 48-51.
11. See, for example, the analysis by Johannes de Graaf, "Kritik av våldets rättfärdigande" in *Vår Lösen*, 1970, pp. 450-452.
12. This is the main thesis of Karl Barth, cf. *Church Dogmatics III:* 4, trans. G. T. Mackay et al, G. W. Bromiley, T. F. Torrance, eds. (Edinburgh: T. and T. Clark, 1961), pp. 116-240.

Chapter II: The Law

1. Concerning the mutual connection between the various utterances in Rom. 1-2, see C. A. Pierce, *Conscience in the New Testament* (London: SCM, 1955), p. 85f.
2. Cf. Daniel D. Williams, *The Spirit and the Forms of Love* (New York: Harpers, 1968), pp. 250-255.
3. Concerning Catholicism, see Bruno Schüller's "Katolsk moralteologi" in the compilation *Etik och kristen tro*, 1971, pp. 104-106.
4. Cf. the analysis of Jesus' proclamation by Joachim Jeremias in his *New Testament Theology, The Proclamation of Jesus*, trans. John Bowden (New York: Scribner's, 1971), pp. 105f., also 108-121.
5. Cf. Anders Nygren, *Agape and Eros*, Part I, trans. A. G. Hebert (London: SPCK, 1932), esp. pp. 41-75.
6. See here C. A. Pierce, *Conscience in the New Testament*, pp. 66-74, 85f., and 111f. The agreement between Luther and the New Testament is remarkable. A short but instructive chapter on Luther's conception of conscience can be found in Herbert Ohlsson's posthumous work, *Schöpfung, Vernunft, und Gesetz in Luthers Theologie*, 1971, pp. 562-570.
7. This guilt depends upon our interdependence as given in our own existence. We are part of each other's life. See Løgstrup, *The Ethical Demand*, pp. 163f.
8. Cf. Heinz Häfner, *Schulderleben und Gewissen*, 1956, p. 7, 133, 178f.
9. Some exegetes have believed that only Luke 12:37, with its focus on an eschatological future is an original word of Jesus. It would then in a secondary way have been the source of the great scene in John 13:4-17, the foot-washing. Compare the well-balanced judgments about this in C. H. Dodd, *Historical Tradition in the Fourth Gospel* (Cambridge: University Press, 1963), pp. 60-63.

Chapter III: Works

1. Here see Emil Brunner, *The Christian Doctrine of Creation and Redemption*, trans. Olive Wyon (Philadelphia: Westminster, 1952), pp. 350-356.
2. More about this in Oscar Cullmann, "The Origin of Christmas" in *The Early Church. Studies in Early Christian History and Theology*, trans. A. J. B. Higgins and S. Godman (Philadelphia: Westminster, 1956).
3. Cf. Regin Prenter, *Creation and Redemption*, trans. Theodore S. Jensen (Philadelphia: Fortress, 1967), p. 435. Also Helmut Thielicke, *The Evangelical Faith: Vol. II, The Doctrine of God and Christ*, trans. G. W. Bromiley (Grand Rapids, Mich.: Eerdmans Co., 1977), pp. 407-415.
4. Luther is typical here. No individual in the history of man, he says, has felt such anguish as Jesus did, and no one will know such anguish in the future: to sweat blood is unique. Out of such unique anguish, comes the resurrection. But Luther affirmed, obviously, at the same time, the statements about the virgin birth, which for us tend to make the anguish illusory.
5. To hold together Jesus' healing and his proclaiming is Einar Bil-

ling's major achievement in *De etiska tankarna*, 1907, see 2nd ed.,
pp. 298-309. The individual stands in the center of both activities.

6. Cf. Alan Richardson, *An Introduction to the Theology of the New
   Testament* (London: SCM, 1958), pp. 81-83.
7. This is the reason that the purely political utopianists have become
   a problem for Marxism itself. See Jürgen Moltmann's interesting
   contribution in the festschrift for Ernst Bloch, 1965, later published also in Moltmann's work, *Perspectiven der Theologie* (Munich: Kaiser, 1968), pp. 174-188.
8. See also Tor Aukrust, *Mennesket i samfunnet* I, 1965, p. 274f.
9. Concerning the combination of ethical rigor and generosity in the
   historical Jesus, see Gustaf Aulen, *Jesus in Contemporary Historical Research*, trans. Ingalil H. Hjelm (Philadelphia: Fortress,
   1976), pp. 42-43, 151-152.
10. See Dietrich von Oppen, *The Age of the Person*, trans. Frank
    Clarke (Philadelphia: Fortress, 1969), p. 194f.

Chapter IV: The Cross

1. Concerning the relation between various ideas of the atonement
   and the accentuation of the divine or the human "nature" see G.
   Aulen, *Christus Victor*, trans. by A. G. Hebert (London: SPCK,
   1931), especially pages 151-154.
2. Cf. Vincent Taylor, *The Gospel According to St. Mark*, 2nd ed.
   (London: Macmillan, 1966), p. 548 (on Mark 14:27). Concerning
   the difficulty of interpreting the original implication of Zech. 13:7
   see further the line of thought developed by Benedikt Otzen,
   Studien über Deuterosacharja 1964, in summary fashion pp. 192-
   194 and 227.
3. See Joachim Jeremias, *Jesus' Promise to the Nations*, trans. S. H.
   Hooke, vol. 24 of Studies in Biblical Theology (Naperville, Illi-
   nois: Allenson, 1958), pp. 41-46.
4. It has always been a leading thought of Regin Prenter, though with
   other motivation than is the case here, that Jesus' death implies
   that he actually is a sinner. See Prenter's dogmatics, *Creation and
   Redemption*, pp. 406, 434f.
5. See also Reinhold Niebuhr, *An Interpretation of Christian Ethics*
   (New York: Harper, 1935), pp. 103-135, where a comparison with
   Marxism occurs.
6. Cf. J. G. Davies, *He Ascended into Heaven* (London: Lutterworth,
   1958), pp. 100-103, 169f., 178f.
7. Cf. Per Erik Persson, "Reformationens nytolkning—sedd utifrån,"
   in *Tolkning*, ed. Olov Hartman, 1968, pp 56-60, where the eastern
   "synergism's" critique of the Reformation is dealt with.
8. Cf. Birger Gerhardsson, *Etik och kristen tro*, pp. 52f., and 49f.
9. See Lars-Olle Armgard, *Anthropologi*, pp. 29, 74, 78.
10. Our problem is clearly delineated in a biblical-theological work
    which deals with the unity between the two Testaments, by Ulrich
    Mauser, *Gottesbild and Menschenwerdung* (Tübingen: Mohr,
    1971), see especially pp. 16f. and 187-190.
11. See Romans 5:19, and in addition Ernst Käsemann, *Romans*,
    (Grand Rapids: Eerdmans, 1980), pp. 155f.

Chapter V: The Resurrection

1. Cf. George S. Hendry, *The Holy Spirit in Christian Theology* (London: SCM, 1957), pp. 55-71.
2. It is just this integration that is commonly lacking in the talk about Jesus' "second coming." See Paul Minear, *Christian Hope and the Second Coming* (Philadelphia: Westminster, 1954), pp. 99-114.
3. Cf. Alfred Wikenhauser, *Die Apostelgeschichte*, 4. Aufl. 1961, p. 123.
4. This idealism is foreign to the Reformation. Cf. Per Frostin, *Politik och hermeneutic*, 1970, pp. 159f.
5. Cf. Hans von Campenhausen, "The Events of Easter and the Empty Tomb" in *Tradition and Life in the Church, Essays and Lectures in Church History*, trans. A. V. Littledale (Philadelphia: Fortress, 1968).
6. Cf. Karl Heinrich Rengstorf, *Die Auferstehung Jesu* (Witten-Ruhr: Luther-Verlag, 1960), pp. 66-69.
7. Concerning the text and the citation from Peter, see E. C. Hoskyns, *The Fourth Gospel* (London: Faber and Faber, 1940), pp. 556-568.
8. The relation between the sun and the sunbeam is a symbol which was used long before the 4th century. See, for example, Bengt Hagglund, *History of Theology*, trans. Gene J. Lund (St. Louis: Concordia, 1968), pp. 44-45 (concerning Tertullian).

Chapter VI: The Gospel

1. The ascension is alluded to in the verb "ascending to my Father" (John 20:17) and is tied in with the fact that Mary of Magdala is forbidden to "hold" him, while Thomas on the contrary is urged to do so (John 20:27). Concerning this see C. H. Dodd, *The Interpretation of the Fourth Gospel* (Cambridge: University Press, 1960), pp. 441-443.
2. The text from Luther which is here cited does not stand isolated. A number of similar statements are brought together by Regin Prenter, *Spiritus Creator* (Philadelphia: Muhlenberg, 1953), trans. John M. Jensen, p. 130f.
3. See the illuminating chapter on the 4th century and its "sanctification of time" in Gregory Dix, *The Shape of the Liturgy* (London: Westminster, 1942), pp. 303-396.
4. Regarding what follows, see my work, *Man and the Incarnation*, pp. 4 and 58, in which typical instances are set forth. It should probably be added that in a book about *credo*, Irenaeus is not just another name. No individual author has played such a decisive role in the production of the tripartite Creed as he has.
5. If one operates with this picture of one God with two hands, the Son and the Spirit, one cannot of course say as the Nicene Creed says in its western form, that "the Spirit proceeds from the Father and the Son *(filioque)*." The image requires that one follow the eastern formula, and only say that "the Spirit proceeds from the Father" (in spite of John 16:14f.). There is more on *filioque* and its negation in the east in Timothy Ware, *The Orthodox Church* (Baltimore: Penguin, 1963), pp. 219-223.
6. See Lars-Olle Armgard, *Anthropologi*, pp. 19, 32, 73 and especially 132, also 205-227.

7. Cf. C. F. D. Moule, "The Judgment Theme in the Sacraments" in Essays honoring C. H. Dodd, *The Background of the New Testament and Its Eschatology* (Cambridge: University Press, 1956), pp. 464-481.
8. See Yngve Brilioth, *Eucharistic Faith and Practice* (New York: Macmillan, 1930), p. 282f. for the "representational feature," an idea that is original with Brilioth.

Chapter VII: The Congregation in the World

1. Cf. Anna Marie Aagaard, *Helligånden sendt til verden*, 1973, p. 257f.
2. Cf. Per Erik Persson, *Att dela Guds hållning*, 1972, p. 72.
3. Cf. Iring Fetscher, *Från Marx till sovjetideologin*, p. 32f. as well as the remarkable citations on p. 42f, and especially p. 47 where "creating life-expression" is directly used as a technical term, of course with man as the subject in the statement. (Trans. note: Fetscher's thought is well presented in English in his *Marx and Marxism* (New York: Herder, 1971).
4. See Rudolf Bultmann, "The Significance of the Idea of Freedom for Western Civilization" in *Essays Philosophical and Theological*, trans. James C. G. Greig (New York: Macmillan, 1955), pp. 307-311.
5. The combination of Spirit and baptism is the main topic of the foundational monograph by G. W. H. Lampe, *The Seal of the Spirit* (London: Longmans, Green, 1951), pp. 33-63. He also brings clarity to the relation between Paul and the gospels on this point.
6. Cf. Hugo Odeberg, "The Individualism of Today and the Concept of the Church in the New Testament," in *This Is the Church*, ed. Anders Nygren (Philadelphia: Muhlenberg, 1952), pp. 52-74.
7. See N. H. Søe, *Kristelig etik*, 5th ed. 1962, pp. 31-41, as well as a number of references to Plato's relation to idealism (look in the name and subject index under "Plato" and "idealism"). Of interest is also Gunnar Hillerdal, *Teologisk och filosofisk etik*, 1958, pp. 19-33, where the individualism of Greek philosophy is set over against the original Christian view of the congregation as a "given" fellowship.
8. The way Hans Larsson in a meditative manner moves Plato over into our time is significant. See his book, *Platon och vår tid*, 3rd ed. 1924, pp. 131f., 179f.
9. For the relation between the book of Revelation and later teachings concerning the Spirit, see Martin Kiddle, *The Revelation of St. John* (London: Hodder and Stoughton, 1947), pp. 99-101.
10. About the Spirit "remaining" on Jesus, in John 1:32f., and about the baptism of the congregation after Easter and Pentecost, cf. Raymond E. Brown, *The Gospel According to John* (New York: Doubleday, 1966), p. 66.
11. Most remarkable in this connection is the "palamistic" tradition within eastern churches. See Anna Marie Aagaard, *Helligånden sendt till verden*, pp. 203-206.
12. Cf. Hans Heinrich Wolf, *Die Einheit des Bundes* (Neukirchen:

Verlag der Buchhandlung des Erziehungsvereins, 1958), pp. 109-113, also 39-47.

13. A very good point of departure is to compare what Bultmann says about Heidegger and the gospel in "New Testament and Mythology" in *Kerygma and Myth, A Theological Debate*, trans. Reginald H. Fuller (London: SPCK, 1953), pp. 24-33, with what Heidegger himself says about conscience in *Being and Time*, trans. John Macquarrie and Edward Robinson (New York: Harper, 1962), pp. 335-348. Heidegger's book came out in its first edition in 1927 and has not been altered since.

14. See John Macquarrie, *Existentialism* (Philadelphia: Westminster, 1972), pp. 215-218, in spite of considerations on pp. 199f. In the area of anthropology, Macquarrie sees no essential difference between existentialism and Christianity.

15. On this, see Gregory Dix, *The Shape of the Liturgy*, pp. 266f., 190-199, and 281-288. See also Alan Richardson, *An Introduction to the Theology of the New Testament*, p. 373, especially note 4. Concerning the true exegesis of the final line in 1 Cor. 12:13 see C. K. Barrett, *A Commentary on the First Epistle to the Corinthians* (New York: Harper, 1968), p. 289.

16. Concerning the Eastern point of view, see Timothy Ware, *The Orthodox Church*, pp. 216-222. Concerning the growing use of the term "filioque" within the Western churches, see J. N. D. Kelly, *Early Christian Creeds*, 3rd ed. (London: Longmans, 1972), pp. 358-367.

17. Cf. Hans Hof, "Att säga det outsägliga" in the compilation, *Myt och symbol*, 1967, especially pages 158-187.

Chapter VIII: Eternal Life

1. Pehr Eklund, *Evangelisk Fadervårsdyrkan*, the pamphlet "Vår barnatro som Andehelgelsetro" 1904, p. 34.

2. It is possible that baptism is already implicit in this statement concerning "new birth." Cf. E. G. Selwyn, *The First Epistle of St. Peter* (London: Macmillan, 1961), pp. 122-124.

3. On Matt. 22:23-33, see Floyd V. Filson, *A Commentary on the Gospel According to St. Matthew* (New York: Harper, 1961), pp. 235-237.

4. See here the noteworthy chapter on "The Resurrection of the Dead" in Tor Andrae's book *Det osynligas värld* (Uppsala: J. A. Lindblads fœrlag, 1934), pp. 104-110.

5. See Oscar Cullmann, *Baptism in the New Testament*, trans. J. K. S. Reid (London: SCM, 1950), vol. 1 of Studies in Biblical Theology, pp. 9-22.

6. Concerning the deeply human interpretation of the final judgment, viewed as the termination of Jesus' prolonged work of restoration, see my *Man and the Incarnation*, pp. 199-201.

7. On John 5:24-25, which is the central text here, see E. C. Hoskyns, *The Fourth Gospel*, pp. 269-271.

8. See Simone Weil, *Gravity and Grace*, p. 30. On Gen. 2:17 and 3:19 cf. Gerhard von Rad, *Genesis*, pp. 80-82 and 101f. See also C. A. Pierce, *Conscience in the New Testament*, pp. 72-74.

9. Karl Barth, *Church Dogmatics* II. 2, trans. G. W. Bromiley et al. (Edinburgh: T. and T. Clark, 1957), pp. 163-168.

10. For the interpretation of 1 Tim. 2:4-6, see J. N. D. Kelly, *A Commentary on the Pastoral Epistles* (New York: Harper and Row, 1963), pp. 62-64. It is important that even 1 Tim. 2:6 is drawn into the exegesis: Christ gave himself "a ransom for *all*." The statement is directed against contemporary Judaism and contemporary gnosticism.

11. Even in texts which are intended for use in the schools it is implied that naturalism actually belongs to the past era. See Gunnar Hillerdal, *Ideer och händelser i religionens värld*, 1968, pp. 78-80, where three very good texts are reproduced.

12. This thesis quite obviously implies an association with Bultmann's position, but without the connection with Heidegger's anthropology which characterizes Bultmann. See his "New Testament and Mythology" in *Kerygma and Myth*, pp. 24-44.

13. Cf. Vilmos Vajta, "Creation and Worship," in *Studia Theologica*, 1963, pp. 29-46.

14. A rich sampling of New Testament texts dealing with external life as a song of praise is given by Paul Minear, *Horizons of Christian Community* (St. Louis: Bethany, 1959), see especially pp. 29-39 and 70-79.

15. This criticism must be directed against Jürgen Moltmann's analysis of a restoration of creation. See his *Umkehr zur Zukunft*, pp. 115-123.

Index of Biblical Passages

Genesis
1:2   18, 27
1:6   50
1:26-30   52
1:26f.   22, 77
1:26   136
1:27   55, 179
1:28   56
2:17   181, 201n.8
3:1-19   51
3:1-15   26
3:4-6   181
3:19   51, 54, 103, 181, 185, 201n.8
3:23   51
4:1   30
6:6   22
6:13—8:22   51
6:14—8:19   52
6:19   51
8:11   51
11:1-9   52
11:4   52
32:22-32   38
32:29   36
44:10   130
50:20   69

Judges
11:12   130

Job
10:9   38
26:14   172
33:6   38
39   90

Psalms
8:4-10   53
19:1-7   172
22:1   84
33:6   145
89:6   172
104:14f.   51
104:16   51
104:20-22   51
104:23   51
104:30   19, 38, 143, 145, 162
119   66
139:7-12   129

Ecclesiastes
3:19   185
3:20   185

Isaiah
6:3   172
11:2   157
29:18-20   101
34:15f.   145
35:4-6   101
40:6   67
42:10   172
43:25   22
48:16   145
53:3-12   99
53:3   80
61:1-2   100, 101

Joel
2:28   145

Micah
3:8   145

Zechariah
13:7   99, 198n.2

Matthew
4:1f.   85
4:2-4   107
4:4   85
4:5-7   107
4:7   85
4:8-10   107
4:10   85
4:23   86
5:13, 14   147
5:45   153
6:26-34   152
6:26-28   39
6:26   89
6:28   19
6:30·   89
7:16-18   75
8:5-13   41
8:10   41
11:2-6   19
11:25-30   101
12:28   146
12:41f.   93
15:21-28   41
15:28   41
16:18   161
16:25   116
19:19   59
19:20   60
21:22   41

22:23-33   175, 201n.3
22:39   59
24:3-36   108
24:24   92
25:31-46   66, 179
25:34-40   103
25:35-40   87
25:45   60
26:69-74   98
27:33-34   107
27:35-37   107
27:38-50   107
28:17   60, 122
28:18-20   122, 130
28:18   129
28:19   129

Mark
1:12f.   18, 85
1:15   86
2:2-11   88
2:5   41
2:7   92, 100
2:9-11   118
2:15-17   60
5:34   41
5:36   41
7:15-23   22
7:26   93
9:23f.   41
10:28-45   176
10:41-45   85
10:42-45   103
10:45   94, 103
14:27   198n.2
14:36   48, 159
14:50   99
15:34   84
16:2   117
16:9-20   128
16:15-18   138
16:15   129
16:19f.   122
16:20   122, 129

Luke
1:35   19
1:39-45   120
3:38   81
4:1f.   85
4:16-21   65
4:17-19   101
4:25-27   93
5:25   172
6:21   160, 186
7:2   93
7:15   89
7:20-23   101
7:22f.   101

9:2   138
10:9   138
11:20   86, 146
12:37   78, 197n.9
12:49-53   176
13:29f.   183
13:30   154
15:18   129
17:6   30
20:38   188
22:44   83
23:34   88
23:43   88, 102
24:44-51   129
24:47   129
24:50f.   122

John
1:32f.   159, 200n.10
3:14   24
5:24-26   201n.7
5:24   174, 180, 186
5:26f.   180
6:48-58   165
6:63   180
6:70   98, 100
6:71   98
8:6   131
8:28   24
9:6   123
12:24   21, 49, 121
12:32   24, 130
12:48   180
13:4-17   197n.9
15:26   166
16:14f.   167, 199n.5
17:3   30
17:12   43
19:26   99
20:17   199n.1
20:21-22   130
20:25   68
20:26   82
20:27   199n.1
20:29   130
21:1   114
21:5-13   125
21:14-19   125
21:14   114
21:15-17   125
21:18-23   126

Acts
1:6-11   129
1:8   129, 130, 144, 167
1:9   122, 127, 129
2:16-21   145
2:22-36   82
3:12-26   82

3:15   118, 180
4:8-12   82
5:29-32   82
7:55-60   109
9:2   131
10:34-43   117
10:40-43   180
10:43   68
14:15-17   38
17:25   38
17:31   117
20:7   82
28:14-31   129

Romans
1—2   197n.1
1:17   30
1:18-32   59
1:18   30
2:5   30
2:6   114
2:14   59, 69
2:15   69, 155
3:19-21   69
3:19   67
3:20   68
5:12-21   196n.5
5:12   37
5:14   89
5:15-19   105
5:19   198n.11
5:20   77
6—8   115
6   177
6:1-14   117
6:2   87
6:3-11   77
6:3   176
6:4   140
6:5   49
6:6   177
6:12   87
7:12   25
8:1-17   146
8:11   19, 143, 174
8:15-27   159
8:18-23   120
8:20-23   183
8:26   19, 25, 166, 186
8:37   122
12   152
13:3-5   69
13:4   46
13:9   59
13:10   25

1 Corinthians
1:23-28   100
1:26   184

1:28   100
4:15   21, 180
8:7-12   69
11:20-22   60
12   152, 159
12:13   165f., 176, 188, 201n.15
12:17   189
12:22-26   153
12:22-24   156
12:25   155
13:3   29
15:1-5   131
15:1-4   82
15:22   49
15:24-26   86, 182
15:25   24
15:26   174
15:31   116
15:32   122
15:33-49   121
15:35-39   166
15:36-38   153
16:2   82

2 Corinthians
3:18   77
4:4   77
5:10   114
5:17   18
12:9   115

Galatians
3:19   77
3:24   68
4:4-6   167
4:4   83
4:24   89
5:14   59
5:16   165f.
5:17   178
5:20f.   179
5:23   25

Ephesians
1:10-23   166
2:14-19   192
2:15   18, 191
4:24   77
4:28   76
5:5   57

Philippians
1:19   167
2:6-8   192
2:8   48, 105, 111
3:10-21   115
3:21   77

Colossians
1:15-22   22
1:15f.   77
1:15   191
1:16-20   166
1:18   188
1:26   30
3:5   57
3:24f.   114

1 Thessalonians
4:11   76

2 Thessalonians
2:3   43
3:12   76

1 Timothy
2:4-6   202n.10
2:4   183

Titus
1:3   30

Hebrews
4:15   77
5:7   48, 83

5:8   48, 80, 105, 111
6:4-6   177
10:22   69
10:26f.   177
11:7, 8   89
11:11   89
11:32-38   89
11:39f.   89

1 Peter
1:3   174
1:23-25   21
3:21   69
4:17   114

2 Peter
1:21   33

1 John
3:2   77
5:6-8   177

James
2:8   59
2:19   36

Revelation
1:4   157
1:7   179
1:10   82
1:11   131
2—3   114
2:7   157
3:1   157
3:6   157
3:22   157
4:5   157
5:5   157
7:9-17   179, 191
12:9   26
20:2   26

Index of Names

Aagaard, A. M.   200n.1, n.11
Andrae, T.   201n.4
Aristotle   51
Armgard, L.-O.   15, 196n.7, 198 n.9, 199n.6
Augustus   78
Aukrust, T.   198n.8
Aulén, G.   15, 198n.9, n.1

Barrett, C. K.   201n.15
Barth, K.   55, 183, 196n.12, 201 n.9
Billing, E.   34, 197n.5
Bloch, E.   198n.7
Brilioth, Y.   200n.8
Bring, R.   195n.1
Brown, R. E.   200n.10
Brunner, E.   197n.1
Buddha   40, 70, 93
Bultmann, R.   118f., 149, 163, 200n.4, 201n.13, 202n.12

Calvin, J.   66, 162
Campenhausen, H. von   199n.5
Constantine   178
Cullmann, O.   44, 176, 196n.4, 197n.2, 201n.5

Davies, J. G.   198n.6
Dix, G.   199n.3, 201n.15
Dodd, C. H.   197n.9, 199n.1, 200 n.7
Dostoyevsky, F.   67
Downing, F. G.   196n.8

Ebeling, G.   34, 196n.9
Eklund, P.   172, 189, 201n.1

Fetscher, I.   200n.3
Filson, F. V.   201n.3
Frostin, P.   199n.4

Gerhardsson, B.   15, 195n.3, 198 n.8
Graaf, J. de   196n.11
Grundtvig, N. F. S.   174
Gärtner, B.   196n.3

Hartman, O.   196n.6, 198n.7
Heidegger, M.   163f., 201n.13, 202n.12
Hendry, G. S.   199n.1
Hillerdal, G.   200n.7, 202n.11
Hof, H.   201n.17
Hoskyns, E. C.   199n.7, 201n.7
Häfner, H.   197n.8
Hägglund, B.   199n.8
Irenaeus   135-137, 195n.4, 199n.4

Jeremias, J.   197n.4, 198n.3

Kant, I.   66
Kelly, J. N. D.   201n.16, 202n.10
Kiddle, M.   200n.9
Kierkegaard, S.   163ff.
Käsemann, E.   198n.11

Lampe, G. W. H.   200n.5
Larsson, H.   154ff., 200n.8
Lindblom, J.   196n.6
Luther, M.   27, 38, 63f., 66, 76, 109, 132, 162, 173, 197n.6, n.4
Løgstrup, K. E.   27-29, 42, 46, 61, 73, 165, 196n.7, n.1, n.5, 197n.7

Index   **207**

Macquarrie, J.   165, 201n.14
Marcion   31
Marx, K.   40, 64, 90f., 107, 116, 148-151, 163f., 200n.3
Mauser, U.   198n.10
Minear, P. S.   199n.2, 202n.14
Moltmann, J.   196n.2, 198n.7, 202 n.15
Moule, C. F. D.   200n.7

Neil, W.   196n.3
Nero   78
Niebuhr, R.   103, 198n.5
Nietzsche, F.   100
Nygren, A.   197n.5

Odeberg, H.   200n.6
Olsson, H.   197n.6
Oppen, D. von   95, 198n.10
Otzen, B.   198n.2

Paul of Samosata   82
Persson, P. E.   15, 196n.10, 198 n.7, 200n.2
Pierce, C. A.   70, 197n.1, n.6, 201 n.8
Plato   51, 154, 200n.7, n.8

Prenter, R.   197n.3, 198n.4, 199 n.2

Rad, G. von   196n.9, 201n.8
Ramsey, A. M.   196n.8
Rengstorf, K. H.   199n.6
Richardson, A.   198n.6, 201n.15
Rydberg, V.   154ff.

Sartre, J. P.   108, 163
Schüller, B.   197n.3
Selwyn, E. G.   201n.2
Socrates   70
Søe, N. H.   154, 200n.7

Taylor, V.   198n.2
Thielicke, H.   197n.3

Vajta, V.   202n.13
Vogel, H.   195n.2

Ware, T.   199n.5, 201n.16
Weil, S.   48, 181, 196n.7, 201n.8
Wikenhauser, A.   199n.3
Williams, D. D.   197n.2
Wolf, H. H.   200n.12